DAVID LARTER

Bowling Fast – the Highs and Lows

David Larter

To Paul

DAVID LARTER

Bowling Fast – the Highs and Lows

BY RICHARD SAYER

Foreword by David Gower OBE

DAVID LARTER

Bowling Fast – the Highs and Lows

BY RICHARD SAYER

First published in 2021 by Albert Publications
in association with
The Society of Old Framlinghamians
www.oldframlinghamian.com

Limited edition of 500 copies

© Richard Sayer 2021
sayer@suffolkskies15.co.uk

ISBN 978-0-9562872-2-9

DESIGNED BY CHRIS KEEBLE, KEEBLE+HALL
+44 (0)7850 183677

PRINTED IN SUFFOLK ON FSC® MIX CREDIT CERTIFIED PAPERS. WOOD
AND WOOD-BASED MATERIALS CONTAINED IN THESE PRODUCTS ARE
FROM LEGAL AND SUSTAINABLY MANAGED SOURCES.

Cricket, perhaps more than any other game, has its ups and downs for the individual, a hundred one day, nought the next. A brilliant catch followed by dropping a dolly. Keeping a sense of proportion and a level head is half the battle.

TED DEXTER OCTOBER 17, 1968.

Cricket is a game of the most terrifying stresses with more luck about it than any other game I know. They call it a team game, but in fact it is the loneliest game of all.

JOHN ARLOTT FROM 'ANOTHER WORD FROM ARLOTT'.

The British have never been a spiritually minded people, so they invented cricket to give them some notion of eternity.

LORD MANCROFT 1963.

INTRODUCTION

———◉◉◉———

I JOINED FRAMLINGHAM COLLEGE in September 1956 from prep school in Essex. I loved my cricket and did well enough in the colts in my first summer term to be included by Norman Borrett (the master in charge of College cricket and a Devon minor county cricketer) in an end-of-term practice match on the College square involving the 1st XI.

I was 14. David Larter was 17. He was also 6 feet 7 inches tall. I had to face an over from him. He was kind, bowling the ball to a full length at much less than his full pace. I saw at least one of them as it sped past my tentative bat.

I did not see David again, on or off the cricket field, for nearly sixty years. And then, quite by chance, our paths crossed. It was Monday, March 23, 2015. David was guest of honour at a lunchtime gathering at the College. There were six of us for lunch. I was there as a Governor of the school.

The lunch was hosted by the College's headmaster, Paul Taylor, who had as a young man been on Surrey's books. It was a special occasion. It was thrown to celebrate David's very generous donation to his alma mater of some of his prized cricket memorabilia. He gave us his England cricket sweater, cap and blazer. We were greatly honoured. They went on display in the College's Fowler Pavilion, where generations of Framlinghamian pupils can gain some understanding of the man who is the College's only Test cricketer in its 156-year history.

At the lunch, having made a brief reference to our meeting sixty years earlier and my terror at the wicket, I asked David if he would be willing for me to write his biography. Overcoming his natural modesty, David agreed. Six years later, this book is the result of that meeting. I hope it captures David's remarkable cricket prowess – and equally importantly, his qualities as a gentle human being.

This is a Suffolk book. Although a minor county, Suffolk has a long cricket history. In 2018 Stradbroke cricket club celebrated the 275th anniversary of the first recorded game in Suffolk. That 1743 match against Finningham was in the days preceding the introduction of a middle stump in the wicket. David Larter is a Suffolk man and the author, designer and printer are all Suffolk based.

RICHARD SAYER 2021.

FOREWORD

———————⬦⬦⬦———————

MODERN LIFE SEEMS TO FORCE US to live our lives all too much in the present with the odd allowance for the immediate past. News is instant, available 24/7, endlessly repeated so that it loses all impact and it as much a boon as a bugbear that there is so much sport available to view across the multiple media channels at our disposal that we can move from event to event without taking the time to savour what we are seeing.

Actually, that's not entirely true. Sticking to sport, one of the sports fan's greatest delights is to be able to recall great moments, favourite events and heroes from a lifetime of following a passion. My early cricketing heroes were Garry Sobers and Graeme Pollock and I have had the pleasure and privilege of playing with huge admiration against some of the greats from the late 70s through to the early 90s.

I saw David Larter play only once (when I was 8 years old), bowling against Pollock in the 1965 Trent Bridge Test, but his name remains familiar to me as are those of the many famous men who feature in this tome as opponents and in every case admirers of Larter's bowling and of the man himself.

At 6 foot 7 inches Larter leads me straight to comparisons with the tall men I have faced, fearsome opponents such as Joel Garner, Curtly Ambrose and Courtney Walsh. Barry Knight is quoted as saying that Larter was quicker than them. Well, if true that's one mighty statement, which immediately gives those of my and later generations something to latch on to. The great Keith Miller compared his on field hostility to that of one of the great fast bowlers of the era, Wes Hall. With 666 wickets at 19.53 apiece Larter was amongst the top English fast bowlers of the 1960s, until he suffered a career-ending ankle-bone injury on his second Ashes trip at the age of 25.

Richard Sayer tells a story well worth reading of the ups and downs of the career of a man described by Peter Parfitt as "amiable, sociable and reserved" off the field but by all as a formidable opponent on it.

David Gow

DAVID GOWER OBE.

CONTENTS

1

THE FIRST TEST

The Oval, Kennington, London.

In his first over, maintaining control over length and line and putting the occasional ball down with some haste, he induced the opening batsman to throw his bat twice at balls short of half volley length; anxious, almost frenetic. With the penultimate ball of his second over, the eleventh delivery he had bowled in Test cricket, the ball deviated off the seam on pitching, so that the batsman, pushing forward in an attempt to steal a single, could only edge it low and hard to first slip, where Cowdrey, quick on feet which had moved swiftly around many a rackets court, took a very good catch down to his right. David Larter had his first Test wicket.

The audience of some 15,000 thundered its approval at this first crack in the wall of the Pakistan innings. For a moment, the 22-year-old fast bowler became the darling of the crowd. The date was Friday August 16, 1962, the venue was the Oval in Kennington, in the London Borough of Lambeth, owned by the Duchy of Cornwall and since 1844 leased to Surrey County Cricket Club; a sacred place.

In 1880 the venue was host to the first Test match ever played in England, between Australia and England. In 1882 Australia toured again, and achieved a dramatic first Test victory – on English soil at the Oval, by seven runs after two days play, provoking a mock obituary notice in *The Times – In Affectionate Remembrance of English cricket which died at the Oval... the body will be cremated and the ashes taken to*

Australia. In Australia the following winter England's tour captain Ivo Bligh, later Lord Darnley, was presented with the ashes of a bail in a tiny pottery urn, and that unimportant piece of pottery has become the symbolic trophy fiercely contested every two years, alternately in England and Australia.

The match being played on August 16, 1962 was the fifth Test between England and the touring Pakistan team. Although England had already won the series handsomely, the chance for spectators to see players in action who would soon be representing their country on the 1962/63 winter Ashes tour to Australia ensured that large numbers attended the dead rubber Oval Test. Over 40,000 people were to watch the match over its four days, in the words of *Wisden Cricketers' Almanack – 'a triumph for England's three amateur batsmen, the Rev David Sheppard, Colin Cowdrey, the captain Ted Dexter, and for David Larter who marked his first Test appearance by taking nine wickets for 145 runs.'*

For David this was a moment which had only ever featured in his dreams. The journey he made to fulfil that fantasy was full of ups and downs, highs and lows.

England had scored 406 for the loss of only two wickets on the first day, the largest number of runs scored in a single Test match day since 1954. Sheppard and Barrington made half centuries, Cowdrey 182, and Dexter played a superb innings of 172. Sir Jack Hobbs, 80 years old in December, was at the ground to watch the match. He told EW Swanton of the *Daily Telegraph* that he could not remember a batsman who consistently hit the ball as hard as Dexter. England's innings was declared closed before lunch on the second day with the score at 480 for 5 wickets. Pakistan, already three down in the series, were determined not to concede another victory to the English.

After Len Coldwell of Worcestershire had bowled the first over all eyes switched to the 22-year-old from Suffolk, making his England debut in only his third season of county cricket. It was a sensational beginning to a Test career, on a wicket which gave no help to the bowler.

Dexter's handling of his young colt was exemplary, conserving his energy and enthusiasm by using him in short spells of 30, 30, 20, 40 and 15 minutes. During the first two spells, championing accuracy over speed, David held back from bowling at his fastest. Standing 6 feet, 7 ½ inches, he approached the crease with 10 easy strides in a run of 20 yards. He swung the ball and occasionally seamed it both in and away – of the three faster bowlers he most often had the batsmen hurrying their strokes. Twice, before bad light stopped play ten minutes before lunch, good length in-swingers from him rapped Imtiaz Ahmed on his pads as he played back.

Surrey County Cricket Club
KENNINGTON OVAL
4d.

ENGLAND v. PAKISTAN
Thursday, August 16th, 1962 (5 Day Match)

ENGLAND

	First Innings		Second Innings	
§1 M. C. Cowdrey .... Kent	c Hanif, b Fazal	182		
§2 Rev. D. S. Sheppard ...... Sussex	c Fazal, b Nasim	57	not out	9
§*3 E. R. Dexter .... Sussex	b Fazal	172		
4 K. F. Barrington .... Surrey	not out	50		
5 P. H. Parfitt .... Middlesex	c Imtiaz, b D'Souza	3		
6 B. R. Knight .... Essex	b D'Souza	3		
7 R. Illingworth .... Yorkshire	not out	2		
§8 J. T. Murray .... Middlesex			not out	14
9 D. A. Allen .... Gloucestershire				
10 L. J. Coldwell ...... Worcestershire				
11 J.D.F. Larter Northamptonshire				

B4, 1-b5, , n-b 2... 11   B 4, 1-b , w , n-b ... 4
Total (5 wkts.) 480   Innings dec.   Total (0-... 27

Fall of the wickets
1—117 2—365 3—441 4—444 5—452 6— 7— 8— 9— 10—
1— 2— 3— 4— 5— 6— 7— 8— 9— 10—

BOWLING ANALYSIS

	First Innings						Second Innings					
	O.	M.	R.	W.	Wd.	N-b.	O.	M.	R.	W.	Wd.	N-b.
Fazal Mahmood	49	9	192	2		2		10	0			
Antoa D'Souza	42	9	116	2				8	0			
Intikhab Alam	38	5	109	0								
Burki	1	0	12	0								
Nasim-ul-Ghani	9	1	39	1								
Saeed Ahmed	1	0	1	0				2	0			
Mushtaq Mohammad								3	0			

Become a Surrey Member NOW.
Ask at the office for details.

PAKISTAN

	First Innings		Second Innings	
§1 Imtiaz Ahmed .... Services	c Murray, b Knight	49	c Cowdrey, b Larter	98
2 Ijaz Butt .... Rawalpindi	c Cowdrey, b Larter	10	run out	6
3 Mushtaq Mohammed ...... Karachi	lbw b Larter	43	b Illingworth	72
*4 Javed Burki .... Rawalpindi	b Larter	3	c Parfitt, b Knight	42
5 Saeed Ahmed .... Lahore	c Parfitt, b Allen	21	c Knight, b Allen	4
6 Hanif Mohammed .... Karachi	b Larter	46	c Dexter, b Larter	0
7 Wallis Mathias .... Karachi	c Murray, b Larter	0	lbw out	48
10 Antoa D'Souza .... Karachi	c Parfitt, b Coldwell	1	not out	2
8 Nasim-ul-Ghani .... Karachi	c Murray, b Coldwell	5	b Coldwell	24
9 Intikhab Alam .... Karachi	not out	3	b Larter	12
11 Fazal Mahmood .... Lahore	b Coldwell	0	b Larter	5

B , 1-b , w , n-b 2... 2   B 7, 1-b 5, w , n-b 1 ... 10
Total ... 183   Total ... 323

Fall of the wickets
1—11 2—93 3—102 4—115 5—165 6—168 7—175 8—179 9—183 10—183
1—34 2—171 3—171 4—180 5—186 6—250 7—294 8—316 9—316 10—323

BOWLING ANALYSIS

	First Innings						Second Innings					
	O.	M.	R.	W.	Wd.	N-b.	O.	M.	R.	W.	Wd.	N-b.
Coldwell	28	11	53	3								
Larter	25	4	57	5								
Allen	22	9	33	1			27	14	52	1		
Knight	9	5	11	1			12	4	33	1		
Illingworth	13	5	27	0		2	21	9	54	1		
Dexter							6	1	16	0		
Barrington							2	0	10	0		

*Captain ‡Wkt.-keeper §Amateur   Toss won by—ENGLAND
Umpires—F. S. Lee & C. S. Elliott   RESULT—ENGLAND WON BY 10 WICKETS
Hours of Play 1st., 2nd., 3rd & 4th days 11.30—6.30. 5th day 11.0—5.30 or 6.0. Lunch 1.30 all days
NEW BALL may be taken by the fielding captain after 85 overs.
Next Match, Thurs., Aug. 23rd (1 day) Y.A. of Surrey v. Y.A. of Sussex

SUPPORTERS' ASSOC. URGENTLY NEED AGENTS. Apply at the Office by Press Entrance
Printed on the ground by the Surrey County Cricket Club Printing Department

After lunch, both David and Coldwell too often pitched short and were hooked. The tide appeared to be turning in favour of Pakistan. David Sheppard later wrote: *'the stand of 82 by Imtiaz and Mushtaq made us feel that we were going to spend a long time in the field but the bowlers all kept at it with great accuracy, gave nothing away and the batsmen duly made mistakes…Dexter gave our giant fast bowler David Larter short spells of about three overs at a time, and he kept at it on a wicket which had little life in it.'*

It was David who achieved the breakthrough with the score at 93 for one. Mushtaq tried to push him off the back foot wide of mid-on, the ball straightened on him and he was lbw. David quickened after the tea interval, bowling fast without loss of accuracy and he comprehensively bowled Burki, the Pakistan captain, with a particularly good delivery. In this, his most impressive spell, his figures were one wicket for four runs in five overs.

I found David very awkward to play, Mushtaq said recently, *he was gifted as he was so tall and he used that gift to maximum advantage. But additionally he was not erratic like some other quick bowlers, he made one play all the time, keeping line and length. It was hard for all batsmen to cope with his steep bounce and accuracy.*

Pace allied to length and line had accounted for Mushtaq and Burki and, thanks to Dexter's economic use of him, David was lively till the end of the day. Called up in the evening for a final fling, David induced Wallis Mathias into edging a fast ball short of a length which lifted from the placid wicket. Coldwell, who until then at his gentle in-swing pace had not looked dangerous, then mopped up the tail effectively. Only Hanif, 'the little master', Mushtaq's elder brother, offered much resistance, before he too was bowled by David for 46 with what John Arlott, writing in the *Guardian*, considered the best ball of the match - pitched on middle on a good length, beating Hanif's shift onto the back foot, and taking the off stump out of the ground. David ended the day with four for 53 from 21 overs.

Dismissed for 183 and forced to follow on, Pakistan did better in their second innings, getting to 171 for one wicket, when Imtiaz Ahmed on 98 attempted to drive David to reach a century which no one would have begrudged. The ball left him off the pitch and caught the edge to provide another sharp catch for Cowdrey at slip. David dismissed Hanif again, caught by Dexter for a duck, then did his best to confound those critics who did not regard him as the best fielder on the team by running out Mathias, backing up too far, with a direct throw from mid-on. He then polished off the innings by bowling Intikhab Alam and Fazal Mahmood.

Arlott was of the view that David's haul had included five of the seven best Pakistani wickets: *'Five for 57 from 25 overs in the first innings and four for 88 from 21 overs in the second are good figures against any opposition on so easy a pitch.'*

Every cricket fan in the country now knew who David Larter was.

ENGLAND BOWLING 5th Test

1st Innings

Bowler	Overs	Mdns.	Runs	Wkts.
Coldwell	28	11	53	3
Larter	25	4	57	5
Allen	22	9	33	1
Knight	9	5	11	1
Illingworth	13	5	27	0

BBCtv   Pakistan at The Oval - 1962

ENGLAND BOWLING 5th Test

2nd Innings

Bowler	Overs	Mdns.	Runs	Wkts.
Coldwell	23	4	60	1
Larter	21.1	0	88	4
Knight	11	3	33	1
Illingworth	21	9	54	1
Allen	27	14	52	1
Dexter	6	1	16	0
Barrington	2	0	10	0

BBCtv   Pakistan at The Oval - 1962

2

EARLY DAYS

David was qualified to play for Scotland, being born on the April 24, 1940 in Inverness. Home, however, was in Leeds, Yorkshire.

David at 1 year old, taken in Melksham, Wiltshire.

My father was an RAF recruiting sergeant trying to convince Scotsmen to join up. Mother had joined him and that is about the extent of my Scottish heritage, but it does make me qualified to play for Scotland and Yorkshire, and after a Suffolk education, anybody else.

Until 1992 Yorkshire insisted on all players being born in the county with one exception – if birth outside the county was due to the war. The news of my Leeds background nearly caused Fred Trueman to have a fit when this came out in a casual conversation during the 1962/63 Australian tour. Indeed, I have wondered what sort of career I might have had as a Yorkshireman.

We moved to Suffolk when I was 10 and my boyhood in God's own county was all sport, and cricket in particular. As part of a local group of about a dozen kids, we played all the Test matches of the period and took on all the characters of our heroes. The local dairy farmer must have been a cricket fan because we cut and rolled and marked out a pitch on his field behind our house (after clearing the cowpats), and we never asked his permission.

David's mother and father in 1943

My mother Edna's father was a monumental mason and builder in Leeds and paternal grandfather was an ostler and coal merchant in Framlingham. He was

On Grandad Larter's coal cart horse.

a widower, my grandmother having died at 28 of a brain tumour.

My father Jack was born in Suffolk at Easton and brought up in Framlingham, and when he left the RAF in 1949 he was drawn back to Suffolk and us with him.

I was nine years old and joined the local primary school, Sir Robert Hitcham's, in Framlingham.

David Boulton was a Framlingham town boy of the same age as David. They grew up together:

My first memory of David is of his first week at Sir Robert Hitcham's. In fact it may have been his first day, but I recall him getting into a fight – more likely a scuffle – with another boy: I don't recall the other's name but he must have been a bit simple since David was already considerably bigger than the rest of us! David and I have been friends ever since.

In September 1951 we both started at Brandeston, Framlingham College's prep school, as day boys, cycling the 4 miles from our homes every day, including of course Saturdays. We never worried too much about cycling that distance in all weathers and in the winter dark: there was no concern about traffic or other potential hazards, and it was only on rare occasions that we used the Eastern Counties bus service, although a few boys came from families with a car.

David Larter was amazed to find that he was, on joining the junior school at the College, a full year ahead of his new friends there.

> The 11 plus later that year seemed easy. I have little or no recall of academic activity, but the games! Organised team sports with basic coaching seemed like heaven. I was already on the large side and thrived on the sports field.

David Boulton recalls the effect big David had on the cricket field:

He soon demonstrated an aptitude and talent for fast bowling and in the two summers we were at Brandeston there were several occasions when opposing school teams were dismissed for very small scores, with batsmen somewhat terrorised by the pace and lift that David could generate. His skill was backed up by several other talented youngsters, notably Michael Spencer, who excelled at whichever sport he tried. Many of us were overawed by the sheer hostility David could generate at well below full pace with the Chingford composition ball we used. His size, strength and ability made him the top guy in the athletics throwing events, where he broke the throwing the cricket ball school record by a distance.

By the time we graduated to the main school at the College in September 1953 David had continued to grow, maintaining his size advantage over all his peers. This ensured that his sporting prowess got him into the Colts teams for more than just cricket. Academically I think David may not have been at the top of the form, but he was fully involved in non-sports activities such as the Combined Cadet Force.

By our last year in 1957 David was not only an established 1st XI fast bowler but also played full back at rugby where he was both a menacing tackler and an awesome kicker: he would attempt, and succeed, with penalties from around the halfway line – using of course the rugby balls of the time which were of leather that absorbed water, got very heavy and behaved like a bar of wet soap in soggy conditions. During the athletics season in the late spring he came into his own in the throwing events – shot, discus and javelin.

There were other interests of course apart from sport in those mid-teens. We had discovered girls and the youth club potential of the Young Conservatives, as well as the gradually evolving music scene as Elvis Presley and Bill Haley started the rock and roll era.

Somehow, we both got enrolled into the Saxtead Green cricket club squad, often playing at the weekends against other local villages; there was much stronger village involvement in team sports in the 1950s than today. The home pitch occupied the whole of the village green – a triangular piece of grass bounded by roads on all three sides, requiring the club to have insurance against broken car windscreens. The other oddity was the pitch: there was no room for a square of mown grass, so the club developed a cinder-surfaced pitch with a mat stretched to cover it, pegged at ends and sides. It was a reasonably true playing surface but could prove quite lively and at David's fastest pace it could be very daunting! We had another Fram College dayboy playing too – Derek Moss - whose father was the publican of the Saxtead Volunteer, where after play we youngsters began training our taste buds for beer.

Derek Moss remembers the Framlingham Young Conservative club, its social side possessing the big attraction of the young ladies from nearby Mills Grammar School:

In the summer of 1957 Mr Davies initiated cricket on Saxtead Green, securing grants to purchase equipment and to lay the pitch. David Larter played during the 1955/6 seasons, before I became captain in 1957 by when most of David's time was taken up by the College 1st X1. I was glad I did not have to face him - he would have been truly fearsome on that Saxtead pitch. As a person he was quite different from what one might expect of a terrifyingly fast bowler: by nature, he was very quiet, almost insular, very modest, and quite private. Despite his physique he was very shy – which might surprise people.

David Boulton resumes the story.

In 1958 David started to play Minor Counties cricket with the Suffolk side and attracted attention from Northamptonshire with a trial. I can remember David being pleased that during his bowling trial he had impressed the coaches by managing to move the ball both ways, in-swing and out-swing.

Back in the '60s the county cricket scene was impoverished; the players were poorly paid, the attendances were small, and both the Northampton and Peterborough grounds were basic, to say the least. The Crawthorne Road pitch at Peterborough doubled as a hockey pitch during the winter, and I played on it a few times for one of the city's hockey teams – most memorably once on the day that our fellow Old Framlingham Andy Hancock scored the famous try for England against Scotland in March 1965.

David's county championship bowling figures are impressive still and I remember his name in the one-day cricket records for a hat-trick. Watching the Northants opening attack of Tyson and Larter, with keeper Keith Andrew standing back halfway to the boundary, was something to behold!

Michael Spencer was in all the sports teams at the junior school and at the College:

David was modest – and well described as a gentle giant. He got on well with everyone. First memories of him at Brandeston were of his prodigious goal kicking at rugby. I rather fancied myself on Junior Sports Day at throwing the cricket ball, but he brought me and others down to earth with a mighty throw which easily

> *David was modest – and well described as a gentle giant.*

broke the record. He was not an immediate star as a fast bowler in those early days probably because coaching was limited. I do remember taking a few catches in the slips off him and probably dropping a few others.

The College magazine noted that at Brandeston in his first year, 1952, David's best bowling for the Under 12s was four for 23 against local rivals Culford, and in the season's averages he came third with 12 wickets at five apiece. In athletics he won the junior Cricket Ball, defeating Spencer with a throw of over 49 yds. Although he appeared in the Form IIA play, *Smugglers' Honour*, the triumph of his performance as Black Bartie is not recorded.

1953 saw him in the second eleven football team playing two matches against St Felix, '*he played well at back, but was not sufficiently reliable to find a place in the first team. In the rugby 1st XV Larter was useful in the line-out* [hardly surprising], *but he doesn't use his weight to advantage in the tight scrums. Tackling weak.*' David, the team's place-kicker, won the place-kicking competition, beating Michael Spencer. At cricket, '*he has increased his speed all through the term and is now really fast with a nice wrist action. If he can learn to control his length and direction he should develop into a good bowler; he has certainly improved a lot since last year.'* David won the house match competition by taking seven wickets for three runs, five clean bowled and the other two lbw, so no help needed from nervous catchers.

He was in this year an outstanding athlete: breaking the prep school records at the high jump with 4ft 3.5ins, and throwing the cricket ball, with a very long 69 yards 6 ins. He was evidently also useful on the billiard table (a skill which was later to prove valuable on rainy county cricket days), a losing semi-finalist in the open event.

> The local authority grant scheme put the College within reach, and I moved on to there from Brandeston in September 1953, when I was 13 and a half. It was quite a lesson, as suddenly I was at the bottom of the pile again, with 300 odd fellow travellers. I also began to realise that as a day-boy I did not conform. Most of the local lads did not really fit in that well – we were a small minority of about 30 in the 1950s, – and we were rarely seen to do well on the sports fields. I loved every minute out of the classroom, and even turned up on some Sundays.

In the Colts cricket team in his first senior summer he was already 6 feet tall, with bowling '*...quite adequate to remove most of the sides opposed to us this year. Larter, surprisingly fast and accurate for his age; a very promising fast bowler who possesses a good action. His batting can only be described as feeble and his fielding is even worse.'* At 15 he was in the second eleven, described as, *'a tall fast bowler who did not have the best of luck, as most of his opponents preferred to stop only the straight ones and leave or avoid the others. Batting: negligible. Fielding: could be improved. Awarded second eleven colours.'*

By 1956, and now in the 1st XI, there was a hint of some future success: '*Larter will undoubtedly improve with maturity. He has the makings of a real fast bowler as he has a good run-up, rhythm and considerable height. At the moment he is far too erratic and wide of the target, but he is young enough for this not to be venial. Must try to cultivate some batting confidence and realise what an asset he has in his height. Usually a sound field.'*

In the last match David took seven for 13 against local club Eye CC: *'a crushing finale to the season in which everybody was glad to see Larter, who has pounded away with unflagging enthusiasm and energy throughout the season, come into his own at last.'* For the 1956 season his figures were 24 wickets at 12.8 apiece. The speed he was now able to generate, and the lift which his height and high action produced, meant that to many of his opponents he was a man amongst boys. Clive Smith,

Framlingham College 1st XI 1957. David Larter seated left. The photo includes two other international players: Andrew Hancock seated second from right (the scorer of the famous try at Twickenham for England v Scotland in 1965) and Norman Porter standing second from right (hockey for Scotland).

a 1st XI batsman, recalls that he had the *pleasure* of not only facing David in house matches but also when David returned to the College to play for the Old Framlinghamians (OFs) when Smith was opening for the College: *a pretty frightening experience.*

He left Framlingham in 1957 after his second year in the eleven. '*The bowling attack has been too dependent on and almost entirely in the hands of Larter and Turnbull. They have bowled manfully and well, but one would like to have seen the spinners bowling more*'. David's 242 overs produced 52 wickets at 9.50 each, a highlight being his seven for 35 against King's School, Rochester. Robin Anderton played in that game, his first for the College: '*My memory tells me that David bowled a full length of in-swing. He was shy, hiding behind his handkerchief when he got a wicket. He rarely bowled short threatening balls in schoolboy matches, or in the nets. His batting was about hitting sixes as he was not expected to contribute a great deal more! He was too good for most schoolboy batsmen, as the King's Rochester game at Buckhurst Hill showed. A gentle giant.*'

The cricket report of the match against local rivals Ipswich School spoke of an unusual talent. *'Ipswich seemed to fear the bowling of Larter, and as a consequence they were all out for 90, Larter taking 7 for 28, a very good piece of bowling, ably supported by Turnbull, who with Larter bowled throughout the innings.'*

David Turnbull remembers happy days:

When I started playing in the 1st XI and David was in his second year in the team, it gave me great confidence to see him thundering in from the College end while I partnered him at the other end. We were in the same house and were usually assigned to practise in different nets, so I was fortunate not to have to face him very often. Fielding at gully to him was a different matter, with the ball often flying in my direction at great speed. During that season we did most of the bowling; his 52 wickets at an average of 9.5 was a fine achievement in 14 matches. I was of course proud to say that I opened the bowling with a future England opening bowler.

At hockey, at full back in the 3rd eleven, he was '*a powerful clean hitter, but slow in recovering'*. At rugby he was versatile, initially playing as a second row forward then in the 2nd XV winning his colours as a full back. He represented his house at cricket, rugby, hockey, and athletics and was said to have made the 'discovery' of tennis in his last term. His main sport apart from cricket remained athletics where he continued the progress he showed at Brandeston. At Sports Day in 1956 and again in 1957 he achieved a rare triple by winning the javelin, discus, and shot put, with College records in the javelin (153 feet) and the discus (129 feet). He also came third in the hurdles. In the classroom David worked hard at his books, winning Form Prizes in 1954 and 1955 before passing five O levels. He proved to be skilled at art, winning the prize for Indian Ink drawing. He was a keen member of the CCF as a Junior Leader and a REME corporal.

David's own modest take on these matters reveals a considerable additional athletic achievement, unrecorded by the College magazine:

> I do not know how many people will recall my great interest in field event athletics, perhaps because I count the master in charge of athletics, Percy Clarke, as one who did not share my enthusiasm. Despite the lack of facilities and coaching I managed to break a few school records in the javelin and discus (the story that I nearly speared housemaster 'Bill' Baly with a long javelin throw is I fear something of an exaggeration). I entered the 1957 All England Schools championships at the White City, London, coming 4th or 5th in both those events. This all during the holidays at my expense.

However, cricket came first for me and after the move from Brandeston to the College my main ambition was to play for the colts. This side was under the sometimes eagle eye of the said Bill Baly. In my first season with him I used the somewhat slingy action I had developed at Brandeston. During the winter I saw a Pathe News item showing the action of the Australian Ray Lindwall. Even though he was stocky as opposed to my height, I decided to try to copy his action, particularly the right arm pumping up and down during the run-up. Even Bill noticed the difference at the start of my second season with him, and indeed the new action was much more 'grooved' and sustainable and, importantly, I bowled quicker. I practised my new action in the early spring evening nets at Framlingham Town cricket club, usually on my own.

David was to meet and also open the bowling opposite Ray on a Ron Roberts Commonwealth tour in 1962 but did not then have the nerve to tell him how important he had been in David's cricketing development.

I quickly moved up to the school first eleven and to the care of Norman Borrett who played cricket many times for Devon, besides captaining GB Hockey to the silver medal at the 1948 London Olympics and for five years being British amateur squash champion. I hugely admired the man and he had plenty of time for me. At that time nets were probably just as important as matches for development. Norman did not try to alter me and all I recall is encouragement and the beginning of a keen interest in me and my cricket.

College contemporary and subsequently successful club cricketer, Dr John Rankin, remembers David did get one bit of coaching: *David had begun to bowl quite inaccurately. Norman Borrett sorted this out after noticing that David was getting his leading arm in the way of his vision as he went into his delivery stride. David was a good listener and soon corrected the problem. I also recall Norman adding a bit of batting advice which David was evidently to apply at number eleven throughout his first-class career. 'Have a go when it's appropriate at the end of an innings - hit the ball on the up and over the top. There's no point in wafting, Larter!'*

What pleasure it gave us all when we had to stop David bowling against local village side Campsea Ashe. They had lost four wickets to David for something like 30 runs and their ex-NZ Test batsman had had to retire with a bruised finger. We took David off simply because he was going to deprive us batsmen of having a reasonable total to chase! I thought that was not bad for a school bowling attack. He was such a quiet person off the field of play.

Michael Spencer knew from playing alongside him that that David was quite special at school. He also had first-hand experience of David's development after leaving:

We played together twice; first in 1958 for the Old Framlinghamians against rivals the Old Ipswichians, who had assembled a very strong side for the local derby. I got some runs, but David literally terrorised the OIs with 5 for 41 and we thrashed them by 100 runs – a very satisfying experience! The second was in a match on the Back, the College pitch, when we both played for the MCC against the College. David had already gained a fearsome reputation in East Anglia as being exceptionally fast. Surprisingly for a game of that status a well-known Daily Telegraph cricket writer, John Thicknesse, covered the game because David had become newsworthy and was seen as close to making the big time.

With an eye to leaving Framlingham on achieving O Levels David began to consider his future.

My thinking then was to follow my father into the RAF. I met the RAF liaison officer at school several times and finished up at RAF Cranwell on an officer training/selection course during school holidays – again an eye-opener to life outside school. My main memory is of my team (some 6 or 8 of us) standing in the middle of a football pitch with piles of rope and some 45-gallon drums. We were informed that a 20-foot-wide river was flowing across the pitch and were asked what we intended to do about getting to the other side – all good fun! I must have impressed somebody because my next stop was RAF Uxbridge and more selection tests.

After one session we were each interviewed by a Group Captain, and as I walked through the office door, I hit my head. I prided myself at that time of being 'all the sixes'– 16 years old, 16 stone in weight, and 6'6" in height. His reaction was one of concern and then the worried question *how tall are you?* His response was that I could never be a pilot because of my height. As he gruesomely put it, I would leave my kneecaps behind if I ever had to eject. He did ask me to consider ground-based jobs, but this did not appeal, so that was more or less the finish of my idea of serving the nation. I must admit that during my later spell with the Legal and General I did obtain joining-up papers for the Royal Marines, the Military Police, and the Paras. But father would not sign anything (I was still only 17), so, sadly, I still did not get to serve Queen and country. I missed National Service by about four months, which was in fact all to the good, because otherwise the cricket might never have happened.

Framlingham College

David's last term at the College, the summer term of 1957, coincided with the Duke of Norfolk opening, as the chief guest at Speech Day, the new cricket pavilion. It gave him, he said, great pleasure to do so in such a lovely setting, and to think of the fun and companionship, *'and the hum and the ring of the ball on the bat, that would go with it. It is for that that cricket was invented, and it is in that spirit that cricket must be played.'* He concluded by asking the Headmaster *'to fit in just one more half-holiday for just one more game of cricket,'* and he offered, if the games master considered the standard sufficiently high, to present a bat and a ball to the batsman and bowler selected by the cricket master at the end of the season. David remembers what happened:

> I recall being introduced to His Grace and presented with a cricket ball (now gone who knows where). The Duke was, somewhat surprisingly, appointed manager of the 1962/63 MCC touring team to Australia, which I was pleased to be a part of. Once we arrived in Perth the Duke treated all of us, in pairs, to dinner in his suite as a way of getting to know us. Once settled, he said *'Now Larter, tell me something about yourself.'* I said confidently that we had met before when he had opened the new cricket pavilion at my school. This was met with a noble but blank face. I quickly added Framlingham and Prince Albert and communication was immediately restored. I suppose someone who owned Arundel Castle and the splendid adjoining cricket ground – where I played in the opening season warm-up game against the West Indian tourists in 1963 – had probably opened more cricket pavilions than I could dream of. It is worth noting that I believe the whole of the MCC touring party were very pleasantly surprised at the Duke's very good knowledge of the game.

1957–1959 FROM MINOR TO MAJOR

1957: All Shook Up is the top song.

Although a Framlingham lad and a member of the town cricket club, David did not play much for them. He was too busy at school. His first ventures away from Framlingham were by courtesy of Michael Ashwell.

> Michael was a lovely man who was a College governor in later life. In the summer of 1957 he used to get a works van from Potters in Framlingham and load me and the kit inside with the spanners and spare parts and off we went to cricket all over Suffolk and a bit of Norfolk. He introduced me to Deben Valley cricket club, based at Woodbridge School. Playing for them led to stiffer opposition and I suppose people noticed me.

David looked for local employment.

I fiddled about around Framlingham town working for an agricultural contractor until Dad put his foot down and said I needed a proper job. I duly took a position at the bottom of the heap at the Legal and General Insurance in Ipswich. I cannot remember my job title – it was that interesting! What was interesting was the purchase of my first form of motor transport – which was to be one of my passions

throughout life. My Harley Davidson 750 V twin motorcycle held a special place in my affections then and is fondly remembered.

From that uninspiring job situation, things looked up in the spring of 1958, when chance intervened.

I was told about a coaching session to be held at Woolverstone Hall School run by Northants players. Long-term Northants batsman Jock Livingston who had emigrated from Australia after the war and having recently retired now acted as a scout for Northants and was running the show. There were several lads there. I was asked to bowl but then very quickly asked to stop bowling as the others were in some danger on a green early season net wicket. Jock put me in another net, and I bowled by myself. Along the way he mentioned that Northants usually held trials at the end of the season and that he would mention me when he got back to Northampton.

That summer David was kept busy in the L&G office, playing cricket for Deben Valley, keeping in touch with the College and the Old Framlinghamians, and playing alongside Michael Spencer in the matches he has described at Ipswich School and for MCC against the College, watched by John Thicknesse.

I was quite quickly picked up by Suffolk – with thanks to a combination of comments from the College, from Deben Valley and from opponents, and I had a successful few games at minor counties level.

David's first match for the full Suffolk side was on August 11 1958 at Felixstowe. Opening the bowling he ran through the Hertfordshire batting, with five wickets in the first innings. The second game was against Norfolk, alongside left-arm spinner Cyril Perkins. Perkins gave David a demonstration of the art of keeping one end tight to enable David, at the other end, to take wickets as batsmen psychologically relaxed from Perkins's tight leash. David got up a good head of steam in his 36 overs in the match taking seven for 109. Geoff Fiddler, who was to play many times for Norfolk and who was undefeated in both innings, confided at the time that none of the Norfolk batsmen was particularly keen on leaving the dressing room to face David's pace. Wicket-keeper Henry Blofeld, later to turn with success to journalism, was defeated in both innings by Perkins, for three and nought.

David's four two-day matches for Suffolk encompassed 12 days and several hundred miles of car travel. It was a foretaste of the stamina he would require in his later career. *Wisden* took note: '... *although Suffolk won only one match, mainly because of inconsistent batting, the bowling was more reliable and JDF Larter, a young fast bowler from Framlingham College, showed considerable promise in four matches. Twice he took five wickets in an innings and at the end of the season was given a contract by Northamptonshire.'*

14 wickets from 88 overs at 20 apiece in those four matches was to be David's Suffolk career record. It was a happy coincidence that whilst he was playing his first and only Minor Counties season, his old cricket master Norman Borrett was enjoying an outstanding season, his penultimate one for Devon, in the College summer holidays, topping their batting with an average of over 100.

> Following my Suffolk games in August Jock Livingston was as good as his word and invited me to a trial. I thought great, a short holiday and then back to the grim reality of my insurance job. The general idea was nets, and then a pick-up match in the middle with a few of the existing staff mixed in. Eventually I was asked to bowl, the batsman being Vince Broderick, a Yorkshireman and left-arm spin bowler not particularly known for his batting. Having learnt that one does not make friends by bowling bouncers at them, I decided to keep the ball well pitched up. Vince did not seem to see the first ball. The second ball was a near perfect yorker, and the off stump was removed. About three balls later the same thing happened. To cut this short I was summoned up to the secretary's office and offered £10 per week for the 22 weeks of the next season, which compared to my Legal and General salary

of £220 for a whole year's work looked pretty good. I took a full second to say yes, but it did not really sink in and I honestly thought this would just turn into a pleasant way to spend the 1959 summer.

The 1958/59 winter went slowly for David, sitting at his insurance desk in Ipswich dreaming of April when he would happily say goodbye to that world and step enthusiastically into another at Northants CCC. The idea of his becoming a professional sportsman was quite a surprise to his parents 'but they were, as always, supportive of my decision.'

My first season with Northants was a constant learning curve. The club found me accommodation and started to get me correctly kitted out, (everything bought and paid for – by me – no sponsorship in those days). Boots were particularly important, and here Frank Tyson helped me out. He gave me some plastic heel pads/cups and steel toe caps, which were to prove invaluable parts of my kit from then on.

He was also pointed in the direction of Albert Whiting's tiny cobbler's shop round the corner from the ground. Northampton's Aussies Jack Manning and George Tribe had set Albert up with the design of boot they wanted. They were handmade buckskin, a design which he was to refine and strengthen for David's size 12 feet.

I played for the county second team and when they did not have a fixture, I was farmed out to different Birmingham League clubs - where a decent standard of cricket was played. I felt that there were, in addition to Frank, many better bowlers than me on the Northants staff, and it was well into that 1959 season before I began to realise that this might be something I should take seriously, and that it was not simply a pleasant way to spend one summer before finding myself a proper job.

His first match for the county seconds was on June 1 at Wantage Road. As the headquarters of a county championship club the Wantage Road ground was not exactly in the first rank. David Lloyd was starting a career which was to lead to Test cricket for England, (for whom he would score a double century) then on to first-class umpiring, to coaching England, and to becoming a popular Sky cricket commentator, after-dinner speaker and author. He played for Lancashire seconds at Wantage Road in the early 1960s:

I remember how we used to go from one end of the cricket ground across the football pitch at the far end to get to the County Hotel, the pub on the corner of Abington Avenue, for lunch and tea on the first floor. There was a widespread view on the cricket circuit that the two most dilapidated pavilions on the county circuit were New Road, Worcester, and Wantage Road. One had to be careful not to get splinters in the feet, walking across the changing room floor.

The County in Abington Avenue.

The ground had little to commend it to the artistically minded. It was set amidst terraced houses and with only glimpses of treetops and of the spire of St Matthew's church. Mike Selvey the Middlesex and England opening bowler, thought the ground *'a soulless place with an industrial feel'* although he did retain a soft spot for the pavilion, nostalgically recalling *'the steep splintery steps down to invariably cold mildewy basement showers'* and the viewing area *'consisting of several rows of red velvet tip-up cinema seats, taken from the local Roxy.'*

The ground was vulnerable to the south-west winds, which did have the advantage of aiding prompt drying of the wicket. The cricket club shared the property with Northampton Town football club. The north end of the cricket outfield overlapped with where the football wingers would ply their skills during the muddy winters, leaving the turf rough when the cricket season started. The football stands would in time be replaced by a custom-built cricket centre, happily leaving unchanged both the charming half-timbered scorebox and Gallone's ice cream van stationed at mid-wicket. David vividly remembers that outfield:

> It was diabolical, particularly in early season when we would be playing first-class cricket during the day and the Cobblers would play soccer at night. It was a great way when fielding to loosen a few teeth, bending for the ball. Most used to stop it with the foot and then pick it up.

All second eleven championship fixtures were two-day affairs. David had met most of his new colleagues in the nets, several of whom he was to know well over the next few years: the Watts brothers, Brian Crump, wicket-keeper Laurie Johnson, fast bowler Mike Dilley and Malcolm Scott the Geordie soccer player and left-arm spinner. The captain was none other than Vince Broderick - David now realising how important it had been for him to bowl so well at him in that trial the previous year.

The game on June 1 was against Worcestershire. David took a wicket in each innings and watched leg-spinner Peter Watts wrap up a ten-wicket home team victory. David managed nine runs in his first innings - possibly giving a misleading impression of his run-scoring ability. As early as his third match he began to take wickets, with match figures of eight for 82 at Wantage Road against Leicestershire seconds.

Brian Crump has good memories of those early days:

Fred, as we called him, after his third forename, was a quiet man with a retiring nature. He was not a bowler with a personality which encouraged an aggressive attitude when bowling. I doubt if this made him any less of a bowler, as each fast bowler has his own attitude and his own dedication…..There was of course in those days not nearly as much aggro on the field as there is today; there was no sledging, and only occasional light banter. David just got on with the job of bowling and did not bother to engage in the banter.

He was a gentle giant of a man, his 6'7" towering over my 5'4". His gentle nature can be demonstrated by a game in which we played together in 1959 at Corby for Northants seconds against Lancashire seconds (David's fifth match for the seconds). Harry Pilling was playing for Lancashire and came out to bat at about number eight, all 5'2" of him. David obviously thought he was a youngster who needed careful handling and cut his run down in order not to bowl too fast at him. Harry top-scored with 36 not out.

David played in 15 of the 20 second eleven fixtures, finishing a promising fourth in the bowling averages, with 38 wickets at 17 apiece. His 13 innings with the bat produced 56 runs and, thanks to four not outs and a highest score of 16, an average of six, a mountain of a figure he seemed unlikely to scale again.

> In that gloriously hot summer I greatly enjoyed myself, travelling the country, playing the game I loved, meeting people, learning a different life, and being paid to do all that.

David was delighted to be told that the county liked what they saw of his bowling and wanted him to become qualified with a view to competing for a place in the full county side the following season, 1960.

> To qualify to play for the county I needed to complete a consecutive twelve-month residential qualification, so I stayed in Northampton for the winter. About this time Northampton Saints rugby team came calling and wanted me to go training with them. The cricket club immediately vetoed this on the grounds that my long legs and other bits belonged to them. A rugby career nipped in the bud!
>
> The club found me a winter job with a local building firm. In 1959 car ownership and driving licences were scarce but I had moved on from my Harley Davidson to a Vincent Comet motorcycle, and to the first of a number of cheap pick-up trucks. I was therefore doubly welcome at the builders because of my driving licence and was immediately promoted to driver of the works bus. I also learnt how to dig drains and lay concrete! I made friends with an Irish groundworks gang and was invited

A Vincent Comet motorcycle replaced the Harley Davidson...

> to join them for a drink. I found the pub, just off the Market Square in town, and walked in. A sudden silence descended on the place, and many pairs of eyes met mine. Then a deep voice bellowed 'David – you found us - what'll you have?' The hubbub started up again. Sadly, after a few visits, I was summoned to the Northants' secretary's office. A club member had seen me going into 'the Irish pub' and I was told to forget my new friends.

in the finest
tradition of
Northampton
craftsmanship

David spend the first winter getting to know the town of Northampton. It had an interesting history. In the 12th and early 13th centuries it had been one of the main centres of England, having been a royal centre in Saxon times, owing much of its growth to its geographical situation in the middle of the country, astride a number of important routes. The shoe industry, the basis of Northampton's future wealth, became important in the second half of the 17th century, and by the 1870s almost half the town's population was employed in that industry. That growth was later to slow as businesses failed to expand and fewer new houses were built. By the second half of the 20th century, the population of 105,000 made it a small market town.

> In what was a small, underpopulated county, the county cricket club had struggled to survive. Having joined the county championship in 1905, the county could only finish higher than second from bottom of the championship on a mere four occasions between 1923 and 1948. That history mattered not at all to me: I was going to become a county cricketer.

At its lowest ebb in the 1930s the playing staff consisted of only 16 players. One of those was locally born Cyril Perkins. He held an unwanted cricket record. In his 56 first-class appearances for Northants from 1934 to 1937, taking 93 wickets at 35 apiece, he was not once on the winning side. That dismal sequence was to continue after he left the staff at the end of the 1937 season – extending to 99 matches without a win up till May 1939. A record of wonderful unsuccess. Perkins moved to Ipswich and played for Suffolk in the Minor Counties championship 1939 and again post war, whilst working as cricket coach at Ipswich School. He retired in 1967, having made 105 Suffolk appearances, four of them alongside David, whose journey between those counties had taken the opposite direction.

After World War II things slowly began to look up for Northants. Two men in particular played a major role in improving the fortunes. Besides being home to a significant element of England's boot and shoe manufacturing Northampton was also home to British Timken, manufacturers of roller bearings for the expanding motor industry. Its chairman Sir John Pascoe was the county cricket club's chief benefactor. His generosity and passion for the game and desire to help Northants to success meant that a number of cricketers were attracted to join what was otherwise an unfashionable club by the offer of winter employment at his company. The other key figure was Ken Turner who served the county club from 1949 to 1985 first as Assistant Secretary and then as Secretary, whose contribution to the success of the club in the 1960s was enormous.

Freddie Brown, 22 times capped by England, left Surrey in 1949 to captain Northants as an amateur whilst working for Pascoe at British Timken. He immediately completed the exclusive cricketer's double of 1000 runs and 100 wickets in a season. He was soon joined by Jock Livingston, a highly skilled player of spin bowling. In his native Australia Livingston had been regarded as a future Test player, a chance he abandoned by emigrating to England in 1947 to play in the Lancashire League, whence he was recruited by Northants in 1950.

The 'small county' perception represented a barrier to the recruitment of top-class players, but there was another factor – particularly for fast bowlers – the Wantage Road wicket. It was naturally slow and required huge effort from the quicker bowlers to extract any lift or pace. A story from the mid-1950s makes this plain: Frank Tyson was for a period in the 1950s the foremost fast bowler not only at Northants but also for England. He was strongly encouraged by Len Hutton and others to leave Northants and to return to his native Lancashire because, so they said, if he was to continue to bowl on the dead Wantage Road wicket it was likely he would be out of Test cricket within two years. He stayed, but by 1960 aged 30 had had enough, retiring after only seven seasons of English cricket.

Spinners and fast bowlers were therefore important items on Livingston's shopping list as he searched the professional leagues for budding talent. He was successful: Australian George Tribe joined from the Central Lancashire league in 1951, University student Tyson from the North Staffordshire in 1952, Keith Andrew joined British Timken as a designer in 1953, and Australian Jack Manning from the leagues in 1954. David was Jock's capture in 1958.

Under Brown's leadership, Pascoe's backing and with Turner and Livingston's recruits, the county broke its traditional mooring to the bottom of the table and began to achieve some table respectability. Brown at 43 handed over the captaincy in 1954 to the long-serving opening bat, professional Dennis Brookes, who immediately took the team to championship finishes of seventh, seventh, fourth and a splendid second place in 1957, the county's best finish since 1912. Livingston and Brookes had recruited as a future captain Raman Subba Row, the Surrey batsman later to play for England, who had been about to retire from the game to train as an accountant but was persuaded to move to a job in Northampton and to play for the county in 1955. Brookes, a popular man both as captain and later as chairman of the local magistrates' bench, agreed, with generous political sensitivity, to hand over the captaincy to the amateur Subba Row in 1957.

By the time of David's advent, the successful team of the mid to late 1950s had begun to break up. A succession of retirements removed Jock Livingston after the 1957 season, Tribe, Manning, and Brookes in 1959 and Tyson to become a full-time schoolteacher in Australia at the end of 1960. Raman Subba Row had taken over the captaincy at a difficult time. Out of the 17 counties, Northants came fourth in 1958, eleventh in 1959 and ninth in 1960.

So much for the recent history of the club David had been asked to join. What cricketing issues faced the English and international cricketing worlds at this time?

First and foremost, the amateur and professional divide was reaching a breaking point. David was about to be thrust into an historically significant period of social change affecting the game. Cricket was the last bastion of class distinction in sport. Its structure maintained the distinction which had begun in the 19th century of two types of player – amateur and professional. The amateurs traditionally were those who were able to play without payment. The professionals were paid to play (particularly in the old days to provide net bowling practice for the wealthy amateurs who employed them). The distinction remained even into the late 1950s, when a few grounds still had two dressing rooms for each team, to enable the amateurs to avoid changing alongside their paid colleagues. Laurie Johnson, who was with Surrey from 1953 to 1958, recalls the room at the top of the Oval stand where amateurs Stuart Surridge and Peter May would have the assistance of the dressing room attendant when changing for the game. When Micky Stewart succeeded May as captain, he declined that supposed entitlement, changing instead with the rest of the team downstairs.

The different image Laurie retains of the consummate professional – Alec Bedser – was exemplified for him by Alec's simple lunch regime: a sandwich and two bottles of Guinness stout. The stereotypical amateur tended to be someone from a monied background, from an independent school and often the product of a university. The professionals were supposedly drawn from the working class. This social divide was fortified by the tradition that the county captain must be from the amateur camp. Lord Hawke, the dominant figure in Yorkshire cricket in the early years of the 20th century, preached a gospel at the 1925 Yorkshire annual meeting which was observed until the 1950s: *'Pray God no professional will ever captain the England side. I love professionals, every one of them, but we have always had an amateur skipper.'*

To improve their chance of captaining England, Hammond (just before the war) and Edrich (just after it) opted to give up their professional status to become amateurs. Although Len Hutton became the first professional to captain England when appointed in 1952 (having declined to turn amateur for the purpose), his county, Yorkshire, did not appoint a professional until Vic Wilson in 1959. Other counties began to take the same route, Warwickshire appointing Tom Dollery, Worcestershire choosing Don Kenyon, Somerset Harold Stephenson, and Keith Andrew in 1962 appointed Northants captain in succession to Raman Subba Row.

There were in the 1950s very few 'true' amateurs. Most would be employed in some manner within the county club or found employment elsewhere by the club. Trevor Bailey was an example of the former - his role as Essex club secretary enabling him to maintain his amateur status – and Freddie Brown at Northants an example of the latter. The process whereby ways were found to finance players who did not wish to be seen as professional invaded not only cricket but other amateur games, including tennis and rugby union. Despite this shamateurism, as it was known, the old regime still had legs. In 1958 an MCC enquiry concluded that *'it was important to preserve in first-class cricket the leadership and general approach to the game traditionally associated with the amateur player… The distinctive status of the amateur cricketer was not obsolete, was of great value to the game, and should be preserved.'*

But this proved to be a final flaring of the dying embers and the end was in sight as David joined Northamptonshire in 1959. Within three years another MCC committee had recommended the abolition of the amateur status, and the 1963 season started with all first-class cricketers as players. The traditional Gentlemen v Players match of the season was to be no more. Norman Preston, the editor of *Wisden*, quoting Sir Jack Hobbs as being sad to see the end of an era, himself commented *'we live in a changing world. Conditions are vastly different to the days of our grandparents; but is it wise to throw everything overboard?'* Viewing it from the comfort of half a century later it seems surprising that this divisive system lasted so long. The amateurs were quickly content with their new status. David quotes one of them:

Trevor Bailey was an old school amateur who made the transition to becoming a professional player easily. He was one of the great all-rounders from just before my time and left a real mark on Essex and England cricket.

The covering of pitches against bad weather was a controversial topic then. It has become a commonplace matter today. In the years leading up to the Second World War MCC as the guardian of the laws of cricket disagreed with the stance of Australia that pitches should be covered against poor weather. Post-war, Australia persuaded several visiting countries to agree to full covering throughout Test series in Australia. It was not until December 1952 that MCC finally agreed to that, as an experiment, for the 1954/55 series.

In the meantime, English pitches remained uncovered. The 1958 English summer was a very wet one, and attendances dropped by half a million from the year before. It was determined that from the start of the 1959 season counties could cover the pitch on each night of the match and if necessary, throughout Sunday when there was no play. In the event of rain during the hours of play, pitch covering was permitted for the duration of that interruption. Ironically the 1959 season proved to be a wonderful summer with days on end of glorious sunshine.

The new covering rule brought a happy change in the attitude of captains and players. More attacking cricket was adopted, declarations were made, and the spectators returned. Test match pitch covering regulations were then brought into line with those in the county championship. But the debate was not over: the fear that the art of leg-spin was being discouraged by this almost total covering meant that from 1963 the whole pitch was covered only before the start of the match and at weekends.

Social pressure built in the late 1950s for a more libertarian approach to sport and entertainment taking place on the Lord's day. The Sunday Observance Act was to remain in full force until amendments in the 1960s permitted Sunday sport. The first step for cricket was the introduction of one day cricket in 1963, in the form of a knockout cup competition sponsored by Gillette. It was to prove a great attraction to the public. The second was a one-day league, started in 1969, sponsored by John Player and Son, the cigarette brand, to be played on the only day of the week not occupied by the county championship – Sunday. The county championship had been the only first-class competitive structure in the country for the last hundred years. Professional cricket was now to become a seven day a week job.

The world David was joining saw attempts being made to deal with two important and highly controversial technical cricketing matters, which particularly affected fast bowlers. The first was throwing: the MCC recommended, and the county captains accepted, that bowling with a bent arm constituted throwing and had to be severely dealt with. It was noted that in England in 1958 not once had a bowler been called for throwing. The laxity was particularly evident in Australia. As James Coyne has noted in *The Cricketer*, Jim Laker, batting on the 1958/59 Ashes tour against two bowlers widely viewed as throwers, Ian Meckiff at one end and Jim Burke at the other, turned around to slip fielder Neil Harvey and said *'it's like standing in the middle of a darts match.'* In 1960, as an experiment, a note was added to the laws to the effect that a ball would be deemed to have been thrown if in the opinion of either umpire there had been a sudden straightening of the bowling arm.

The second issue was drag – the practice of fast bowlers dragging their back foot across the bowling crease in the delivery stride. It had bedevilled cricket around the world for some years. It arose from the fact that the no-ball rule was based on the back foot. So long as the fast bowler brought down his back foot behind the bowling crease, he was permitted to drag that foot through the crease, usually aided by the wearing of a steel toe cap, before releasing the ball, without regard for the landing position of the front foot. This meant that the ball was often released from 20 yards or less, giving the batsman less time to play his shot than if no drag was permitted. *'Having the ball thrown at you from 18 yards blights the sunniest disposition',* wrote Peter May.

> *Having the ball thrown at you from 18 yards blights the sunniest disposition...*

Attempts were made to eradicate this unfair advantage by requiring the bowler to land his back foot some distance behind the bowling crease, at a point marked by the umpire with a white disc. In 1963 this unsatisfactory no-ball rule was dramatically rewritten – so that the position of the front rather than back foot was the determining factor. From then on, a ball would be judged legitimate only if some part of the front foot landed behind the front, popping, crease. It was to have an effect on David's progress in the game.

David was set to play in a decade which saw more change than any decade since the late 19th century. Lack of money in the game led to sponsorship, TV rights, overseas players, one day cricket, air travel tours, and the end of the amateur.

1960 HOME SEASON

National service ends.

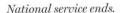

Several well-known players had retired from the county scene in the winter, including notably Jim Laker, Godfrey Evans, Cyril Washbrook and the Northants duo of Brookes and Tribe. Alex Bannister of the *Daily Mail* named some youngsters aiming to fill the gaps, including *'David Larter of Northants, Barry Knight of Essex and the Watts brothers of Northants, all emerging from their apprenticeships'*, and Tom Cartwright of Warwickshire and Butch White of Hampshire as youngsters to watch out for.

After the blissful sunshine of 1959, the cricketing summer of 1960 was bedevilled by appalling weather, causing gates, which had revived, to fall away. It was also beset by politics. Anglo-South African relations were at their worst for 50 years, just as the South African cricket team prepared to tour England, a tour described by John Arlott as *'the unhappiest ever made by a party of overseas cricketers in England,'* plagued by anti-apartheid protest. The fact that South Africa lost the Test series outright in the first three Tests - the last two Tests being drawn – was an additional debit factor.

The litany of woes did not end there: South Africa's opening bowler Geoff Griffin had twice been no-balled for throwing in South Africa, and it was a very poor decision by the South African Cricket Association to choose him for the tour of England, fully aware of the topicality in England of the throwing issue. Opening the bowling at Lord's in the second Test he achieved the first ever hat-trick in a Test there, but was called eleven times for throwing by umpire Frank Lee, the first instance of penalised throwing in any Test in England and only the third in all Tests. He did not bowl again on the tour.

David Sheppard, the only ordained minister to play Test cricket for England, and as cricket writer Rob Steen remarked, *'the only man to achieve the double of England captain and Bishop of Liverpool,'* publicly refused to play against the visiting South Africans, an all-white team representing a country of which their skin colour was a tiny minority. His view was that *'apartheid drew cricket into one of the great issues of humanity, and a great issue of justice for the Church of England.'* In 1968 he called for and spoke at a special general meeting of the MCC at which a vote of no confidence in the committee for its handling of the d'Oliveira matter was debated but defeated.

Sheppard's commitment to his church work meant that he played only 10 games during the period 1958 to 1961. In 1962 he was to return to the crease for half a season, on the strength of which he was selected for the 1962/63 tour, his third Ashes Test series, in which he scored the second of his two Ashes centuries.

In the county championship the greener pitches made it a vintage year for quicker bowlers, nine out of the top ten in the averages being medium-pace or above, the only spinner being Ray Illingworth. England's opening attack in the five Tests against South Africa consisted of Trueman and Statham, with help from Alan Moss in two Tests, and Ted Dexter as a seamer in the other three.

For David this was a season of high expectation. Could he do well enough for the county second eleven to graduate from apprentice to full county player? Frank Tyson was due to retire at the season's end, and David wanted to get the call to fill those very large shoes. He started the season well; after half a dozen games for the seconds he had taken 17 wickets at 16 apiece.

Then came June 4 – David's red letter day. The *Guardian* noted the event: *'David Larter makes his first county championship appearance for Northamptonshire at Derby today. At 6 foot 7½ he will be the tallest man in first-class cricket. He is a fast bowler.'*

Derbyshire batted first and were bowled out for 191, David conceding 10 runs from his 10 overs, without a wicket. Northants batted and declared at 286 for 7 wickets. When Derbyshire batted again David took his first wicket in first-class cricket by bowling Derbyshire's opener Charlie Lee for nine, and went on to capture two more, delighted to end with three for 35. Northants were set 159 to win in just under two hours but with Derby's veteran fast bowler Les Jackson wreaking havoc, making the ball both fly and creep as he took all five wickets to fall, Northants struggled to 51 before rain intervened and the match was drawn.

It was an early masterclass for David. He was eager to learn. In the margins of the match he had the chance to talk not only to Les Jackson but also to the great man – Frank Tyson. The first impression was a little disappointing:

> For a man who was a trained schoolteacher, he did not communicate that well. Perhaps I was too far down the food chain to bother with. Do not get me wrong, he was perfectly friendly, but cricket-wise little was forthcoming. Frank did introduce me to Les Jackson, and after having bought them both a beer, a sort of mangled discussion about the art of fast bowling ensued. A cricket ball appeared, and fingers were wrapped around it and wrists cocked, but as the Australian Jeff Thomson has said, it appears the secret is to 'wang it down the other end as quickly as possible'. All Frank's pace came from a massive pair of shoulders and a very pronounced 'windmill' arm action. Amazingly for an intelligent man he did not seem to know how he produced such speed. Swing and pace variations were strangers to Frank. In the county nets he frightened all our lads as he just could not bowl slow.

Tyson was as quick as anyone in the world in 1954/5 on the MCC tour to Australia. Bradman believed then he was the fastest bowler he had ever seen, and Bradman had been Larwood's specific target in 1932/3; Charlie Elliott, a first-class cricketer who became an international umpire, thought that Tyson was the first bowler he had seen to equal Larwood's speed. Eric Russell, who opened the batting for both Middlesex and England, remembers the story of Tyson bowling a bouncer at Old Trafford in 1954 which hit the sightscreen without bouncing again beyond the bemused batsman. To show how the day and the conditions can create different experiences Geoff Smith of Essex says: *I faced Tyson but did not find him as quick as the South Africans Adcock and Heine.*

In English domestic cricket Tyson suffered from the six-day weekly grind of county cricket and from the slowness of the Wantage Road pitch, but on away wickets he was lethal. He wrote: '*to bowl quick is to revel in the glad animal action; to thrill in physical prowess and to enjoy a certain sneaking feeling of superiority over the other mortals who play the game. No batsman likes quick bowling, and this knowledge gives one a sense of omnipotence.*' A credo shared by David but expressed in Jeff Thomson's blunter phrase.

In his second county match, on June 9, David earned an early first national newspaper headline – from the *Daily Telegraph*: *'Larter claims 3 Lancashire wickets'*. Old Trafford was a pitch which suited the faster bowlers, particularly with rain to freshen it. David was able to make the ball lift alarmingly from a good length, removing three batsmen for a cost of only 12 runs during an opening day limited by rain to less than 3 hours.

I remember the feeling which ran through the team, Jim Watts recalls, *watching Tyson bowling at one end and David at the other: that this was something very special. Lancashire's Alan Wharton said afterwards that he had been unable to decide which was the safer end to bat from.*

Lancashire were bowled out for 156, with Tyson taking two for 64 and David three for 32 from 23 overs. Northants batted well to take a first innings lead of 139. David's batting, upon which this account will not often dwell, did not last long. Going in, as he invariably did, at number eleven 'next to the roller', his first knock for the county resulted in a score which would recur throughout his career – 0 not out.

A grim rearguard action by Lancashire, saving a draw at 113 for nine, ended a grim Whit weekend match, cold and dull, in front of almost empty spectator stands. But for David the sun had been shining, and the crowd had been huge. He had found good rhythm and lift, dismissing Lancashire's first three batsmen for only three runs, including Alan Wharton to a stunning catch by Barrick in the gully. Both he and Tyson bowled throughout to eight close fielders. David's six wickets in the match for 65 came from a very economical 36 overs. He was described by the *Telegraph*, embarrassingly for David given the identity of his opening bowling partner, as *'the new Tyson'*, whilst England and Lancashire local legend Cyril Washbrook wrote that he looked *'a fine prospect with a splendid easy action'*.

David's third match, his first at the Wantage Road headquarters, was against Gloucestershire, captained by the commanding figure of Tom Graveney. David failed to take a wicket in Gloucester's 302 for five declared, although Robin Marlar, Sussex's former captain, in his newspaper column, noted that Gloucester's opening stand of 134 had been achieved 'Tyson and Larter notwithstanding'. Thanks to a gritty display from all-rounder Brian Crump on his first-class debut Northants narrowly averted an innings defeat. Crump was to become David's opening bowler partner for the rest of his career.

David hoped his nerves would not show as he bowled to Graveney, one of his schoolboy heroes:

Tom Graveney was the one man you did not want to see walking out to bat. It seemed to be so easy, indeed, one could only admire the grace and style.

Gloucestershire's opening bat was another remarkable sportsman. Arthur Milton's first match for the county had been against Northants in 1948. He was capped by England ten years later, scoring a century on debut. As an Arsenal wing forward he won a single England soccer cap against Austria in 1951, deputising for Stanley Matthews and Tom Finney.

David's fourth match was away against Leicestershire, by a strange coincidence captained by the only other England cricket and soccer double international then playing, Willie Watson. Watson had played soccer for England four times. His debut was in 1949 when England defeated Northern Ireland 9-2. Picked for the 1950 World Cup squad to Brazil, he did not play, and his last cap was against Yugoslavia in November of that year. He played the first of his 23 cricket Tests the following summer, scoring 57 in his first innings against Dudley Nourse's South African side, and his last against the visiting New Zealanders in 1959.

The *Telegraph* produced another headline for David: '*Larter bruises Dickie Bird's ribs*' as Jim Swanton took his first look at the new boy:

'*At Grace Rd, Leicester, Tyson and the 6'7" former Framlingham College fast bowler David Larter, bowled three overs each, with Bird being hit in the ribs by Larter. Bird was caught in the gully to a wide ball short of a length from Larter who was operating towards the livelier end, as he forced the Leicestershire innings onto the rocks in an eight over spell which brought him four wickets for one leg-side boundary. His height and the batsmen's understandable apprehensions about the pitch were jointly responsible for the collapse. At the moment Larter is learning his trade. All one can say as yet is that his action appears to offer more scope for improvement than those of Sayer and Rhodes, who are the leading members of England's junior fast bowling squad. Also, he is never likely to bowl an over in less than three minutes given his follow-through ends almost within handshake of the batsman, and he has 40 paces to go before he's back to his mark.*'

... including the heartening spectacle of breaking Terry Spencer's middle stump...

The first innings gave David his best figures yet with five for 20, including the heartening spectacle of breaking Terry Spencer's middle stump, as he and Tyson demolished Leicestershire for 100. Rain again kept Northants from that elusive first victory, and they remained stuck fast to the bottom of the table, with three losses and seven draws from their 10 matches.

Four consecutive home matches followed. The first, at out-ground Rushden against Kent, for whom England opener Peter Richardson scored 96, was drawn. This was followed by the first win of the season, by six wickets over Yorkshire at Northampton, from which David was rested, his place in the side being taken by Gordon Williamson, whom David had originally displaced, and who did well with five wickets in the match. Buoyed by this change in fortunes, the side, with David restored, then recorded an uplifting victory over Worcestershire by five wickets.

Clement Freud, reporting for the *Guardian* under the headline *'Makings of a giant'*, noted that the Worcester match was the first to be played on a new pitch, part of the square at Wantage Road having been dug up and relaid during the winter in the hope of getting more life from it. The pitch was certainly livelier than its long-held reputation for docility. David took great advantage of this putting in his best performance to date, tearing through Worcester's batting as they were dismissed for 115. Tyson surprisingly conceded half that total in his nine overs, Dick Richardson taking 28 off him in two overs. In Freud's words *'while Worcestershire took 54 runs off England's old typhoon, a new hurricane got the wickets at the other end. Larter, 6 foot 7½ inch Suffolk-born fast bowler, claimed 6 for 26.'* Stephen Chalke in his biography of Keith Andrew was blunter: *'…David Larter out-bowled the ageing Frank Tyson…a new generation was tasting its first successes.'*

Stirred by this lese majeste, Tyson, long a sufferer from the passive Northampton pitches, responded to the new more sporting wicket in the second innings by taking four of the first seven Worcestershire wickets. David took the other three to give him his best match figures to date of nine for 85. Worcestershire's formidable opening pair of Jack Flavell and Len Coldwell took 10 wickets between them.

Ray Illingworth is of the view that as even Frank Tyson's fearsome speed was negated by the slow wicket at Wantage Road, David would have done better to have played at Lord's, Hove or Trent Bridge. Barry Knight expressed the same opinion, adding that David would have got stacks of wickets on Essex's green pastures.

David agrees:

> I managed to survive the Wantage Road pitches, made for batsmen and spinners, although I would of course have got more help from the tracks named by Ray and Barry. Ray's suggestion of Lord's is the best one: Alan Moss retired after the 1963 season. Wouldn't it have been great bowling in front of the selectors and the crowds at HQ! Dream on!

A three day break – a rare occurrence in the relentless county schedule of the 1960s – was followed by a trip to out-ground Peterborough for the return match against Leicestershire, memorable for David only because he scored his first runs for the county, two not out. In Leicester's brief knock David rather than Tyson took the first over, but only three overs were possible before rain saw an end to proceedings.

It was at this point that the popular press began to show signs of over-excitement about the new fast bowler. Norman Ford in the *Daily Mirror*, pointing out that England must soon find replacements for Statham and Trueman, invited the selectors to pick 20 year old Larter, *'who last month shattered the cream of Lancashire's batting and pulverised Worcester with 6-26'* for the third Test against the South Africans instead of Statham.

The *Daily Telegraph* was more restrained in respect of a cricketer who had only played seven first-class matches: *'Young David Larter must surely be a strong candidate for MCC's winter tour of New Zealand.'* The tour was to be funded by the New Zealand Cricket authorities, keen to renew interest in the game there. MCC had agreed to assist in this endeavour by sending a side to play three unofficial tests and several other matches, using the trip as a testing ground for promising young English cricketers.

On July 12, taking advantage of play being rained off in the Leicestershire match, the county set off for its West Country tour, with nine days of consecutive cricket against Gloucestershire, Somerset, and Glamorgan. From Gloucester, where Northants notched up their third win of the season, the *Telegraph's* Ron Roberts commented: *'One is eager to see Larter on a quick wicket for he has a nice action and moves well for such a big man'*. Whilst the Northants spinners dominated, David in the second innings removed three of the first four Gloucestershire batsmen.

David's first visit to Cardiff on July 20 saw Northants well beaten by an all-Welsh Glamorgan team captained by Welsh rugby international Wilf Wooller, with off-spinner Don Shepherd taking nine for 48 in a remarkable 49 overs. David conceded 38 runs in Glamorgan's second innings plus eight in wides. Wicket-keeper Laurie Johnson recalls the event: *David was striving too much for pace on the wet wicket and I was throwing myself around so much to reach some of the wide ones that I had to leave the field with a leg injury. Our opening batsman Brian Reynolds had to take my place.*

I was fortunate to catch the end of the distinguished career of Glamorgan's Allan Watkins – this was the last time he was to play against us. He was a great all-rounder. After retirement he was to become a much-loved cricket coach at Framlingham College.

With 15 Tests to his name Watkins was famous as a close fielder. He could 'catch flies' at short leg. In Arlott's words *'he caught the uncatchable so often as to have made the impossible his normal standard.'*

A quirk of the fixture scheduling meant that the day after the Cardiff match the two teams resumed hostilities in the return match at Northampton. The proceeds went towards Des Barrick's benefit after 10 years with Northants. This time Northants won by three wickets off the last ball of the match. David encountered fellow fast bowler Welshman Jeff Jones, with whom he was to room both in Australia and in India, where they developed a friendship, in David's words *swapping hints and bits and pieces about bowling.* David had a high opinion of Jones's bowling, genuinely quick and *'really bringing left-arm over the wicket fast bowling to the fore.'*

It was only my fifth first-class game, Jeff Jones, 60 years later, recalls. *I was 18 years old. I had been bowled by the slow left-armer Mick Allen for a duck in the first innings. I was very nervous as I went out to bat in the second innings as Tyson and David were bowling. Our England all-rounder Jim McConnon was 20 odd not out facing Tyson who had built up a fair head of steam. As the ball yet again passed the outside edge of Jim's bat he would smile and say 'well bowled' to Tyson. Tyson was infuriated by this and bowled even faster. At the end of the over I was more than happy to tell Jim he should continue to take Tyson's bowling whilst I faced David. David clean bowled me second ball, but at least I didn't have to face Tyson. I guess it was fair enough – I had bowled David for a duck when he had batted!*

David's cricket education was furthered by watching the performance of former England bowler Alan Moss as he demolished the Northants batting at Kettering in the last week of July. Moss, finding more pace in the pitch than any other bowler during the match, removed six batsmen for 13 runs in 13 overs as Northants were dismissed for 58, Moss ending with a career best of eight for 31.

Peter Parfitt, the Middlesex and England all-rounder, remembers facing David in that Kettering match. *He livened me up; had me jumping around a bit. He had prodigious bounce. If anything, it wasn't a quick track – probably heavily marled. I survived his attack and went on to score 78, caught Larter bowled Crump. We scored 297 with Bob Gale scoring a century, which makes David's figures of 2 for 40 in 17 overs a good reflection of how well he bowled. Tyson also took two wickets but went for 73 from his 23 overs.*

Tyson was certainly the quickest I have faced; the most lethal was undoubtedly Charlie Griffith when he toured here in 1963. Trueman was the best of the lot, swinging the ball at pace and as strong as a bullock. Fred had aggression whilst David was the opposite – amiable, sociable, and reserved, although I would not call him shy. His great strength was that he could get bounce from a length. Both Snow and Jones could be very quick at times, as could Rumsey. David could certainly generate quite fearsome pace. He got his Test wickets at 25 apiece, which compares favourably with Trueman at 21, Statham 24 and Snow 26.

I was to play with David in his first Test when he got nine wickets – a very good performance. He was later to get seven against South Africa. In fact, I played in seven of his 10 Tests and toured with him four times – two Ashes tours plus East Africa in late 1963 and India in early 1964 – so I got to know him reasonably well. In Tests I fielded either gully or second slip to Colin Cowdrey (which was a bit of a nightmare as he didn't go much to his left or right, which meant wicket-keeper Jim Parks had to cover to his right and I had to cover to my left). So, I had a pretty good view of David's speed and accuracy. I would not call him inaccurate, like Harmison for example. He had this laid-back approach, but he was always a trier.

Northants ended the season strongly, losing only one of their remaining seven matches and winning three. In the early August visit to Leyton to play Essex David took three wickets in the match, one of which was that of Essex opener Geoff Smith, caught by Frank Tyson:

This was the first time I had faced David Larter, Geoff recounts. Over the next five years I was to face him seven times in four different championship matches and he got me out four times, lbw twice and caught close in twice. He was not in the mould of many quick bowlers, who would give a display of histrionics each time you played and missed, or in rare cases, like Peter Loader of Surrey, a volley of personal abuse – pretty unpleasant. In David's case he would just turn on his heel and get back to his mark for the next ball. He was a very nice, decent, man. And make no mistake he was quick. An example of this was the match at Clacton in July 1965 when David tore into us on a wicket which bruised each time the ball pitched, an effect of the tide coming in alongside the ground. David had me lbw in the first innings and caught by Prideaux in the second. I actually edged the ball firmly on to my pad for the lbw; my opening partner Gordon Barker smiling as he said he was not sure if I had instead been given out caught behind.

Attitudes were different then. We all walked if we snicked the ball to the wicket-keeper. In fact our skipper Doug Insole, for whom I had the highest regard as a captain, used to say to umpires that as we always helped them by walking, he hoped for some reciprocity from them on doubtful lbw calls.

The marquees were up amongst the tree-fringed boundary at Wellingborough School for the visit of Sussex on August 6. The Sussex opening batsmen came out of the thatched pavilion and stepped onto the field of play from the WG Grace paving stone, rescued by the school's geography master from Grace's home in Bristol before it was demolished in the 1930s. The process became a procession as Brian Crump and David with four wickets each rolled Sussex over for 182. Six wickets from left-arm spinner Mick Allen dispatched Sussex for 91 in their second innings to give Northants an eight-wicket victory within two days.

Opening the bowling opposite Tyson, David found himself for the first time up against Ted Dexter, as well as Jim Parks and the Nawab of Pataudi, both of whom he clean bowled. Tony Pawson in the *Observer* noted that Pataudi handled the Northants attack well but was *'less happy against Larter's speed... Larter's persistence soon ended the innings, despite some great batting by Parks'*. David's career highest batting score leapt to 10 before he was caught by Dexter:

> Ted Dexter was a brilliant attacking player, physically imposing and always keen to dominate the bowling. Jim Parks was one of the nice guys. He was to keep wicket to me quite a lot and he somehow always seemed to be in the thick of any party going on. He could bat a bit as well.
>
> Tiger Pataudi was an attractive and stylish batsman, brilliantly overcoming the handicap of little vision in his right eye as a result of a road accident in Hove whilst captaining Oxford University. He was schooled in England and was very anglicised. Although in India he was the equivalent of royalty I found him very approachable and friendly. He was to make his Test debut at 20 during MCC's tour to India in 1961 before being catapulted into the captaincy in 1962 in his fourth Test, taking over from the badly injured Nari Contractor in the West Indies. At that time he was the youngest captain in Test history.

The return match against Sussex at Hove took place only five days later. Ian Peebles, the old Middlesex and England leg-spinner, liked David's action – *'his run up is smooth but lively and his action is high and wheeling. A very fine prospect.'* Alan Ross of the *Guardian* was viewing David for the first time: *'Larter, newly nominated for New Zealand, was downhill whilst Tyson bowled uphill from the sea. At present not much body comes into the rather hurried, loose, and uncoordinated action but steepness of trajectory and an evident ability to swing either way makes him an interesting proposition for the future. Dexter was nearly bowled by a beauty from Larter that darted away off the seam, and twice just stabbed yorkers out of his stumps.'*

Hove was another of those venues where David might have liked, in an ideal world, to have plied his trade, a wicket to give speed bowlers encouragement. To bowl downhill there meant running down a ten foot slope towards the sea end, whence borne on a southerly wind the sea fret would blow in to freshen the wicket. The bowler, turning back towards the north to his mark would view, in front of the stern blocks of flats, the customers in their deckchairs pausing their consumption of ice creams to offer polite applause for the bowler's efforts. A family ground, Hove befitted a club adorned by families of cricketers: Gilligan, Tate, Langridge, Cox, Oakes, Parks, Griffith, and still they come – Lenham, Buss and Wells.

The match was drawn. The Northants coach then pointed north for the return journey to Northampton where Lancashire were to be the visitors the next day.

Travel was a major part of a cricketer's life. In the early 1960s, when there were two championship games each week, with Sunday off, half the counties would hit the roads every Tuesday and Friday evening for their matches starting the next day. The mileage covered was huge, journeys often involving more than 100 miles.

> Our club policy was that the team would travel to and from away matches by coach, following one player's career-ending private car accident some years before. Most of the other counties allowed players to travel by car. I was to get exemption when Test and other matches often put me in vastly different places for me to rejoin the lads.
>
> We were blessed with a regular extraordinary driver called Chris. A very good driver, affable chap and budding operatic tenor, we were often treated to his efforts, in Italian. He forgot the words regularly, but we found that with La La La we could all join in. He was a lot older than us and could occasionally be persuaded to tell the odd hair-raising story of his war as a special services operator – if we supplied the beer! Card games (but no money) were a way of passing time, as was listening to Colin Milburn's assessment of the local crumpet as we went through towns. I remember Crumpy had to sit up front next to Chris, otherwise he was as sick as a dog.

At Wantage Road Lancashire were dismissed for 246, of which Test opener Bob Barber scored a powerful 146. Tony Goodridge of the *Guardian* saw David *'following up his own bowling at such enormous speed that one almost feared for the safety of Keith Andrew and his slip fielders. Larter achieved the desired effect and took the return catch which ended Barber's great effort'.*

> It was strange to think of gentleman Bob in the 60s Lancashire set up, but he made a great success of it and furthered his own international career as a very destructive left-hander.

The match ended in success for Northants, a well-judged century by opener Mick Norman taking them to victory with five minutes to spare. For David there was the success of three top order wickets, but also the frustration of his first injury, the fast bowler's perennial nightmare of a pulled muscle in his side. It was serious enough for the medics to advise that he should rest the muscle and should not play in the county's remaining three championship matches. His season was over.

Northants finished the championship in ninth position. It was a disappointing end after the earlier sixth position, but still two places higher than the previous year. They had won eight, lost six and drawn 13 of their matches.

David's end of term report, from Gordon Ross, editor of the *Playfair Cricket Annual*, was along the lines of a very promising start: '*Although raw and inexperienced, Larter became talked of as Tyson's natural successor. He played in 16 of the 31 Northants' matches, scoring 33 runs with a highest of 10, he took 46 wickets in 325 overs, a strike rate of seven, and an average of 16.3 runs per wicket. He twice had five wickets in an innings.*'

... *Larter became talked of as Tyson's natural successor.*

He topped the Northants averages, his best bowling being his six for 26 against Worcestershire, and ended a very creditable fifth in the national averages behind Statham, Les Jackson, Alan Moss and Trueman. Frank Tyson, in his last season, was a little way down the list, with 73 wickets at 26.10 each.

In the 1960 Second Eleven championship, in the second season of its existence, Northamptonshire won by a margin: playing 26 matches (six more than any other county) they won 12 matches and lost only two, a good augury for the county's future success. 18-year-old Colin Milburn hit the ball very hard in scoring over 1,000 runs and David's early season 17 wickets at 16 apiece came at the same strike rate as his first-class wickets – a wicket every seven overs.

> The 1960 season was when the dream became a reality. It all started with second team games, but it became obvious that I was going to get a first-class game before long. This turned out to be against Derbyshire. Fairly uneventful except that I was playing with names I had only read about. The press was picking up my height (generally reckoned to be 6'7 and half) but nothing special about the bowling. This changed with a home game against Worcestershire a few games later. I took six for 26 and this got noticed, both by the press and other sides.

It was somewhere around this time that I realised I was bowling faster. I was stronger, but there was something more: I think a mixture of the new experiences and the desire to compete with the opposition bowlers I was seeing. At this time and probably for the next five years there were some six or seven bowlers who merited the description of fast. From North to South these were Fred Trueman of Yorkshire, Brian Statham and Colin Hilton at Lancashire, Harold Rhodes at Derby, Frank Tyson at Northants, David (Butch) White at Hampshire and Peter Loader of Surrey. I made up my mind to join their ranks. I like to think that I got close to doing that the next season.

There were no speed guns then but from what I know I rated all these bowlers, and myself, as capable of speeds above 90 mph. If one ever saw Butch White bowl then one would not doubt my judgment. His charging run, whirlwind action, coupled with his impressive physique made him genuinely quick and seemingly indefatigable. He was also a great chap to have a pint with! Fred Rumsey, David Brown, Jeff Jones and John Snow joined this category during the '60s. From overseas there were Hall and Griffith (not to mention the terrifying Roy Gilchrist), Rorke and Meckiff, Adcock and Heine, all definitely very quick bowlers.

My overriding thinking is that my bowling speed developed as the level of cricket was raised. At school I was fast for a boys cricketer, at club level fast for some players, minor counties somewhat faster, county second team I was learning the craft, first-class I was fitter, stronger, experienced, and hugely competitive. For Test match level I had to rack up the intensity of the performance yet more. It actually became a problem to bowl slow. I much preferred bowling in an empty net at full speed, rather than worrying about the ability of someone at the other end, who might be a team-mate.

WINTER 1960/61 MCC TOUR TO NZ

*9 December 1960 Coronation
Street is aired for the first time.*

In the late summer speculation had built in the press as to which of the up and coming cricketers would earn selection for the MCC's winter tour to New Zealand. Having only started his first-class career in June, David had no such aspirations. It was therefore a real surprise to him when the MCC selectors included him in the 14-man party announced on August 8 and trumpeted by the *Daily Mail's* headline *'Giant Larter Gets his Chance'*.

> My selection for the MCC side to tour New Zealand at the end of 1960 was again a schoolboy dream come true!

With a mere 16 first-class matches under his belt David was one of twelve young county cricketers in the tour party. Two senior figures led the youngsters. The captain was Dennis Silk, Millfield headmaster and Somerset batsman in the summer holiday period, with Willie Watson, the highly experienced Yorkshire and England batsman as the senior pro. The twelve had been well-chosen, for nine of them were to become Test cricketers. Parks, David Allen, Russell, Prideaux, Barber, JT Murray, Don Wilson, David Smith and David. Three pace bowlers were picked, the three Davids – Larter, Smith of Gloucestershire, and Sayer of Kent. The one surprise omission was John Edrich, one of England's brightest batting prospects, Russell, more experienced and a better fielder, being preferred.

'I look forward to watching the enormous Larter very shortly,' was Jim Swanton's comment in the Telegraph. 'Of the three fast bowlers Sayer might be potentially the fastest, even though he does not at present have very impressive mechanics for the job. Like that of Tyson, his is essentially a strong man's action not specially well coordinated and rhythmic.' He then named Barry Knight, Ken Higgs and Ossie Wheatley as potential future fast bowling rivals to the three Davids.

Former England selector Cyril Washbrook wrote that Larter and Sayer 'could easily be the successors to Trueman and Statham in the short space of two years. Sayer has genuine pace now and I think that Larter can be developed, if wisely handled, into the greatest find for years.

David was thrilled to be recognised so soon in his career. He was a young colt inexperienced both in cricket and in life: indeed, he had never been abroad before.

> This was a great trip, good cricket, good people, and a mind-boggling country. Backward at the time in terms of infrastructure investment and modern living styles, but magnificent, with much brought up to date today.
>
> We were billeted with families as an economy measure for most of the trip, and this ensured a much better understanding of life in New Zealand. I recall a tour of a sheep farm, grimly hanging on to the back of a Ferguson tractor, and Jim Stewart of Warwickshire being treated to two 4 a.m. milk rounds with his proud host.
>
> Part of any tour are functions, and I remember one for the wrong reason. It was a reception given by the Governor General at Government House in Auckland. It was dragging on a bit, when a low whisper in my ear invited me out into the garden. Turning I saw a grinning David Sayer slyly revealing a full bottle of champagne under his jacket. Suffice to say we polished it off, but the real reason for the memory is trying to disguise the hangover which lasted for two full days! We were beer drinkers and definitely not used to the good stuff. 'Slayer' Sayer gained a fearsome reputation while at university. His bowling was courtesy of a very fast arm and a splendid physique.

Sayer was a bespectacled, self-deprecating man of a retiring nature. He evidently saw a kindred soul in David. As Ivo Tennant has written, Godfrey Evans, having previously kept wicket to Frank Tyson, thought Sayer in 1958 was faster for the first five overs of his spell than any bowler in England. He called everyone 'maestro' which

FR Malden (baggage master), JT Murray, DR Smith, D Wilson, JDFL, DM Sayer, RM Prideaux,
WE Russell, WJ Stewart;
DEV Padgett, DA Allen, JH Phillipps (Manager), DRW Silk, W Watson, JMParks, RW Barber.

as Tennant pointed out could backfire on him. At a cocktail party on an MCC tour of Argentina Sayer mistook the British ambassador for a waiter, and tapping him

'Say, maestro, where is the vino?'

on the shoulder said *'Say, maestro, where is the vino?'* Cue embarrassed pause and nervous laughter.

There were no official Tests but interest in the game, which had been flagging in New Zealand, was revived by a series of three four-day Representative Matches (referred to as the 'unofficial tests') among the 22 fixtures. Revived interest also came from the way Silk and Watson led the team to play bright, entertaining, and cheerful cricket. It was a happy coincidence that the December arrival of the tour party in New Zealand came only days after the conclusion of the Australia v West Indies tied Test in Brisbane, a match, and a series, played by both sides in a spirit of adventure, which Ron Roberts for one felt *'had ignited a torch of hope for Test cricket the world over.'* The tour lasted two and a half months, including Christmas, the first match being played on December 24 and the last, the third 'test' on March 10.

Dennis Silk was a complete surprise to most of us. We were full time professionals with some bloke we had only just heard of, in charge. Must admit the old amateur/professional era was very near to its end, but still very evident. Most counties managed to have an amateur captain, even if some of them did not know which end of the bat to use - there were of course some good ones around - Cowdrey, Dexter, Subba Row, and others.

Dennis was already a well-known sportsman playing cricket and rugby to high standards who seemed to be firmly in the amateur camp. His cricket did not particularly stand out on the tour, but between him and Willie Watson everything ran like clockwork. He was a polished after dinner speaker and had NZ audiences in stitches with some of his rugby stories. Needless to say, the lads soon warmed to him and even respected his intellect (those that could spell it). I was suitably impressed with the way he fitted in as if cricket were all he had ever done. A man to inspire and to admire.

Cricketing highlights for David, with quotes from Ron Roberts in the *Daily Telegraph*, included the following:

Seven wickets in his first first-class match against a Wellington side which included a number of NZ capped players (*'Larter bowls MCC to first tour win'); another seven against Central Districts ('Larter bowls well')*; five wickets in the match against a strong Canterbury side and five against Otago.

In the first unofficial test, before a crowd of 5,500 braving the cold, he took four wickets, Roberts with encouraging words*: 'from his enormous height Larter made the occasional ball dig in even on this easy paced surface, and though carefully used in short spells, took three good wickets as he worked his way through 21 overs, an indication of improving stamina'.*

In the second test there came another four. The *Guardian* reporter was impressed: *'while he is being nursed along carefully at the moment, he is undoubtedly improving on this tour both in stamina and general control'. Roberts agreed: '[Larter] is having an excellent first tour and his return of 4 for 20 off 16 overs is his best work yet....Larter's present speed would not be above Higgs of Lancashire, but he must make a fearsome sight as he comes boring in towards the batsman, and he does not waste the striking asset of his 6'7". He both dug the ball in and moved it a little off the seam and his control is improving.'*

David naturally gained most satisfaction from successes against opposition batsmen of high reputation. In the first tour match against Wellington on December 31 he came up for the first time against New Zealand's leading batsman and captain John Reid, and was delighted to have him caught behind by John Murray for a duck in the first innings and to bowl him for three in the second. In the second test Reid was again amongst his four first innings victims, bowled for eight. David had less fortune against Bert Sutcliffe, New Zealand's greatest post-war batsman before John Reid, who scored fifties against MCC for Otago and for the Governor General's XI, although David took four for 44 in the Otago innings.

John Reid held the NZ side together for years.

He was a good, very forceful, right hand bat who really seemed to enjoy a hard game of cricket. I got to know him pretty well over the years. He was New Zealand. It may sound unkind, but there was nobody else walking out to the crease who caused the same "buzz". I am talking about our team, not the crowd. Everybody sharpened up and knew full well that they were in for a hard battle. I was very happy to field at fine leg or third man, any closer and he was a danger to life and limb. I got stuck at gully once (at Wellington – I cannot now remember if it was a Test or not) and he square cut a delivery. It bounced but even so hit me straight between the eyes before I could get my hands moving. All were most concerned, not least John, but I have a solid skull and no damage was done!

John Murray, David Sayer, Jim Parks, Willie Watson, Roger Prideaux, Don Wilson, JDFL; Doug Padgett, David Smith, Micky Bear, Bob Barber.
New Zealand Colts. Ashburton January 11 1961.

After retiring from playing Reid became a much-respected Test match referee. *I loved the way the mighty John Reid went about his ICC match referee duties,* says cricket writer David Frith. *One evening he showed me his match report, and it included reference to players who frequently spat on the field. 'Expectorating is a disgusting habit...'* he wrote. *I bet that the majority of the cricketers would not have known what he was referring to – but I liked his attitude.*

Apart from the three unofficial tests the most important match of the tour was that against the Governor General's XI on February 27. Over 50,000 spectators attended, by far the largest crowd which David had experienced, and was just what the host country had dreamt of when it first extended its invitation to MCC to tour. The match ended entirely appropriately with the Governor General himself, Lord Cobham, no mean cricketer, taking a brilliant running catch to dismiss David. The game gave David the excitement of bowling against former and present NZ captains Martin Donnelly, Geoff Rabone, Sutcliffe, Reid and – a special bonus – the Australian fast bowler Ray Lindwall.

It was a thrill to chat to Ray, one of my heroes, who despite the generational gap was very friendly. I told him I remembered how back in May 1956 a party from Framlingham College went to see the Australian tourists play against Cambridge University. I had been looking forward to seeing him bowl, but instead had to be satisfied with him getting a hundred, his first in England, and in only

... 'dipped their bread and filled their boots'

106 minutes. As they say up north, he and several others 'dipped their bread and filled their boots' that day!

David generously found time to remember the old school. The editor of the Framlingham College magazine received a letter from David written from Nelson on March 3 while the match there was held up by rain:

New Zealand is a wonderful country and a land of opportunity for young people who were prepared to work hard and use their initiative. At the beginning of the tour I found the wickets too slow to generate any real pace. For this reason too the New Zealand batting and bowling was somewhat negative and defensive. However, the MCC side by forceful methods set an example which the New Zealanders were quick to follow with the result that in the second 'test' they beat the MCC at their own game. I am enjoying the tour

Mail from home.

immensely, and much appreciated being entertained by a number of former pupils now resident in New Zealand. Lloyd Kenyon met me at Waimate, reaching the ground in time to see me bat, taking guard with meticulous care before despatching my first ball into the next parish. The next ball saw my middle stump arrested in flight by the wicket-keeper standing back. I was reminded of the detail of this innings that evening by Kenyon during a motor tour round the countryside.

The tour came to its end, with David very much on the up. But around the corner came a down. The last tour fixture was the third test at Christchurch commencing on March 10. Rain washed out most of the match, ensuring New Zealand ended the three-match series one up. Such play as was possible was enhanced by what *Wisden* described as an heroic innings from Willie Watson, played with a broken hand. On the

Don Wilson (photographer), Parks, Padgett, Larter, Sayer (in front), Russell.

third morning, March 13, David, in some discomfort with stomach pains, was taken to a Christchurch hospital; there his appendix was immediately removed.

This kept him back from the tour party's departure for home. But as David recounts it there was no need to feel sorry for him:

> The end of the trip was memorable in that I left a bit of me in Christchurch – my appendix – but it did allow me to enjoy the company of some charming nurses and the MCC were very generous and flew me back in first class. I broke the journey for two day stays in Honolulu and New York. In 1961 back home this gave me pretty impressive bragging rights, particularly as I saw Elvis Presley at Honolulu airport - admittedly from about 200 yards!

Playing in nine of the ten first-class matches David topped the first-class bowling averages, his best bowling being five for 56 against Central Districts at Wanganui. Including the non first-class fixtures he played in 17 of the 22 matches on tour, coming second in the tour averages with 49 wickets at an average of 14. His strike rate was one wicket every seven overs, compared with 12 and 15 from fellow pace bowlers David Smith and David Sayer, and eight from the leading spinner Bob Barber whose 45 wickets were taken at 23 runs each.

Wisden picked out David as *'perhaps the great success for MCC.'* Encouraging words also came in the end of tour summaries. Interviewed by Terry McLean for the *Observer* Dennis Silk praised the bowling of David Allen, Bob Barber and David Larter: *'It is going to take Larter two or three years to develop, and he will never be really fiery. But he uses his great height most sensibly and because of it I feel he will turn into a genuinely hostile bowler. No pitch we have encountered in New Zealand has resembled a green top, but Larter has nevertheless bowled some menacingly good overs.'*

Interviewed by the *Daily Express*, Willie Watson thought that David would not reach his peak before 1963, but *'the skipper and I are very pleased at the way David has come along. He has the happy knack of nipping in for a wicket just when we want it. He is very keen and willing to learn and his control has been improving all the time on this tour. But he's only 20 and being so big it would be a mistake to rush him.'*

England selector Doug Insole, writing later in *The Cricketer* magazine, was full of praise for Silk's side, playing attractively and successfully, scoring runs quickly, bowling overs at a cracking pace, and generally playing crowd-pleasing cricket. *'The tour has been an outstanding success. One interesting aspect of the early-season cricket will be to watch for signs of improvement among the younger players who made the trip.'*

David looked a very promising bowler on this tour, says Jim Parks, *with the ability to get disconcerting bounce. A nice fellow. I later asked him to write a chapter on touring for me for the book I later put together, the Commonwealth Book of Cricket, and he chose the New Zealand trip.*

David's contribution was the following:

> In New Zealand, on my first tour, I found conditions very similar at first to those in England. As a bowler, I found the atmosphere and light alike. The ball swung in the air; the pitches were a bit lifeless but had some juice in them and would respond to seam. It was, in fact, just like home – at first.
>
> As the New Zealand summer got underway, however, and we worked our way back north, I had my first experience of real warmth on the cricket field. Higher temperatures mean that a bowler, particularly a fast bowler, needs to measure and pace out a day spent in the field. Here is where the young tourist can derive much benefit from a senior professional. In New Zealand, we were lucky to have had Willie Watson with us. He was, of course, widely travelled both as a cricketer and soccer player. He advised me profitably on how to handle myself. In hotter conditions, for example, at eleven a.m. you must try to project yourself into thinking how you will feel by the time four or five o'clock comes along, and plan accordingly. At home, in England, you are apt to get stuck straight into your bowling stint without the same regard for conserving energy.

Ron Roberts in his tour summary observed that David Sayer had days, when he found his rhythm, when he was as fast as many batsmen in England know and fear him to be. He dwelt on his appraisal of David Larter: *'He had done well, returning to Northants without his appendix but a better bowler…. Prideaux and Larter proved to be distinct finds, well worth further encouragement…. Larter is relatively supple for such a large man, and, carefully groomed on this tour, the colt responded with consistently good performances. He nearly always took an early wicket, developed his stamina to the point where he could get through 20 overs in a day (if in short spells), coming back quite brightly, and exercised better control than at home last summer. At 20 he should give excellent service to Northants, and perhaps at higher levels, though his pace is never likely to be more than fast-medium, and his value greatest in the lift that comes from enormous height that is properly used in an orderly action.'*

6

1961 HOME SEASON

The E-type Jaguar is born.

The brighter cricket played by the young MCC tourists in New Zealand would, it was hoped, herald a breakthrough from the style of play which had prevailed in the county championship over recent seasons. At least some serious debate was starting. The Advisory County Cricket committee met on March 15 with one item on its agenda: to discuss ways of improving the current slow tempo of the game. The statistics showed that the pre-war runs per over rate of 2.7 had dropped by 1960 to 2.54; the pre-war runs per hour of 59.4 was down to 43.7; and finally, that per day runs had fallen from 365 to 274. The 22 overs bowled in an hour had become 18.

By mid-season, the pressure for brighter cricket had produced some benefit. Runs per over were up to 2.63, per hour to 52.6, per day to 315, and overs bowled were back to 20. The weather had made a contribution: whilst the 60s decade was to be largely cold and wet, 1961 was a welcome exception. Batsmen scored more runs more quickly on the firmer wickets.

Batting rates were of little importance to David. With bat in hand he did not often trouble the scorers, and if on occasion he did so it was usually an action-packed episode. But the bowling rate was a serious matter. Press comment about the length of his run was frequent, though he did not dawdle, getting through his overs fast enough to enable Northants to perform at 20 overs per hour - high speed indeed when compared to the pedestrian 21st century rates of 14, even 13.

David was pleased at the speed of his recuperation from the appendicitis. He was back at the county ground on April 16, a week later than most of the players. He continued with a course of remedial exercises at Northampton General, and had a gentle bowl in the nets for the next two weeks, building up muscle strength.

> I felt generally fit, and pleased with my improving stamina having bowled more than 20 overs in a day on three occasions on the New Zealand tour. That was more than I had done for the county so far.

Training was minimal by today's standards. Jim Watts recounts the seriousness of the regime:

In those days we did not go in for fitness – we made ourselves fit by bowling and batting. We did no loosening up or other exercises. For a week or two before the season started we would play football in Abington Park and then a few days' sessions in the nets. We all smoked. I still have the memory of David sitting down on the dressing room bench at the end of a day in the field, loosening his boots and then lighting up a Senior Service cigarette.

As for treatment for injuries, in my first county match, at Rushden, I pulled a hamstring. I was told to play on. Afterwards you would just get a rub and some heat. I remember Frank Tyson was on the massage table at the time and of course he got priority so I got only cursory treatment. There were no scans or x-rays in those days. If we had a problem we would play on if at all possible.

> 'There were no scans or x-rays in those days. If we had a problem we would play on if at all possible...'

Coaching was very basic. What there was focused on sideways action and follow-through, but paid little attention to the physical attributes of the individual. There was too much bowling in the nets on practice days and too little fitness training. One would learn from watching. I learnt to swing the ball watching Harry Kelleher at Northampton, the seam position, the wrist position. We bowled ourselves cricket fit. No films or analysis at all.

Tyson had retired at the end of the 1960 season, so David was propelled into the role of the county's main, and usually only, strike bowler – a massive responsibility. Tyson had led the Northants attack from 1952 to 1960, taking 767 first-class wickets at 20.89, at a strike rate of 50. 41% of his championship appearances were at Wantage Road, on the dodo-dead Northants pitch, yet he took 168 wickets there at 23.27. He had a short Test career, playing in only 17 of the 40 Tests during that period. Injuries and illness were to cost him dear – a sore heel, an ankle strain, a leg bone fracture, and tonsillitis were some of the many reasons why he missed matches. In Tests he took a wicket every 45 balls at a cost of 18.56 – a strike rate superior to any of his English contemporaries, including Trueman.

Tyson had offered to remain at Northants for the 1961 season to assist in David's development but was turned down. Referring to his injuries Tyson said 'I often wonder if modern footwear and present-day medical science would have prevented or cured quicker my various injuries.' David was to repeat that thought years later.

David was ready to go by the first match of the season, against Middlesex on May 6. It was the first time he had played at Lord's.

Donald Ramsamooj, Roy Wills, Gordon Williamson, JDFL, Peter Watts, Brian Crump;
Mick Norman, Keith Andrew, Raman Subba Row, Brian Reynolds, Michael Allen.
May 6 at Lords.

Desmond Eagar in the *Sunday Telegraph* was pleased to *'enjoy some fine bowling between the showers at Lord's on Saturday... Larter bowled with an aggressive field 2 slips, 2 gullies, and 4 short legs.'* It took David some time to adjust, bowling from the pavilion end, to the slope of the ground and of the pitch, from left to right, and his opening overs were rather off target. Middlesex's Eric Russell helped himself to two fours off balls he could just manage to reach. David then got his radar working and as

Eagar noted *'began to look dangerous and a bit quick, as they say, having Eric and Syd Russell and Gale caught close to the wicket, and Ted Clark bowled, so that at lunch with the score at 64-5 his figures were 4 for 24.'* David ended with seven wickets in the match as Northants completed a thrilling win by three wickets with 10 minutes to spare, only their fourth win over Middlesex in 30 years.

Middlesex's Ted Clark b Larter 35.

Eric Russell was to face David on numerous occasions thereafter. His opinion was that David's height was a great asset as it enabled him to gain lift off a good length. *He wasn't an aggressive character but that did not matter – he was a natural bowler. On the circuit he was known as being quick with lift. Not as quick as Jeff Jones or perhaps John Price. I don't think he was particularly regarded as injury prone – all fast bowlers miss games through injury.*

Eagar commented on Northants' over rate. *'By lunch Northants had got through 35 overs which, considering the length of run of the three bowlers used, and that five wickets had fallen, was no slouch.'* David's lengthy run-up was the subject of a careful study by the *Daily Mail's* Crawford White. He noted that with David running in 31 yards and the keeper standing 16 yards back, bowler and keeper were 69 yards apart at the commencement of the run up. *'He is the tallest player in cricket, and he takes the* longest run. Running and walking he covers a quarter of a mile every over.'

David's captain Raman Subba Row wasn't concerned by this: *"David has to find his own rhythm. At the moment he needs this run, and as we average 20 - 21 overs per hour I do not mind it a bit. In fact, I do not want David to alter his run. I want him to settle down. He is a great prospect. He is not a tear-away fast bowler – he swings the ball both ways and is aiming at accuracy as well as speed.'*

For the season's second match David translated from the lively Lord's wicket to the slow surface of home - Wantage Road. Hampshire were the visitors and they batted first. John Arlott was there for the *Guardian*: *'Marathon rolling has given the Northampton wicket a new greenness of look if not of character – which has raised its pace from dead slow to easy. Larter, the long-legged, long-running, white-hope fast bowler persisted with out-swing in face of some vividly unfriendly strokes by Marshall.'* David got through 38 overs in the match, a sign of his increasing stamina, as Northants struggled to a draw.

With the Australians as the tourists 1961 was an important year for all English cricket followers, let alone for young fast bowlers with ambition. As early as the third match of the season the newspapers were already speculating as to the make-up of the England team for the first Test at Edgbaston on June 8. Crawford White asked rhetorically if England's selectors still held the past against bowlers who had once been called for throwing – Lock, Rhodes, and Butch White, the latter two having been ignored for selection for the 1960/61 winter New Zealand tour party. He hoped the selectors would look at Moss, Rhodes, Higgs, Loader and Larter to support Trueman and Statham, or even in due course to replace them.

Cricket can be a dangerous game. It was not for another 14 years that the wearing of a protective helmet to face fast bowlers was introduced. For David May 18 at Peterborough was a low point. He broke the back of the Gloucestershire innings with four wickets for three runs in a spell of 24 balls, but one of those wickets arose, most unfortunately, from a low full toss which broke the jaw of Tom Pugh, Gloucester's skipper, in two places.

> I thought Pugh would anticipate me bowling a bouncer, so I tried a yorker, but it went a little too far and he ducked into it. I intended to appeal but stopped when I saw he was hurt.

Wicket-keeper Keith Andrew did however appeal and Pugh was given out lbw, walking back to the pavilion in a daze. *'I lost the flight of the ball and turned my head into it. I was not knocked out – just given out.'* Pugh was lucky that this very uncomfortable injury was not ultimately more serious. The incident rather took the gloss off David's five wickets in the first innings. Thanks to a fine knock by Arthur Milton Gloucestershire then chased down 304 to win with two balls to spare.

David's season was building well. With only three matches played, he was 13th in the national bowling averages with 16 wickets at 18 runs each. He added only two more to that tally the next day at Wantage Road as left-arm spinner Mick Allen won the match by bowling out Derbyshire with 13 wickets. JJ Warr of the *Sunday Telegraph*, recently retired as a Middlesex and England fast bowler, was familiar with the unhelpful nature of the wicket for faster bowlers: *'The post-war wicket here has been notoriously slow, transforming even typhoon Tyson into a gentle zephyr.'*

Derbyshire's Harold Rhodes nevertheless claimed nine wickets in the match with fast bowling well up the Beaufort scale, his genuine pace and sustained hostility doing his prospects of an England recall no harm in front of the watching Gubby Allen, now in his last year of seven as chairman of selectors. Warr noted that *'Larter showed flashes of real speed, particularly when Mr Allen feinted to be leaving the ground.'*

David's batting did not often make the papers. The *Daily Mail* did however think it important to let its readers know that *'Larter's one run for Northants in the drawn away game against Lancashire on May 24, came from his second scoring shot of the season.'* Denys Rowbotham in the *Guardian* reported that David, whilst not always keeping strict control of his direction, looked *'ominously fast, lively in bounce, and dangerous every time he pitched to a length.'*

The MCC selectors' choice of players to face the tourists at Lord's on May 27 was, as always, of considerable interest, the match being viewed as something of an early Test trial. Gubby Allen's visit to Wantage Road had been significant – both Rhodes and David were chosen. Swanton felt Northamptonshire *'had done their best to husband [David's] strength and to encourage him to do something with the ball, until his physique begins to match his frame. Everyone seems to agree the speed is there if called upon.'*

The Australians won the encounter by 63 runs after a brave declaration by skipper Benaud was followed by some fine leg-spin from him. Australia made 381 for five, and 186 for no wicket, both declared. *Wisden* noted *'some excellent bowling by Larter and Mortimore.'* Former Australian all-rounder Keith Miller, covering the tour for the *Daily Express*, was typically forthright:

'I like Larter – the best bowling prospect I have seen for seasons. My tip to the England selectors is to pick him for the first Test against the Aussies at Edgbaston. He is only 21, inexperienced, and took only one for 74 for the MCC at Lord's. But he had

YES ENGLAND, I LIKE LARTER

DAVID LARTER
fierce and fast

He is the best pace prospect for seasons

By KEITH MILLER

I LIKE Larter. Yes, the 6ft. 7½in. Northampton speed merchant is the best bowling prospect I have seen for seasons. My tip to the England selectors is to pick him for the First Test against the Aussies at Edgbaston.

He's only 21, he's inexperienced, he took only one wicket for 74 for the M.C.C. at Lord's but he had Norman O'Neill dropped three times, and in his torrid opening overs he reminded me of Wes Hall.

"Whirlwind" Hall is the most feared man in bowling today. It was Hall who undermined Australia's batting in the series against the West Indies. David Larter could upset them now. He bangs the ball down with the same challenge and hostility.

When his accuracy improves his lifters will test not only the broadest bat but also the toughest heart.

The Aussies respect Brian Statham and Freddie Trueman but they know them. Larter is not known and with his resemblance to "hoodoo man" Hall it would be a big psychological victory for England to give him a chance as the third speed man.

NEED SPEED

After all, England must bank on speed, and Harold Rhodes didn't look a Test man at Lord's. He tried to bowl too fast. He would be much better off cutting his pace a little and concentrating on accuracy.

There is no Laker waiting to send Australia crashing to defeat this season. Of the off-spinners Ray Illingworth is the most likely Test candidate and I would bring back Tony Lock to support him.

While Larter was impressing me at Lord's, Bill Lawry was consolidating his place as Australia's Test opener. He is currently the most reliable runmaker in the team.

Brave words, I know, when you remember I would be a foundation member of any Norman O'Neill and Neil Harvey fan club. But despite O'Neill's dashing 122, there has been more solidity about Lawry in his recent innings than any other Australian.

Norman O'Neill dropped three times and in his torrid opening overs he reminded me of Wes Hall… the most feared man in bowling today. Larter bangs the ball down with the same challenge and hostility… It would be a big psychological victory for England to give him a chance as the third speed man. After all, England must bank on speed, and Harold Rhodes didn't look a Test man at Lords. He tried to bowl too fast…'

Another former Australian Test player journalist, Jack Fingleton, was equally impressed: 'Larter had no luck at all. What impressed me most was the number of times he rapped the batsmen on the leg. This was a sure sign that the Australians were not picking up his pace from the pitch. He gave them all anxious moments.'

Michael Melford in the *Sunday Telegraph* pictured himself as a batsman: *'6 foot seven of him rushing towards you at speed must be an awesome sight when he is on target and for 20 minutes he bowled with accuracy and hostility, repeatedly lifting the ball to the batsmen's gloves from around a length…Larter's performance after a moderate opening spell was an encouragement to those wondering where a successor to Statham and Trueman is coming from.'*

Swanton too was positive: *'the best English aspect of the day was the promise of Larter who has filled out over the winter and is now a fine figure of manhood, vastly tall but not disproportionately so. He at present controls the old ball better than the new. It must be remembered that at only just 21 he has taken a mere hundred first-class wickets as yet.'* The *Guardian's* Denys Rowbotham looked ahead: *'in an extremely hostile spell…[Larter's] formidable pace and fiery lift from his great height made him an exciting prospect for the next MCC tour to Australia.'*

Northants' victory over Derbyshire on May 23 was their last until June 30, a run of nine matches of which five where lost. The side was in transition. The successful team of the 1950s had broken up with the retirement of stalwarts Brookes, Manning,

MCC v Australia 27 May 1961. Both Mortimore and Rhodes at silly mid-off – 'a Dexter theory'.

Tyson and, most of all, the former Australian Test player George Tribe who held the team together: he could bat, doing the double seven times in eight years, but his bowling was of the highest class. A master of chinamen and googlies he could spin the ball like a top, a skill witnessed often by Laurie Johnson: *I recall keeping to him in a game at Wantage Road against Derbyshire where the groundsman had cut the wicket too close to that used the previous day. George put so much spin on the ball that he was landing it on the next-door track and still hitting the wicket on our track.*

The 1961 team was probably the youngest the county had ever fielded. Only Keith Andrew at 30 was over 29 years of age. *Wisden* felt Crump, bowling off-breaks, disappointed, as did Allen and Peter Watts. There was some hope for the future in the shape, all 18 stone of it, of 19-year-old Colin Milburn. Ken Turner, Northants chief executive, had persuaded Milburn to join the county from Durham in 1959. Finding out that other counties were prepared to offer £10 per week, Turner upped the ante to £10.50 a week and captured his man. David had been asked, when Milburn first arrived at the county from Durham, to help the team's Geordie, Malcolm Scott (who had played left wing for Newcastle United) to keep an eye on young Milburn.

This we duly did and found Colin to be a delightful but rough character. At that time, he did not drink. I am afraid to say that we soon introduced him to good old Northampton bitter beer and the facts of life re the opposite sex. We operated as a gang of friends and all started to climb the ladder as professional sportsmen, seeking to enjoy the freedom that this gave us as opposed to working in a bank or whatever. That is the Colin I knew. His talent was obvious then, but it took some time for people to realise he was not just a bit big, but that he was also a bit special. I stayed close right up to the start of his international career, but this took off just about the time that I retired. The different reputation he then developed (or had thrust upon him) was not something I knew. I was back in Suffolk by the time of his accident, and I followed his painful efforts to come back, but I never met him again.

> *'We operated as a gang of friends...'*

Middlesbrough was one of several out-grounds for Yorkshire, their policy being to take championship cricket to as many parts of the county as was financially feasible. Between them in 1961 the 17 championship counties played in no less than 81 venues, Kent, Glamorgan and Essex topping the list with eight each. The pitch on June 24 did not help the batsmen. David took 10 for 69 in the match, including that of Brian Close in each innings. But hopes of a return to winning ways for Northants were dashed as their batting in turn collapsed to the seam bowling of Mel Ryan, whose 10 wickets gave Yorkshire an 89-run win. Close was quoted in the press: *'[Larter] could have a great future in this game. He certainly had me worried on that Middlesbrough wicket.'*

Former England fast bowler and renowned coach Alf Gover offered his *Sunday Pictorial* readers a prescient assessment of David's immediate future: *'There is no likelihood whatsoever that Larter will hurl them down at the Australians in a Test match this summer…I expect the selectors will give David a feeling of Test cricket in a match or two against Pakistan next summer. But it will be in the sterner atmosphere of the 1962/63 Australian series that he will be ready to take on the role of Goliath.'* A slightly unfortunate analogy: Goliath didn't do too well in battle.

Northants were now bottom of the table with a run of seven championship defeats. On June 30 they finally achieved a win. The match against Worcestershire pitted David against Jack Flavell and his fellow opening bowler Len Coldwell, who were to lay claim to being the most potent opening attack in the country during the 60s. They took 11 wickets between them but could not dislodge Lightfoot, who produced a brilliant century, and Crump who saw the county reach the target of 381 with seven minutes to spare. Northants were finally off the bottom rung of the table – now occupied by Nottinghamshire.

At a small dressing room presentation after the match skipper Raman Subba Row presented David with his county cap. Not only was this confirmation that he was regarded as a leading player in the side, it represented some financial security: David's earnings went from £10 per week to £650 per season. Good, but nothing to compare with what Middlesex were prepared to pay. *'At Lord's not only were the capped players paid three times more, also they got to change in the home dressing room and consume a lavish lunch in the players dining room, while the rest had to change in a glorified cupboard and survive on a ham sandwich from the Lord's Tavern.'* A picture that would be difficult to believe had it not been written by Simon Hughes as editor of *The Cricketer*.

Northants returned to losing ways in the next fixture, unhappily against Notts, at Trent Bridge. For David, it was impossible to escape the strong feeling, playing at the world's third oldest Test venue, of the history of the place – the Larwood and Voce stand, the vast Australian-style data-filled scoreboard, the magnificence of the red-brick balustraded 1886 pavilion, and the elm tree behind George Parr's stand, named after the mid-19th century batsman who reached it with a famous hit. It was

Parr who had strongly recommended young cricketers not to forget to pay attention to the umpire. *'First of all, enquire after his health, then say what a fine player his father was, and finally present him with a brace of birds or rabbits. This will give you confidence, then you will probably do well.'*

David performed well in this theatre, if a little daunted, capturing five wickets in the match – the absence of any lbws perhaps suggesting a failure to provide an appropriate brace of game. He did dismiss Notts' captain and former Test player Reg Simpson for an elegant 66. Pace bowler Mike Dilley, back in the Northants side after two seasons, performed a hat-trick, but poor batting in their second innings left David playing a crucial batting role as last man, needing to hold out for the last 10 minutes of the match to stave off defeat. Almost but not quite a hero he succumbed to Notts off-spinner Bomber Wells to the fourth ball of the final over.

Following the second Test at Lord's, where 33 of the 35 wickets to fall went to pace bowlers, debate arose as to a supposed Nursery End ridge just short of a length which had made life hard for all of the batsmen. It was said that batsmen were aware of quicker bowlers getting very uneven bounce if the ball on occasion hit the ridge. Eric Russell, who had batted at Lord's for Middlesex since 1958, had no doubt that the ridge existed: *it was on the top half of the square nearer the grandstand, and just short of a length when bowling from the pavilion end. The ridge made David Larter even more awkward to play, particularly as with his accuracy, being there or thereabouts all the time, he would hit the ridge often.* MCC called in experts to survey the pitch and promised to eradicate the problem before the 1962 season began.

> I had heard all about the ridge, as we all had, but when bowling at Lord's I cannot say I experienced any evidence of it at all.

It was not the ridge that led to Mike Brearley being bowled by David. In his book *On Form* Brearley discussed the question of being 'in the zone'. *'One may be in the zone for a moment, achieving in a single stroke perfection of timing and placement. I remember opening the batting for Middlesex against Northants at Lord's in the 1960s. I faced the first over from David Larter, a giant of a fast bowler. The sun was out, the pitch benign. Early in the over, I played a cover drive with minimal use of the feet. I timed the ball perfectly and it bounced back off the front of the Grandstand. A zone moment – but unreliable: a couple of balls later, I missed a straight ball and was bowled by him for four.'*

Interviewed recently, Brearley recalls that David was feared, both for his height and pace: *He had a reputation of being a gentle giant, someone who lacked that ruthless killer instinct that the great fast bowlers often had, even if they were mild off the field.*

Lancashire hosted the Australians at Old Trafford on July 1, the proceeds of the match going towards Brian Statham's benefit, the ultimate total of £13,000 reflecting his great popularity. He strained side muscles and was unfit for the third Test at Leeds, which was to follow two days later. The selectors, ever prepared to surprise, recalled as his replacement one of the great county cricket warhorses, Les Jackson of Derbyshire, whom David had encountered in his first championship game.

Now 40 years of age, his only previous Test appearance had been at Old Trafford as far back as 1949. He was one of the many fine county bowlers denied more Test caps by the coincidence of their career with those of Trueman and Statham. In his case it had also been said that the eminence grise of English cricket, Gubby Allen, did not like Jackson's less than classic action. David rated him highly:

> Les Jackson was a legend and something of a throwback to the old professional days. His fame on the county circuit was only partly due to his ability to balance a full pint of beer on his forehead before swiftly consuming it. You threw Les the ball and he bowled all day, with a murderous nip-backer that flattened many off stumps. Like me he took more wickets than runs scored (many more than me!).

In fact, 1,733 wickets, at a miserly 17 each, in a career of 418 matches.

Swanton balked at this retrograde selection step, pointing out the selectors' inconsistency by not going back to either David Smith or Knight from the second Test, and repeating his preference for Moss, Larter or White. But Jackson justified the selectors' faith, helping England to a win with some expertly accurate seam bowling. Although the Test became known as Trueman's match, the Yorkshireman taking 11 wickets for 88, the persistent Jackson did very well with four for 83 in 44 overs.

The selectors made no friends when they unceremoniously dropped Jackson for the fourth Test at Old Trafford. He was not to play Test cricket again. Changing the customary attack strategy of two fast bowlers with Dexter as support plus two spinners, the selectors dropped Tony Lock and included three fast bowlers, Trueman, a fit again Statham, and instead of Jackson, Jack Flavell of Worcestershire, for his first cap at the age of 32. The new bowling strategy failed as England snatched defeat from the jaws of victory, Australian captain Richie Benaud's brilliant six wickets of leg-spin winning the match by 54 runs.

Keith Fletcher recalls that in the 60s and 70s there was a fair chance that one would be dropped if one had two bad Tests. For the fifth Test at the Oval the selectors took that line, dropping Close. And they went further, dropping Trueman after 24 successive Tests, in favour of Flavell. This resulted in a rare event - no Yorkshireman in the team. The draw meant England could not level the series.

Fletcher makes the further point that because of that unsympathetic selection policy even established players were nervous of losing their place in the side. *This in turn meant that established players tended not to give advice to young incoming batsmen – for example as to what tactics opposition bowlers might employ in a particular situation.* David shared that view:

> There was a bit of a 'them and us' mentality. In my case I rarely started any cricket conversation, so some fault was my own.

Northants hosted the Australians in a wonderfully exciting contest. They had been the first county to beat the 1960 South Africans and now came within a hair's breadth of becoming only the second one to beat the 1961 Australians. When Alan Davidson started the last over, with four minutes remaining in the match, Northants needed four runs to win with six wickets in hand. That became one run off the last ball with five wickets in hand, when the stalwart Lightfoot, who had scores of 80 not out and 57 not out in the match, declined a – possibly suicidal – winning run and his partner Malcolm Scott was run out. The county had given the Australians one of the biggest frights of the tour.

As Ron Roberts wrote in *The Fight for the Ashes 1961*, it was curious that a team who had won only once in their previous 15 games and were bottom of the championship should have taken the Australians to the very mouth of defeat after losing only 12 wickets in the match. David had a good game with match figures of four for 90. He claimed opener Bill Lawry twice, once with the second ball of the match for a duck, and in the second innings caught behind by Keith Andrew for 100. He had the other opener and future captain Bobby Simpson lbw and only struggled against Norman O'Neill who made a brilliant century.

MCC's 1961/2 winter tour to India, Pakistan and Ceylon was in the news in mid-July as MCC released the names of those players from whom availability to tour had been requested. The total of 29 included David's name – a significant endorsement of the progress he had made over the last year. There were seven other opening bowlers on the list: those (except Jackson) who had represented England that season – Statham, Trueman and Flavell – plus Butch White and Alan Moss, together with the uncapped Knight, Alan Brown, David Smith, and, hearteningly, David's Northants colleague, Brian Crump.

Northants requested, and MCC agreed, that David should not be selected for the tour. Ken Turner explained: *'David has had a tough season on top of the tour to New Zealand last winter. We don't want him to be burnt out before he is 23 – and by the time of the next tour to Australia. He did not turn down the tour. We did, for him.'* Trueman and Statham declined the invitation and the selectors chose Brown, Smith, Knight and White.

Swanton wrote that he was *'not sorry personally that neither Larter nor Gifford has been picked as they are both so young and short of experience. Broadly speaking, batsmen are rarely too young, but bowlers can certainly be. These are two real hopefuls who might perhaps be ready for the Australian tour a year hence.'* Brian Crump was another one overlooked, although he was not unhappy at that, worried as he had been that his constitution would not stand up to more than a month of curries.

The occasional talk in the press of David's apparent vulnerability to injury because of his willowy frame received a firm rebuttal from Andy Wilson in the *Sunday Telegraph* on July 26 reporting from Grace Road Leicester:

'Northants were never in control of the game despite the honest endeavours of David Larter, who exploded the old-fashioned myth that modern fast bowlers lack stamina. He almost dismissed Leicestershire before they reached what might be a match winning total. In this hunting shire they believe in horses for courses and on this ground last year Larter took 5-20. Today his 6 for 55 in 19 overs included three wickets after tea at a time when he might justifiably have been resting. 5 minutes before lunch when nothing seemed likely to disturb the flow of runs Larter made two lift quickly and had Willie Watson playing a shade late to the next which kept comparatively low and had him lbw'.

Watson, returning to the Leicestershire team after skippering the Players against the Gentlemen, set a fine personal example, dominating the match with two polished displays, and was according to *Wisden 'in a class apart and alone mastered the pace of Larter.'*

With supreme irony David was injured the very next day, bowling against Somerset at Wantage Road, as Somerset racked up 420 before declaring. 41-year-old Bill Alley struck 156, on his way to a wondrous season's total of 3,019, and to the accolade of one of *Wisden's* Five Cricketers of the Year. Northants lost by an innings. It was small consolation to David that he drove a ball from Langford out of the ground for six, only to be castled next ball. This was Northants' eleventh defeat of the campaign.

He remained out of action – through injury – for three weeks, missing five matches, returning for the last four matches of the season. Captain Raman Subba Row had suffered a leg injury scoring a six-hour century playing for England in the fifth Test. Due to retire at the end of the season, Subba handed the mantle of captaincy to Keith Andrew, a role Andrew took to with ease, unbeaten over the last four matches with two draws and two wins. The decision to appoint him full-time captain for the following season was to prove inspired.

At Swansea, the ground where in 1968 Sobers was to strike his 6 sixes in an over, Glamorgan, set 203 to win in 140 minutes, were bowled out for 130. Northants' victory margin would have been much less if, as reported by Swanton, *'it had not been for a vigorous and unexpected last stand in which Northants' fast bowler Larter played a notable part, adding 46 in 25 minutes with Scott. His 34 with three sixes and 2 fours was the side's top score and his personal best, his previous best being 11.'*

The team coach left Swansea as soon as possible. They had to get to Dover that night for the last match of the season – against Kent the following day. It was a journey of some 250 miles. Stephen Chalke quoted Brian Crump: *'we got there about two in the morning and when we reported into the hotel, we found the secretary had booked us in for the following week. We finished up in Folkestone with several of us sleeping with blankets on a stage.'*

It says a lot for the players' fitness and fortitude that after that journey from hell they beat Kent, by four wickets, despite a splendid 132 from England opener Peter Richardson. Northants was a county against whom Richardson regularly filled his boots. In the six matches David played against him between 1960 and 1965 he scored 96, 132, 120, 105, and 64 not out, the only failure being at Kettering in July 1963 when Reynolds caught him off David for three. He played 34 times for England during a period of heavy competition for the opening batting positions. In 1957, in a rare family event, he and brother Dick played together for England in the third Test against West Indies.

He was a fine bat and an inveterate practical joker, specialising, as Ivo Tennant has recorded, on EW Swanton *'to whom he would send fictitious letters from retired colonels in the hope that their content would be mentioned in Swanton's Monday morning column.'* Once, with help from Colin Ingleby-McKenzie of Hampshire, Richardson persuaded one of the umpires to hold up play at Canterbury and to walk to the commentary box to ask Swanton to keep his voice down as the noise was unsettling the batsmen.

Their end of season flourish meant that Northants finished the season 16th out of the 17 counties, just behind Surrey but just ahead of the wooden spoon holders Notts. They had won five, lost 13, and drawn 10 of their 28 matches. The vagaries of cricket were amply demonstrated by Surrey's lowly position, relatively soon after their seven championship winning sequence in the 1950s. Laker had retired but they still had Alec and Eric Bedser, Loader and Lock to bowl and Stewart, John Edrich, May and Barrington to bat. Yet they won only four games in the season.

Wisden highlighted Northants' inadequate attack. *'In a season when 15 of the 17 counties boasted at least one bowler with over 100 wickets, Northants best was 77 by Larter. Even Notts had Wells on 99. Larter would no doubt have shown better figures but for injury and lack of the type of support this young, tall, willowy bowler must have to conserve his energy.'*

David topped the Northants bowling averages with 70 wickets at 19 apiece, from 556 overs, a figure second only to the spinner Mick Allen, despite missing five matches. His final tally for all first-class games was 77 wickets at 22 each. Of his batting little need be said, although his average improved to 4.23 from 26 innings in which he scored 72 runs, thanks to that 34 at Swansea.

> For me 1961 was something of a settling and proving season. I was consistent and took wickets, surprising a few household-name batsmen. The club had got it into their head that I should not be exposed to any undue hard work and made this known (without asking me!). As a result, I played for a couple of MCC teams, but little else outside of the county side.

His modest 'little else outside of the county side' was in fact much more. Apart from representing MCC against the tourists in May, David was selected to play in two games at the season-ending Scarborough Festival.

IMAGE: DAVID PICKERSGILL

Bowling for the Players against the Gentlemen, David and Barry Knight were handicapped by a wet ball, conceding 31 in four overs but, as noted by the *Telegraph*, *'to their credit they did not wilt and with a firmer grip on the ball managed to call a halt to this dash, and then between them rounded up the tail with the new ball.'*

The next day, September 6, David played for TN Pearce's X1 against the Australians. 1,499 runs were scored, then the second largest aggregate for a three-day fixture. There was the traditional lighthearted aspect, in which only the original new ball was used, a shiny red apple was bowled immediately after the lunch interval, every batsmen was given a run to get off the mark, and no lbw decisions were demanded; there was also some serious hitting to entertain the crowd, including a blistering 64 minute Dexter century, and centuries from Edrich, May, Geoff Smith of Essex and Bobby Simpson of Australia. 21 sixes were hit on the third day, as Australia scored 357 in 220 minutes to win with 10 minutes to spare. Amidst the mayhem David's 15 wicketless overs for 75 runs represented relative containment.

Unserious to a degree it may have been, but this was a big match for David, a second opportunity to play in front of a large crowd – 15,000 on each of the three days – as well as to appear alongside the great and the good. Apart from the century makers, there was MJK Smith, Parks and Trevor Bailey, with local hero Fred Trueman opening the bowling with David, against such as Benaud, Simpson and Norman O'Neill.

In end-season summaries Crawford White in the *Daily Mail* named David as one of the eight outstanding future Test prospects, whilst the Australians nominated him and Yorkshire batsman John Hampshire, as the two best young England players they had seen. And when the captains of both England and Australia were interviewed by Ron Roberts at the end of the Test series, Benaud offered this reply to the question of young English cricketers he had seen during the tour:

'I saw some good players around the counties. I liked the look of Gifford, the Worcestershire left-arm spinner, Brearley and Tony Lewis (though he had a bad knee), Alan Jones, a fair-haired left-hander with Glamorgan, Langridge, the Sussex opener, Larter, though he has a terribly long run, Russell of Middlesex, and Geoff Smith the Essex batsman.'

FEBRUARY 1962 – COMMONWEALTH TOUR TO AFRICA AND PAKISTAN

February 20 – John Glenn is the first American to orbit the earth.

MCC had accepted Northants' request that David be omitted from the MCC winter tour to India, Pakistan and Ceylon, to permit him a winter's rest after his tour to New Zealand the previous winter and a heavy summer's workload. It was to prove a very sensible decision. The tour commenced on October 7, only four weeks after the end of the domestic season, and lasted four months. *Wisden* described it as one of the most strenuous tours ever undertaken by any country, comprising eight five-day Tests and 24 matches in all. India defeated England for the first time whilst England defeated Pakistan in their three match series. As *Wisden* noted, *'without top-class fast bowlers capable of making an early break, England had to work extremely hard to dismiss India for a reasonable total on the dead, easy pitches found in three of the Tests.'*

My digs in Northampton was a small furnished flat in the middle of town. I was later to realise this lifestyle was not very healthy – it was too easy to fall into bad habits living on one's own, so for the last few years of my time I was a paying guest at Mrs Watson's boarding-house in Abington Avenue, just round the corner from the ground.

The flat was therefore my base for the summer cricket routine from April to early September, and also in the winter of 1960/61, whilst I completed my county residential qualification, although of course the tour to New Zealand took up part of that winter. As soon as the 1961 cricket season had finished, now residentially qualified, I was free to push off back to Suffolk for the winter to work for Father in his small agricultural haulage business. It was just what I needed, after 650 overs of summer fast bowling. I returned easily to the country life which I had enjoyed since childhood.

Virtually all our trade was with E.G.Clarke and Sons Ltd around the Suffolk and South Norfolk area, meeting the odd Old Framlinghamian farmer on my travels. One would think cricket occupied my thoughts, but I must be honest and say that this was a hugely enjoyable time. I loved driving lorries and the physical work involved.

David benefited from the break and from his winter agricultural work. Then out of the blue came a letter. It was an invitation from Ron Roberts to join a whistle-stop Commonwealth XI tour to East Africa. Roberts was a popular cricket journalist who reported on many overseas tours for the *Daily Telegraph*, and himself arranged and managed numerous tours to different parts of the Commonwealth, the USA and Greece. His death in 1965 after a long illness, aged only 38, robbed cricket of a great contributor. Northants were happy for David to accept the invitation given that the tour would last only one month. It gave David the chance to earn some money – £300 plus expenses.

Just before David departed on the tour, in early February 1962, he was tracked down at his father's farm by the *Daily Mail's* Crawford White. It is worth quoting the interview in full:

> 'David Larter, the giant Framlingham College boy who seems sure to succeed Trueman in the next few years as England's most ferocious fast bowler, flicked 2 hundredweight of corn of his shoulders as easily as feather pillows. It seemed odd that this was his way of tuning up for fast bowling in Rhodesia in 10 days' time and, I believe, in Australia next winter. But it made sense to quietly spoken Larter who has been a Northants professional for the past three years.
>
> "I've been doing this work all winter to build up the body and back strength you need for fast bowling and I've never felt fitter or stronger in my life. These

sacks of corn are not the toughest to handle – I often have to load 21 stone sacks of beans and peas, and they had my knees buckling last year. But I can cope with one fairly easily now… I would like to stay in county cricket for another 10 years – if I'm good enough", he says. "But I am not thinking of myself as an England player yet. If an Australian tour came my way it would be wonderful. But right now my objective is to get 100 county wickets this summer. I had 77 from 21 games last season and I want to improve on that. My interest is in speed. I want to bowl fast – really fast. I do not mean as a wild tear-away – I aim at control.

I admire Trueman and Statham as great bowlers but if I could choose, I think I would prefer to develop Trueman's exuberance rather than Statham's precision. I do not want to be predictable. I like to let the occasional bouncer fly and I like to try the yorker and even the occasional full toss. And I like to have an especially fast one up my sleeve, even if it is occasionally wide."

Some critics fear Larter is too tall to be a really great fast bowler. They prefer to see the compact power of a Larwood, a Lindwall or a Trueman. On the whole they are probably right. But Larter's great virtue lies in the excellence of his sideways-on action and the genuine speed he develops from his great height. If he builds the body strength needed to control his height, I believe his potential is unlimited.

"I've been lucky" he says. "I've had my present action since I was 13 and the experts have not tried to alter it. I am trying to cut down my run to save energy and develop greater body action by a better follow through. I am going up to the nets at Northampton for three days next week before flying to Rhodesia for four weeks with the Commonwealth team. I want to start bowling again."

Does Larter ever get clothes ready-made? "Only ties and handkerchiefs" he says sadly. "I even have to have my cricket boots (size 12) specially made. I tear the heels off an ordinary pair in one match." I wager Larter, the boy no batsman likes to face, will be ordering extra boots for Australia next August.'

The tour of the Commonwealth side, under the title of the International XI, lasted a total of eight weeks between February and April 1962 and took in some 40,000 miles in air travel. In deference to the MCC's principle that players should not be overworked on unofficial tours Roberts, with masterly efficiency, arranged for all players to be picked up and dropped off at points en route most convenient to them, rather than keeping the whole party together for the entire time. The vice-captain Everton Weekes was one of six players to remain with the party throughout, logging nearly 50,000 miles to and from his Barbados home. In this way Roberts involved 25 players in all, drawn from six countries, of whom 19 were Test cricketers. 17 matches were played, including eight which were granted first-class status, and only one match was lost.

Two Australians, Lindwall and Benaud, shared the captaincy, Lindwall leading the first part of the tour to Kenya, Rhodesia, and East Pakistan with Benaud taking over in Sydney for the second phase, encompassing New Zealand for two matches, then India and Pakistan, via three non-first class matches against Hong Kong.

> I was a surprised but thrilled member of this rare gathering – a tour party straight out of my childhood dreams: Everton Weekes, Ray Lindwall, Sonny Ramadhin, Hanif Mohammad – the list goes on. You could say some of these were old-timers and that the rest of us were there to do the running about, but what company!
>
> On February 8, a number of those who were heading for the first phase matches, in East Africa, met up on February 8 at London Heathrow. I shook hands with the London contingent, the four mentioned (less Lindwall who was resting a leg injury) plus Colin McDonald the Australian opening bat, the West Indian Hampshire opener Roy Marshall, and my fellow Englishmen Tom Graveney (now of Worcestershire), Derbyshire fast bowler Harold Rhodes, Somerset keeper Harold Stephenson and Worcestershire's left-arm spinner Norman Gifford.

The motivation for Roberts's endeavour was the fostering of fellowship between the multi-racial members of the party, and between them and those they would encounter on their travels. He believed that political separations could be ignored and defeated by human interaction. His post-tour report highlighted how satisfying the team spirit built up had been, particularly by Benaud. *'The way that the West Indian Everton Weekes and the South African Roy McLean, for instance, struck a genuine friendship was a fine example of how the cricketers themselves can transcend cricket politics.'*

Weekes had played 48 Tests for the West Indies between 1948 and 1958. His Test batting average of 58.61 remains the 10th highest in cricket history - and he played in a period of uncovered wickets. He made a century in five consecutive Test innings (a feat that remains unmatched), and was out for 90 in the sixth, when, as he told this author in 2010, *I was run out by my partner.*

Playing for South Africa between 1951 and 1964, Roy McLean gained 40 caps and still holds one unofficial and unusual record: he scored the highest percentage of his team's runs while he was at the crease over his entire Test career; often batting with partners who had strike rates in the low 30s (from 100 balls). His strike rate was 58, unspectacular by modern standards but outstanding in his day, which meant that he made 62% of South Africa's Test runs whilst he was at the wicket during his Test career.

After landing in Salisbury on February 10 the Heathrow party moved to Nairobi where they were joined by Pakistanis Hanif Mohammad and Saeed Ahmed, by the Indian spinner SP 'Fergy' Gupte and by the South Africans Basil d'Oliveira, Neil Adcock and McLean. After one match in Nairobi the caravan went back to Salisbury and on to Bulawayo before heading for Dacca in East Pakistan. For the second phase Benaud and his Australians, Craig, Simpson, Meckiff and Ford the NSW keeper, joined at Sydney. Cowdrey and Subba Row then flew from England for the final matches in Bombay and Karachi.

Colin McDonald, Saeed Ahmed, Harold Stephenson, Norman Gifford, JDFL, Harold Rhodes, Roy Marshall, Fergy Gupte, Sonny Ramadhin;
Ron Roberts, Basil d'Oliveira, Tom Graveney, Ray Lindwall, Everton Weekes, Hanif Mohammad.

Born only three weeks earlier than David, Norman Gifford was the other baby of the party: *The flight to Salisbury from London was my first international flight - great excitement on the famous Comet aircraft. Ron Roberts had put together a wonderfully varied tour party of different nationalities and backgrounds. The team and party spirit was just great. I loved the changing room conversation between all these great players.*

The first fixture was a non first-class game against a local Nairobi scratch side. David and Derbyshire's Harold Rhodes opened the bowling. The *Telegraph* reported that the hosts found the pace of these two, balanced by the spin of Ramadhin and Gifford, too much for them.

On February 24 the first-class matches in Rhodesia started with fixtures in Bulawayo, Nkana and Salisbury. Both David and Norman Gifford were awestruck by the arrival of Ray Lindwall for the game in Salisbury on 3 March. David had the honour, but also the nerve-wracking experience, of opening the bowling opposite him. For Norman *it was just magical standing at mid-off watching Ray run in to bowl. We had seen wonderful players in the county championship – not least Trueman and Statham, but this was a real-life Australian legend, playing with us. I roomed with another great Australian Colin McDonald, the opening bat and it was wonderful listening to him talk about some of his Test experiences and watching him play a fine innings of 82.*

48 from Weekes and 43 from Lindwall enabled the Commonwealth team to reach 294 against a strong Rhodesia Invitation X1 captained by South African skipper Jackie McGlew. David did not occupy his habitual spot as the last batsman, his promotion to no.10 saying quite a lot about Sonny Ramadhin's batsmanship. Evidently buoyed by this plaudit David struck Colin Bland for sixteen in one over, including in Roberts's words 'two gigantic sixes befitting a man of his size', before being caught off Bland for 30.

> I was lucky to have seen Neil Adcock bowl as he abruptly retired when the ill-thought-out front foot no-ball law was introduced. If Peter Heine was the bludgeon, then Neil Adcock was the rapier that finished the job. He was very tall and fearsomely quick with a high whirling action. He accelerated up a long run and I could have watched him all day.

It was in Salisbury that David had his first glimpse of racism in Africa.

> A group of us were in the hotel lobby in Salisbury when Sonny Ramadhin walked in looking pretty shocked and angry. He told us that he had gone into a nearby hairdressing shop and had sat down to wait his turn. The hairdresser finished with his customer and then motioned to a white man, who had come in after Sonny, to sit in the barber's chair. Sonny started to say that he was next, to be brusquely told that he was not going to get a haircut in that shop. The fact that he was probably the greatest spin bowler in the world at that time made no difference – apartheid in action.

Norman Gifford experienced a similar revelation at the next stop on the tour – Bulawayo. *A party of us went into a bar and ordered a round. The barman told us that he could not serve Everton Weekes, a lovely man who was our skipper for that match. Tom Graveney, who would always be happy to have a drink, turned on his heel and led us all out. It was my first experience of racial discrimination and it was very unpleasant.*

Ron Roberts recounted another incident involving Weekes, this time at the end of the trip, in Sydney. Weekes, sharing a Sydney taxi with Adcock and McLean, was asked by the driver if they were all members of the South African cricket team. *'Man, are you colour-blind?'* Weekes enquired.

It was not long before the party was to see another side of the coin – overseas governmental reaction against apartheid. It was the first hitch in Roberts' carefully constructed tour plan. On March 3 Roberts reported in the *Daily Telegraph* that *'the International touring side, due to play two matches in Pakistan, have received a directive from the Pakistan government that the South Africans McLean, Adcock and Goddard cannot play. It is hoped that the young English bowlers Larter and Gifford will be available for the Dacca match.'* David and Norman (and the Rhodesian Colin Bland) happily agreed to extend their participation beyond the intended East African leg to take the places of the visa-denied South Africans for the Dacca fixture.

In Bombay Roberts was worried how Adcock and McLean, not playing there but who had to pass through transit, would be treated: *'after all there was one hotel with a sneering notice: "dogs and South Africans not allowed".'*

The Dacca match was the first time the two young Englishmen had visited Pakistan, memorable for that but more significant for the fact that it was Ray Lindwall's last first-class match. In a 21-year career Lindwall played 61 times for Australia, taking 228 wickets at an average of 23 per wicket, and forming with Keith Miller one of the most potent fast bowling partnerships of all time.

Lindwall captained us against the East Pakistan Governor's XI, says Gifford. *Whilst he bowled 19 overs in the searing heat, he made sure us 21-year-olds earned our keep on a very flat wicket, 27 overs for David and 32 for me.*

It was hard, not just for the two young English bowlers, to keep the opposition's world-class batsmen from scoring at will. Hanif Mohammad made 77, passing 10,000 first-class runs in the process, his older brother Wazir Mohammad 100 and Test player Saeed Ahmed 149, out of a total of 385 for 5 declared. David loved the thrill of it all and was satisfied with his work. He dismissed both Saeed and Mahmood Hussain, his 27 overs for 68 runs giving him a foretaste of what was to plague him in two years' time, the difficulty of getting batsmen out on flat sub-continental pitches.

Hanif, to whom I had also bowled in my first Test at the Oval, was a small quiet man who held at one time or another almost every batting record. Perhaps a bit cautious but he knew what he was doing and took some shifting once he was at the crease. He was quite different in approach from his other brother Mushtaq who joined Northants during my time, who was an attractive and attacking batsman and a very skilful leg-break bowler.

Tom Graveney was the batting star of the tour, with 1,000 runs in the eight first class matches, with two centuries and three scores in the nineties. He had spent the 1961 season in Worcestershire's second team, serving out the qualification period ungenerously demanded by his previous employers Gloucestershire, and was raring to bat in top company. David had the good fortune to room with Tom.

> We were mostly billeted – I shared with Tom Graveney. He was some 13 years older than me and represented a level of professional cricket that I only knew from sports news and film clips. To actually play with him, against him, to tour with him and laugh and joke with him, and ultimately to share a room with him, was hard to imagine. He was an urbane, gentle man (except when he fell out with Gloucestershire) and to watch him walk out, take guard and start playing as if he had been there for a week, was a privilege.

Norman Gifford had started his career with Worcestershire the year before Graveney joined the club from Gloucestershire. Norman soon delighted in the study of his batting at close range.

He just loved scoring runs and would never treat batting lightly; even in a benefit match, and even just in the nets, he would want to score runs. He made a huge difference to us. When we won the championship in 1964, he averaged 55 each time he batted, whilst the next best, Ron Headley, managed 34.

There was another – future – Worcestershire player in the party, an outstanding Cape Coloured South African all-rounder, relatively unknown to Norman:

It was the first time any of us in the tour party, other than the South Africans, had seen Basil d'Oliveira. It was not until 1964 that he came over to England to live, initially playing at Middleton in the Lancashire league and then for us at Worcestershire. On the tour we could immediately see what a powerful player he was - hitting the ball hard and, at that stage in his career, bowling quite a lively pace off a longish run. When he got to English conditions, he worked out that he could move the ball about off a much shorter approach.

David saw a remarkable talent:

> Basil showed his great natural ability. I suppose he could be thought to have started the move away from conventional coaching-manual batting to more adventurous and sometimes jaw-dropping strokes. Although he took wickets with some skilful medium-pace bowling it was his batting which brought him fame. Towards the end of the decade he was to become a cause celebre, subjected to parliamentary questions and much fuss back in his native South Africa. I thought he handled it very well, just shrugging it all off and getting on with playing his cricket. He fitted in well on the tour.

'Basil... more adventurous and sometimes jaw-dropping strokes.'

On a tour like this where the socialising was an important element 'Dolly', who was quite a character, played his part. Like many cricketers he liked a drink at the end of the day. David liked Dolly and had no problems with him. Jeff Jones on the 1968 MCC tour to the West Indies was to experience the fiery side of Basil: *he was nose to*

Players pretend the bus in the Dacca hotel forecourt is their official transport: McDonald (in hat), Graveney leaning, Lindwall, Bland and Stephenson inside.

nose one evening with Rohan Kanhai, both of them on whisky; I got him out of a few scrapes. David did the same for me on our tour – he got me out of a few scrapes!

Recollection of Dacca takes Norman Gifford back to his second visit to the city: *It was with Joe Lister's Worcestershire side in 1964/5 when our visit to the stadium coincided with the declaration of Bangladesh's independence from Pakistan. A mixture of celebration and opposition rioting turned the stadium into flames. We were locked within the ground by the police for some four hours until it was safe to leave. The joys of foreign cricket travel.*

In his four first-class matches David performed creditably taking eight wickets at 28 apiece. His opening partner Harold Rhodes, who did the entire trip, bowled in seven of the eight first class matches taking nine wickets at 44 apiece. Norman played in three matches and finished with nine wickets at 37 each.

For the Suffolk youngster the trip was educational, not only in racial and political terms but of course in cricketing terms it was a masterclass. And he also had fun:

> We had a few days off. It was on one of these that our hostess in Nairobi – the very glamorous wife of the chairman of the East Africa Coffee and Cotton Board – decided to take us to the zoo. When in Rome... ! The visit was OK, but remember I am 21 and not too enthralled, when something caught my eye in a large enclosure. To get a better view I stood on a convenient large earth hump. Within seconds the said glamourous lady is screaming at me to get off this hump and to get my trousers off! This I duly did to find bloody big ants all over my legs and inside my trousers, with a few bites to emphasise the invasion. When calm was restored, she laughingly told us that many an evening garden party was enlivened by guests rapidly shedding clothes when the ants joined in (more later about trousers off for ants, in India).
>
> The air travel also brought its exciting moments, I recall a flight from Karachi to Dacca on a four-engined Constellation plane, carrying all our party and then full to the brim with Pakistan nationals. We were on the tarmac and engine no.1 started, then no.2 and no.3 and then came a huge bang accompanied by smoke and flames from no. 4. I swear the Pakistanis went down the aisle two deep, whereas our lot gathered our hand luggage and walked calmly off the plane and back into the airport lounge. The trip was a huge experience for this somewhat naïve and new world traveller. I will add that it was brilliant to see central Africa before all the name changing and mindless violence that followed.

He also encountered aspects of this physically demanding sport which were new to him:

> The heat we encountered on the tour was something I had not experienced before, and I quickly learned I had to conserve energy. This led to my learning to bowl off a shorter run. Being a chap of unusual height, I developed a habit in England of bowling off a long run of around 30 paces. I know this seems a devil of a distance, but I have long legs and felt I had to go back all this way to achieve the right rhythm in my delivery.
>
> When I arrived in Nairobi, I discovered that we were not only playing at several thousand feet above sea level, which must affect the breathing, but the bowling involved a sort of three-dimensional operation – all at ground level! What I mean is that there were three different surfaces underfoot. The start of a fast bowler's run was on grass, then the approach to the stumps was a concrete-type substance, and finally you finished up on a matting surface, and moreover, one that tended to slip away when your feet came down with any force.

A further adaptation that had to be made involved footwear.

> Freddie Trueman had once bowled in his normal spiked boots on the mat at Nairobi, and they had to buy a new mat afterwards! The spikes ripped the mat to shreds as he followed through with his full weight and speed. Any quickish bowler thereafter was asked to bowl in crepes. What with the three different surfaces, and the rubber soles, I could not cope with my long run. I shortened it by half and although I was never happy bowling on the mat, I persevered with the shorter run later, on turf wickets in Rhodesia, and have found it useful ever since. So, of necessity, touring has helped me a great deal in this respect.

David had not previously taken much note of the need for close attention to looking after the body.

> Bowling in Africa, high above sea level, knocks up some bowlers. Brian Statham, I was told, used to take a whiff of oxygen to aid his respiration during the intervals of matches in the Transvaal. Fortunately, I got used to the rarefied air fairly quickly and it did not upset me.
>
> Apart from conserving energy I learned the hard way to take care of my body. In England, if a day starts cool, the odds are it will stay that way. Overseas, it can be blazing hot at noon and at three o'clock it can become

remarkably cool. That is when lumbago and fibrositis can stab you in the back. On the Commonwealth tour Ray Lindwall often sweatered up if he took a wicket during an over – which of course meant he was often sweatering up! My lesson about taking this precaution was learnt after I had taken the wicket of a number ten batsman late one evening. It was cool and draughty, but I did not notice it as I was keen to get at the number eleven. Without putting on my sweater, I suppose I cooled off too quickly. Anyway, I tore into my first ball at the new batsman and pulled a muscle.

For David the tour was an important step in his career, playing with and against a number of the world's foremost players, a greatly enriching experience from which he learned a lot about his profession but also about life in different countries and different cultures. This privileged exposure to racial and political issues gave him insights into the human condition which would stay with him for life. He was fortunate in that in many ways he was taking part in a groundbreaking event. The success of the multi-racial team's three matches in Rhodesia was shown when the home authorities invited a further International XI tour later that year. David's trip was the first time that any of the great West Indian cricketers had been permitted to play in southern Africa, and the first time they had played alongside South African cricketers such as McLean and Adcock. Friendship transcending the political divide, a divide David saw at first hand.

8

1962 HOME SEASON

The Cuban missile crisis threatens a nuclear confrontation.

Returning in mid-March from the steamy heat of Dacca in East Pakistan to the North Sea chill of Suffolk David reported back for farming duty with his father. But not for long as he was off again to Northampton in mid-April, for pre-season training.

> 1962 was to be very important as my performances were beginning to create not just a thought, but something of a clamour to push me up to international status. But it is a pity that the idea that I needed building up persisted. I weighed 17½ stone, stood nearly 6'8" and bowled 20 plus overs every other day for Northants. I was not pleased with the so-called protection, but had to wait.

The clamour came from some respected sources. John Arlott in the *Observer*, listing young fast bowlers of potential Test class who might give support for Statham, included David *'a real hope but perhaps not yet quite ready, White, Flavell, Rhodes (if the umpires approve him), Higgs, Colin Hilton, John Cotton, David Smith, Knight and Terry Spencer.'*

It also came from the other side of the world: Richie Benaud, Australia's captain, not long returned home after captaining the Commonwealth International XI in the

Bombay and Karachi leg of the international tour, under the heading 'Storm Warning' started his newspaper column with these words:

'Remember the Typhoon called Tyson – who with his colleague George Statham ripped the Australian batting apart on the 1954/55 tour of Australia? Tyson is finished… but the new name on the horizon is Larter – David Larter. This young Northampton quickie played against us at Lord's last year and bowled fast. At 6 foot 7 ½ he ran in just on 33 paces to deliver the ball. Tyson shortened his run after a poor first Test in Brisbane. Larter is almost a blueprint of this. The England camp are pinning their faith to a fast bowling combination this year and are keeping fingers crossed that Larter will spearhead it. They still have Statham and Trueman. There will be a third genuine fast bowler chosen – Larter. He was not considered for the recent MCC tour of India and Pakistan because his county club asked that he be allowed to mature more before being subjected to the strains of a Test tour abroad.'

Ray Robinson writing in the *Guardian* from Sydney quoted Benaud's article and added some context: *'Benaud's expectation that the MCC selectors will choose four pace men comes close on the heels of offers to four West Indian fast bowlers to play and coach in India next season to develop potential speedsters there and to improve Indian batsmen's performance against pace. Fast bowlers are entitled to carry themselves proudly at all this evidence that they are at last being recognised as the most dominant force in the game.'*

Benaud's reference to Brian Statham as George arose from an old Lancashire tradition, stemming from the 1920s, when wicket-keeper George Duckworth was regarded as a good luck charm in the Lancashire teams which won the championship several times in that decade. It was therefore deemed important to have a George in the team in the post-war period. First Winston Place took it on and then Statham, since when it has lapsed.

David's pre-season training had included significant work on shortening his run-up. On the Commonwealth tour on the hard grounds in the heat of Rhodesia and Pakistan he had had bowling success with his run reduced by 8 yards, and he decided to continue with that approach. The *Daily Mail*, referring to David as a possibility for selection for the 1962/3 Ashes tour and as the most likely successor to Trueman and Statham, revealed that he *'had been discreetly advised by Lords to use a shorter run'.* David had not:

This was so discreet that I never heard it. From Lord's or anyone else.

The *Mail* continued: *'Ken Turner, Northants' secretary was asked to comment: "Larter's long run was spectacular and helped to build up his reputation, especially among opposition batsmen, but playing 6 days a week, it took a lot out of him. Now it remains to be seen if his new run will be effective".'*

The fast bowling contenders for selection for England were out in force in the two important early season matches at Lord's, starting on April 28. Flavell and Knight opened the attack for MCC against Yorkshire, whilst for MCC against Surrey immediately afterwards David was picked alongside Alan Moss. It was David's first match of the season and it was a tough assignment. Although he managed to jar Micky Stewart's fingers a couple of times early on, neither David nor his fellow sufferers Moss, Garry Sobers the West Indian star all-rounder, and Fred Titmus the England off-spinner, could make much of an impression on Stewart (137 not out) and his opening partner John Edrich (76) as Surrey cruised home by 6 wickets. Surrey's Peter Loader, hopeful of recall to the English colours eight years after his debut, was at his hostile best, claiming 10 for 90 in the match. The only good memory of the encounter for David was of his only scoring stroke in the match – a straight six off Sydenham, struck with apparent ease.

On May 9 the final of the new Midlands Knock-Out Cup took place at Grace Road, Leicester. This was a one-day tournament between Derbyshire, Nottinghamshire, Northants, and Leicestershire, sponsored by Leicestershire, the brainchild of their secretary Mike Turner. It provided a useful template for the one-day knock-out Gillette Cup which was due to start in 1963.

> We were supposed to play 65 overs a side, but in the final against Leicestershire, I rather messed it all up by taking three early wickets so that we bowled them out for 218 with nearly eight of the overs unused, winning by five wickets. It was fun at the time. We had of course no idea it would grow into today's monster. Modern day ODIs with their screaming crowds, pyjama style dress, reduced fields of play which render records obsolete, incoherent music, obsession with anthems and interviews with sweaty players, all add up to an unattractive scenario for me. There is some interesting cricket: the 2019 World Cup final was exciting, but did we really need all those ex-cricketer experts telling us how they would have done it? Bring back John Arlott or even Richie Benaud both of whom knew it was called tele-vision and that silence is golden. I am not daft enough to ignore the huge amounts of money, nor the crowd numbers, and if this gets youngsters playing, then long live one-day cricket – so long as Test cricket is held up as the ultimate game to play.

Wantage Road home advantage counted for little in Northants' championship game against Worcestershire, with Len Coldwell taking nine wickets to give the visitors a clear win. David got through 43 overs in the match for six wickets. They included some important England scalps – Tom Graveney (in both innings, caught behind by Keith Andrew), Dick Richardson and captain Don Kenyon. The first day saw a huge 407 runs scored from a remarkable (by today's standards) 118 overs. Eric Todd writing in the *Guardian* reported on the paradise awaiting batsmen on the county ground:

'Northamptonshire has become a green and pleasant land for those sides who win the toss and are rich in batting talent. No visitors will believe that the groundsman was once a fast bowler. The measure of his fiendish triumph was revealed in two previous matches this season at Peterborough and Northampton, where eight innings produced 2,040 runs for the loss of 48 wickets, and there were six declarations. "No wonder you wanted to come here", observed Tom Graveney to Roger Prideaux, once of Kent but now of Northants. The best of Larter will not be seen until he has harnessed consistent accuracy to his many other admirable attributes.'

> Roger Prideaux was a strong aggressive front foot player, who never quite got to the top. Perhaps a complicated domestic life did not help, but he should have played regularly for England.

Although David had struggled to make much impression for the MCC in the match against Surrey, the selectors persevered with him for the important MCC game against the Pakistan tourists, another chance for the selectors to see Test candidates in action. Swanton's opinion was that *'Larter would seem to have all the mechanics for the job and for two seasons has seemed the likeliest hope among the budding fast bowlers.'*

In the first innings of the big match David, Knight and Dexter did not bowl well, disappointing Alex Bannister in the *Daily Mail*: *'Pakistan's batting exposed England's second rank attack as very ordinary. Knight did not improve his prospects, and Larter, tipped as a future replacement for either Statham or Trueman, was lifeless, often lacking in control and not as fast as last year; the spinners Gifford and Savage were no more impressive.'* In the second innings David did better, with much more hostile bowling giving him the wickets of Alim and Saeed, persuading Denys Rowbotham that he was showing promise for MCC *'and perhaps even for England.'*

Alec Bedser thought that England's young bowlers were guilty of bowling too short and wide, *'the chief offender being England's brightest fast bowling hope, Larter, who has much to learn.'* Swanton, previewing selection for the first Test at Edgbaston on May 31, believed that *'Larter is a possibility, whilst Coldwell is at the moment very much on the crest of a wave.'*

Under an overblown *Daily Mail* headline *'Selector Bedser Grooms Larter for*

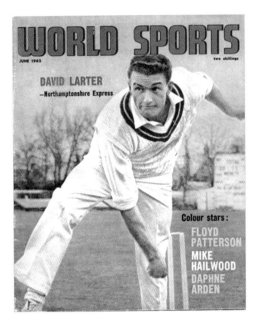

Australia' Alex Bannister wrote that on advice from Alec Bedser, holder of the world Test bowling aggregate of 236 wickets, David was spending lonely hours trying to master control by bowling at a single stump. *'Bedser told him the only way to learn control was constant practice, advising that: "even when I was in Italy in the war I bowled anywhere at any odd moment and at anything I could knock into the ground." He advised Larter to attack the off stump and to bowl a fuller length – "he is pitching too short because he tries to bowl too fast". Last year he used a 35-yard run and in 600 overs (400 less than the average aggregate in the championship), covered 125 miles.'*

Dear old Alex Bannister must have dreamt quite a bit of this. Alec Bedser – whom I greatly admired – hardly said a word to me at any time.

The panel of Test selectors was appointed on an annual basis by the Board of Control. For some years, the panel had been led by MCC grandee Gubby Allen. He and his colleagues Herbert Sutcliffe and Wilf Wooller having resigned, a new panel was appointed for 1962, led by Walter Robins with newcomers Alec Bedser and Willie Watson, plus Doug Insole of Essex as the only one remaining from the previous panel. The panel was faced with three choices for Test captain for the Pakistan series: the previous winter's tour captain Dexter, Cowdrey, or the Rev David Sheppard who, having retired from cricket five years previously to concentrate on church duties, had now been persuaded to return to first-class cricket with the idea of leading MCC on the forthcoming Ashes tour. As it turned out, Sheppard was not free to pick up a cricket bat until June. The selectors voted for Dexter, but only for the first two Tests, after which Cowdrey would be given his chance.

In choosing the 12-player squad for the first Test the new panel took no chances, standing by the old firm of Trueman and Statham, with Dexter supporting them as third seamer. Knight was chosen in the 12 but, as at Edgbaston one year earlier, was discarded on the morning of the match. Trueman did not have a good match and

Rowbotham thought it likely that Larter would supplant him for the second Test.

In 1962 Northants were slow starters. It was not until their sixth game that they secured their first win of the term. The team had retreated into its shell - as shown by its performance at the Oval in the fifth game, a miserable draw with an average hourly scoring rate between two sides over the first three innings of just over 40. David bowled tidily for his four wickets but the highlight of the match for him was, on the last occasion he was to play against him, to watch Peter May unfurl a number of his favourite cover drives in an innings of 71. He also eased a couple of boundaries through mid-on, shots which in Eric Russell's view highlighted his status as one of the greats, *the only batsman I ever saw hit the ball regularly past mid-on with a straight bat.*

> I remember bowling at him with some trepidation, as he was an England captain with such a reputation and Lord knows how many runs. I did sneak one past his outside edge and he flashed me a smile and a 'well bowled'. I doubt if that happens these days!

On June 1 came that first victory, over Glamorgan at Wantage Road. Reynolds and Norman put on almost 200 for the first wicket in two hours and a half, a welcome improvement in the run rate. David had four wickets in the match, but the match winner was Peter Watts, his leg-spin accounting for nine victims.

In the next match, against Gloucestershire at Kettering, David, having taken five wickets in 31 overs in the first innings, pulled up with injury after one over in the second and went off. Keith Andrew enquired of his team whether anybody could bowl seamers. He was told that off-spinner Brian Crump used to bowl them in the Staffordshire league and he was therefore thrust into the role. He nearly won the match in his new style with four for 60 but Gloucestershire, eight down, held out for a draw. David was relieved to see Tom Pugh's fractured jaw fully mended as he scored a feisty 54.

Northants were lying 11th in the table after seven matches. David missed just one match and was fit again for the Trent Bridge fixture on June 15, a match he was to remember. On a green pitch Nottinghamshire's bowling had Northants in trouble at 154 for 9 when David joined skipper Keith Andrew at the wicket. One hour later Andrew was dismissed with the score at 239, David being left 51 not out, his first and only 50 in first-class cricket, including two raking sixes off Bomber Wells's off-spin. His innings put Northants back in the game and his three wickets then helped dismiss Notts for 233, to give Northants four points for a first innings lead in a drawn game. When asked why he had managed to hide his batting light under a bushel for so long, David could only offer:

As they say – 'every dog has his day'! Seriously, I just seemed to see a very big ball that day and everything connected.

David was now ninth in the national averages with 35 wickets at 20. He took five wickets in the match against Middlesex, a game watched by Test selector Willie Watson, and eight against Yorkshire, which included a few overs against the obdurate Geoff Boycott, playing one of his early games for Yorkshire. Northants victory by six wickets, achieved with only five minutes to spare, was the last defeat Yorkshire were to suffer in their championship winning season. Continuing his good run of form, David then dismissed seven Leicestershire batsmen in the next match, away at Grace Road on June 23, putting in another serious shift of 45 overs in the two innings.

The *Guardian*, noting the selectors' decision not to change the team for the second Test, expressed the view that David was the most likely candidate to be selected as backup to Statham and Trueman in Australia. Trueman had silenced his critics with fine bowling on a lively Lords wicket much to his liking by taking six for 31 as Pakistan were dismissed for a paltry 100. Len Coldwell in his debut Test, chosen on the back of a purple patch of 66 championship wickets at nine apiece, replacing the injured Statham, had an outstanding game with match figures of nine for 110 as England cruised to a nine-wicket victory.

Alex Bannister could now see the vacant places for the Australian tour filling up. *'If one added David Sheppard and JT Murray to the Lord's 12, this would leave only three places left to fill on the Australian tour party. Of the bowlers, the main contenders are Knight, Loader, Larter, Coldwell, Gifford, and Barber. Coldwell has made phenomenal progress in the last two years, when 'Crash' Coldwell as he was known to his Worcestershire colleagues, was thinking of giving up the game because of a painful knee damaged in a car crash. Instead, he had an operation on the knee and resumed cricket, taking 140 wickets last year and coming sixth in the averages. This year he has been the first bowler to reach 50 wickets. His steadiness has won him a place in front of Larter and Butch White for chief supporting role to Trueman and Statham.'*

Pakistan's next game after the Test was at Northampton. Regrettably the Wantage Road track was at its deadest. David prised out the century-maker Saeed Ahmed, caught behind, before persuading Wallis Mathias to hit his own wicket and clean bowling Intikhab Alam. Pakistan declined to attempt 175 to win in two hours and the game petered out into a draw.

Worcestershire had back in May given Northants their only defeat of the season to date. The return fixture, at Kidderminster on July 2, brought sweet revenge with an eight wicket victory for Northants. But it came at a cost. Bowling in the second innings, David felt a sharp pain in his side:

I had torn several intercostal muscles – the bane of a bowler's life – not funny, and devils to mend. It meant I missed six county games over the next three weeks up till July 23, right in the middle of the season.

Statham, fit again, resumed his place instead of Coldwell for the third Test at Leeds starting on July 5. Pakistan were again defeated, giving England, this time under the captaincy of Cowdrey, the series victory after only three Tests. Trueman and Statham took 10 wickets between them and third seamer Dexter five.

The selection panel, joined on this occasion by two MCC representatives, ex-chairman Gubby Allen and assistant secretary Donald Carr, wrote in early July to 29 county cricketers asking if they would be available for selection for the winter Ashes tour. The fast bowlers on the list were Coldwell, Flavell, Trueman, Statham, Knight, and a very delighted David. Interesting names amongst the batsmen include AR Lewis, Prideaux, and the Rev David Sheppard. The absence from the list of stock bowlers Shackleton and Cartwright suggested to EW Swanton that the selectors had more or less settled on taking Coldwell *'who has the great merit of strength and heart'.* He also thought that the naming of Flavell, 33, together with Knight, as a possible auxiliary to Statham and Trueman, *'indicates how England's fast bowling resources have declined.'*

The selectors would announce the fourth Test team for Trent Bridge, on Sunday July 22, with the match starting the following Thursday, before meeting again on July 29 to finalise their selections for the Ashes tour. That gave those contenders who had indicated their availability three weeks to press their case. The Gentlemen v Players match at Lord's on July 18 thus took on the mantle of a virtual Test trial.

Swanton had been interested in how the Lord's pitch would play. He had seen the Varsity match played there only one week earlier: *'no one quite trusted the wicket especially at the Nursery end. The ball just short of a length was still inclined to fly, and one would not have been inclined to fancy the Gentlemen's chances of making many today against Trueman and Larter'.*

That thought was not to become reality as David's intercostal rib injury forced his withdrawal from the Players' team. He was replaced by Shackleton, who had just become the first bowler to 100 wickets in the season. A high-class century from David Sheppard cemented his claim for inclusion in the side for the fourth Test, as well as – at least according to the popular press – his role as captain of the forthcoming Ashes tour party. His main rival Cowdrey withdrew as captain of the Gentlemen due to kidney trouble, to be replaced by the second choice Dexter. It was a considerable surprise when on the second day of the Players match Dexter was announced as the captain for the Australia tour. That appointment was to have a significant effect on David's career.

The Lord's game finished on July 20. Fred Trueman drove the next morning from there to Taunton for Yorkshire's next game. He was late reporting there and as a punishment was dropped from the game by his skipper Vic Wilson. Fred was less than impressed by his captain's decision. He drove straight back to the north, announcing that after such treatment (in his benefit season) he would not be driving south again to Bristol for Yorkshire's following match against Gloucestershire starting on July 25, assuming, he said, *'as is on the cards, the selectors decide to give Larter a run and I am rested from the Test side.'*

But David was still unfit and at the next day's selection meeting the selectors could not 'give Larter a run', retaining Statham and the irate Trueman, bringing in Barry Knight as a third seamer. The selection which captured the headlines was the recall of the Rev David Sheppard.

David's return to action, after three weeks of treatment from the county's physiotherapist Jack Jennings, took place the day after the selection meeting, in a county second eleven match against Somerset seconds. The intercostals stood up well enough to enable him to return to the full county side on Wednesday July 25, the day before the start of the fourth Test at Trent Bridge.

Rowbotham in the *Guardian* wrote: *'it is a reasonable assumption that had Coldwell and Larter been fit enough they would have played in the fourth Test. This implies that Coldwell has already earned his passage to Australia and Larter will probably be taken on trust, whilst Knight is being considered as an all-rounder.'* As Swanton put it: *'the injuries to Larter and Coldwell are most inconvenient for the selectors.'*

The July 25 game was against Derbyshire at Buxton, the parkland ground over 1,000 feet above sea level, famous for the loss of an entire June day's play in 1975 to a snowstorm. Anxious to prove his fitness and to keep in the Australia tour selectors' eye-line David delivered a hostile spell full of pace and lift from a length, taking three wickets for one run in eight balls. He could not have chosen his second victim better – Donald Carr – Derbyshire's captain but more importantly a co-opted selector of the Australian tour party. In David's view 'a very nice man – one of the last old amateur captains.'

The game was awash with fine individual performances. Derbyshire's Derek Morgan claimed ten wickets in the match, the venerable Les Jackson five and David seven, not sparing himself with 43 overs in the match. But those performances were outshone by an innings from Colin Milburn, now a slim-line version having lost three stone over the winter by regular visits to the gym. On a green-top, with the ball seaming both ways, in fading light and with no sight screens, he scored 102 out of a second innings partnership with Mick Norman of 152, with 18 fours. Norman scored 58 and no one else scored more than five. Of all the wonderful innings he was to play in his short career this was in Milburn's own view the best. Keith Andrew called his team members out from the changing room to watch Milburn's knock, rating it the greatest innings he ever saw (*'all the years I played cricket were worth it just to see Colin at his best'*), and he had seen many around the world. As Keith expressed it in Stephen Chalke's fine biography: *'Dexter had a touch of genius, but Milburn was one.'*

> ## 'Dexter had a touch of genius, but Milburn was one.'

In separate action on the same day at Bristol, the Brian Close 'hard man' canon was given another chapter when during Gloucestershire's innings against Yorkshire, opener Martin Young was caught by Phil Sharpe at slip off Illingworth, the ball having rebounded six yards off the head of Close, fielding at short leg. Close went off with a cut head, but of course soon resumed his position at short leg.

The crowd at Wantage Road for the county's next match against Hampshire was smaller than it might have been, given that at Trent Bridge along the road Graveney and Parfitt were hurrying to their centuries in the fourth Test before Dexter's declaration at lunchtime on 428 for five, and Fazal Mahmood, flown in from Pakistan four days earlier to reinforce his beleaguered colleagues, was still bowling. It is doubtful whether Fazal had anticipated back home in Karachi that in four days' time he would be bowling 60 overs, and taking three wickets for 130, whilst five of his colleagues managed 74 overs between them.

John Thicknesse in the *Telegraph* reported that *'Larter was quite a proposition for Hampshire. His direction was good today and he looks more in control from a 20-yard run. From his great height he was able to get lift more than the others and once Andrew, 15 yards back, had to stand on tiptoe to hold down a bouncer.'* David's fiery two for 54 from 26 overs included the wicket of Roy Marshall, a batsman David greatly admired:

> Roy was the one everyone came to see. I recall him late-cutting Frank Tyson once for six over third man, and I think it was in the first over; a wonderful entertainer and a truly laid-back character popular wherever he went.

No first-class cricket was played on Sundays. But rather than resting, David played, as he often did on Sunday rest days, this time in a charity match at Exning near Newmarket, a ninety-minute drive from home. Ian Wooldridge was there: *'After bowling 3 overs for 5 runs and no wickets he was some 20 yards from the pavilion walking in for the tea interval when his agonies were ended by a loudspeaker* announcement: *"I am happy to tell you"* came the Australian accent of Jock Livingston *"that David Larter is in the England tour party". 2,000 Suffolk and Northamptonshire spectators cheered, and players gathered around to shake his hand.'* When he went out to bat, he hit a six and three fours in a celebratory innings of 27 before driving off to a contented sleep in the specially made bed installed for his 6'7" frame in his Northampton digs.

Despite his sub-editor's over-used headline humour attempt *'Larter – a giant gamble'*, Alex Bannister agreed with Rowbotham that the big surprise in the MCC party was not David but Ray Illingworth instead of Tony Lock. This meant that the party included three off-spinners, with no left-hand bowler for the first time in 100 years of England's Ashes visits. It also meant that the selectors had decided to make do without an eighth batsman, preferring to take all three of David, Coldwell and Knight instead of only two of them. Only David and wicket-keeper Alan Smith had not yet played for England.

Bannister liked the choice of Larter – *'a justified risk, for he has tremendous potential and with his great height he should make the ball lift disconcertingly on the hard Australian pitches. Tyson had less than half the number of county championship wickets already credited to Larter, when he was sent to Australia in 1954. Coldwell will, with Barry Knight, serve as a stock bowler.'* Swanton did not shy away from expressing his overall concern: *'the party is weakish in the bowling department but with hardly anyone to hide in the field. Perhaps there will be some slight reservation over the selection of Larter, who was unable to prove his place for the Players because of injury. Such men as Titmus and Coldwell are among the most willing of workers, apparently happiest when hardest at it.'*

From Australia came a comment from a doyen of Australian cricket writing, Ray Robinson: *'Neil Harvey said today that England's attack is going to depend a lot on the development of David Larter'.* Harvey was an Australian hero, who had first toured England with Bradman's Invincibles in 1948; he was to retire from Test cricket after 79 appearances after the MCC tour that winter.

David's father, now a successful 51-year-old fertiliser haulier living and working at Framlingham was interviewed by Ian Wooldridge. *'Jack Larter must advertise for a new strongman to hump hundredweight sacks around the local farms this winter. The last one gave notice by phone last night. "He went off in an old farm pickup in the first week of April and we haven't seen him since" said his late employer. But he said it proudly. "He writes to us once a week, but we never see him" said his mother Edna. "You see, he's married to cricket. He plays six times a week, but he still cannot wait to play on*

Sundays. He says he will not get married until he is finished with it all. It wouldn't be fair to cricket or to the girl".'

On August 8 at Old Trafford David was on top form. Lancashire collapsed before his hostile bowling and Keith Andrew's brilliant catching. *The Times* reporter was impressed that David wisely bowled from a shortened run and at half pace on the greasy turf, without losing his effectiveness. In his second spell David ran through the innings, taking the last four for 18 in 6.1 overs.

Wally Grout of Australia had created a world record in 1959/60 when for Queensland he caught eight Western Australian batsmen wickets in an innings. The Northants men were aware of this record as last man Ken Howard faced the first ball of David's 20th over, with Keith Andrew having caught seven of the nine wickets to fall. Howard edged it and was caught by Andrew who threw the ball up in a rare moment of celebration. Joy was however confined when it was spotted that the off bail was lying on the ground, evidence that Howard had in fact been bowled by David rather than caught behind, and Andrew had to be content with equalling rather than beating the world record. David finished with seven for 48, the best performance of his career.

> *'David finished with seven for 48, the best performance of his career.'*

When asked what I regard as my most satisfying bowling performance, I would choose this match against Lancashire. In the early 1960s the Lancashire side had a clique at its heart who loved to play the 'Northern hard lads' role – even worse than the Yorkies! – and they let it be known that I represented the poncey southern public schoolboy type that they could roll over for a pastime (how on earth Bob Barber stood it I don't know – well, he did eventually clear off to Warwickshire). Anyway the seven for 48 quietened them. In those days, the wicket faced the 'right' way and the view from the pavilion was side on. A little bird told me that not one of them left their seats, as they had never seen the ball whistling through so quickly. Keith caught seven that innings.

Ian Wooldridge described David's effort as *'one performance that will echo all the way to Australia.'*

Keith Andrew became Northants' full-time captain in 1962. It was a role in which he excelled. No one knew better than him the chemistry and personality of the close-knit group which formed the team for the early years of the 1960s. Stephen Chalke, in his biography of Keith, persuaded him to take the reader into the sanctum of the dressing room as he, and other team members, looked back fondly on their exploits. David Larter is given more column inches in that book than anywhere else, and with Stephen's permission here are some extracts:

'Fred, as he was called by his teammates, was a shy man, capable of bowling at great pace, but he was not, says Malcolm Scott the left-arm spin bowler, steeped in cricket like Brian Crump. If a leg-spinner were swept by the batsman to fine leg and you or I were fielding down there, we would make allowance for the spin – but not David! The ball would hit the boards and the crowd would shout ''Boards! Take him off!''

I'd got to look after Larter, said Keith, and treat him with kid gloves. He was a good bowler. In fact, he was probably a better bowler for Northampton than Frank Tyson. But getting him on the field was the problem. Better than Tyson? At his best he was lethal, one of the best I've ever kept to. He swung the ball more than Frank did. Frank used to think he was swinging it – 'did you see that one go?' he'd say, and I'd always agree 'My god yes Frank' and he motion with his fingers as if he'd just bowled a leg cutter, but really with Frank it was purely pace.'

The Northamptonshire records support Keith's point: Tyson 170 matches, 525 wickets at an average of 20.95. Larter 134 matches, 511 wickets at an average of 18.19.

Keith Andrew again: *'I never attacked much with Crumpy. He was a ploy to stop them scoring so they would try to hit Larter. I had a little mathematical formula. I thought if I could keep Larter on his feet for 6 or 700 overs, he will get 100 wickets or thereabouts, and Crump will get the same, bowling a thousand overs. I think Brian got Larter a lot of his wickets. 'Yes, well,' Brian says, 'David got me a lot of my wickets as well.'*

Jim Watts finds Keith's quoted comments surprising: *I assume Keith's reference to looking after Larter and treating him with kid gloves must be a reference to him being physically fragile – but I never regarded David as injury prone. I really cannot recall any major injuries prior to the one that finished his career in Australia. He no doubt had his share of injuries but that's what happens to all fast bowlers.*

I agree with Keith's comment that Tyson did not swing the ball, whereas David had a natural away swing. I have the highest regard for Brian Crump's bowling – accurate and very useful. I remember Arthur Milton of Gloucestershire saying that they would give Northants £50,000 to get Brian Crump to come and play for them – 'no one will ever score off him at Bristol'. But Brian was not the type of bowler who batsmen wished to get away from and get down the other end – where they would have to face David. It was in fact the other way round – David got a lot of wickets for Brian.

Both David and Jim thought highly of Keith Andrew. David commented:

> In my view Keith was the most polished and probably the best but understated keeper of the time. He caught a lot of my victims and became a thoughtful and successful captain.

Alan Knott recently spoke of Keith as one of his wicket-keeping heroes, and quoted a tip he received from him: *he told me he always used keeping gloves without webbing, as they helped his one-handed catching.*

Three-nil up in the series, the selectors announced six team changes for the fifth Test. Out went Trueman, Statham, Titmus, and Lock. In came David, not just as one of the 12 but certain of his first cap, opening the bowling alongside recent debutant Len Coldwell, with Barry Knight and Dexter adding seam options and Ray Illingworth, the surprise choice for Australia, and Allen as spinners.

The Times correspondent saw a parallel with 1954 when the touring party to Australia having already been chosen, Tyson and Loader were blooded against Pakistan at the Oval, just as Larter would be now. *'Here is a side which will give Dexter a foretaste of his touring problems: Illingworth bowls like Allen, and Knight like Dexter, Coldwell is the same pace as Knight, only Larter is quicker than anyone else and the main interest will lie in the form he shows'. Alex Bannister made the same point: 'it was eight years ago that Tyson made his debut on the same ground against the same opposition. He was then regarded as much the same gamble as Larter is today.'*

> At long last the call came, and I headed to the Oval in August to play against Pakistan in the 5th Test. The results fortunately showed that I was ready for this level. This debut match brought me into close contact with Ted Dexter as the England captain. I was too focused on what I had to do to get excited about his captaincy, but it was the start of a frustrating period for me.

The day before the Test David bowled for an hour into an empty net at Lord's under the direction of Alec Bedser. He had been critical of David bowling short of a good length during the MCC match against Pakistan at Lord's in May. He was now quoted as having some concern that David's speed was reduced by his newly shortened run.

> The protocol for the Test was that players were to arrive the day before the start, treating it as a training/nets day. Dinner with the selectors the night before a Test was the usual, accompanied by a sort of pep talk. I say sort of because none of the selectors I knew were hilarious after dinner speakers!

On the morning of the match Swanton treated his *Daily Telegraph* readers to a gentle lecture. *'No doubt the focus will be on the fine manly figure of Larter. Estimates as to his fate in Australia vary from those who predict that his supposed proneness to injury will scarcely survive the deck games on the boat, to the flat pronouncement that he is 'a gamble'. As to this one might comment that remarkably few England fast bowlers have broken down in Australia and as to the gamble that phrase might be applied, so different are the conditions, to every single cricketer being sent out for the first time.'*

The details of the Oval match, and David's contribution to it appear earlier in the first chapter. The match generated a considerable amount of press comment. The following represents a dip into that large pool.

The *Guardian* thought that, David apart, the bowling and fielding did not generate much confidence for the Australia tour. *'Ijaz Butt seemed determined to commit cricket suicide. Twice in Larter's first over he threw his bat at balls short of half volleys and drove no less wildly in his second over to be caught off the edge at first slip. Imtiaz and Mushtaq showed how easy it was to score without rest. Larter was controlling his length and direction to the sacrifice of pace, and Coldwell at little more than brisk medium was achieving nothing more than genial short of length in-swing.'*

One spectator that day was 16 year old David English, later to be dubbed the Godfather of English Cricket for his work in developing budding young cricketers through the annual Bunbury Cricket Festival. 1,043 of those Bunburys went on to play first-class cricket and 114 for England. *'I watched David Larter capturing five for 57 in his first outing and nine for 145 in the match.... a brilliant debut for England. I remember also watching him hurling them down for Northamptonshire from a great height of 6 feet 7 inches, terrifying the opposition batsmen. In 1963 he was second only to Fred Trueman as an English fast bowler. His non-stop career finally came to a stop with injury on the 1965/6 Ashes tour, after he had captured five for 68 against South Africa at Nottingham, over-shadowing John Snow in the process. ... I remember as though it was yesterday!'*

Swanton commented on England's fielding: *'this oscillated from good to not so good. At one end of the scale is Parfitt who took a beautiful catch at cover point, at the other Larter. He of course has a long way to get down, but so have other tall men. When he does find the ball in his hands he has as might be hoped a swift low throw.'*

Swanton added: *'...all concerned...had an excellent example from the captain [Dexter] whose fitness and energy have to be seen to be believed.'* But he was impressed by David's bowling: *'on so unresponsive a wicket 9 for 145 are fine figures* which at least will give some encouragement to Larter and to the captain an added confidence in his possibilities. Larter is not fast yet and I do not say his success in Australia is necessarily dependent simply on speed. He might be extremely useful at his present pace which is fairly described as brisk fast-medium. One feels that this splendid piece of machinery, if he will excuse the metaphor, might be capable of a high-grade performance in terms of mph if it would be tuned by an expert mechanic. Maybe Alec Bedser will prove to be that mechanic.'

The *Daily Telegraph's* JJ Warr was against over-enthusiasm: *'Larter is, on the evidence here, not the force 10 typhoon that his Northants colleague Tyson became in Australia. However, his tremendous height clearly poses problems for the batsmen and he should prove difficult to see, bowling with the Melbourne stadium roof as a background. For me, I would have been happier with the choice of Shackleton rather than Coldwell, Shackleton being one of the all-time great bowlers in the history of the game. Indeed, apart from the age difference it is hard to see what Coldwell has got that Shackleton hasn't.'*

Some members of the press corps did not think England's bowlers finished off their Pakistani opponents as promptly as they might have, without commenting on the blandness of the Oval wicket. Walter Robins quashed these out of hand: *'Larter bowled extremely well and in Australia he will have the benefit of the advice of Alec Bedser, one of the greatest bowlers in Test history. Larter carried out everything Bedser told him to do and very successfully. He will make the ball bounce much more in Australia than at home, and I think he will do very well indeed.'*

Dexter added his weight to Robins's point by stating that he would not have minded batting against Australian bowling on that wicket. *'Our bowlers could not have had a more searching test. Larter with his great height was the only one who did make the ball bounce much above stump height. It was a magnificent performance for him to achieve 9 for 145 in the match. I had not seen much of him before this match, but he was an eye-opener to me. He showed that he is a bowler of the highest potential. Knight and Coldwell were steady, and the few overs I bowled made me realise what difficulties our bowlers had.'*

As the Oval match finished on the fourth day, David had a rare two days break before resuming his championship duties for Northants against Nottinghamshire at Wantage Road. His three wickets in the first innings put him on 99 wickets for the season, and he achieved the magic target of 100 for the first time when Notts' opening bat Alan Gill edged a ball which left him to Keith Andrew. David picked up a second, giving him five of the nine Notts wickets which fell in the match, but still insufficient to prevent a Notts victory. The final match of the season was at Bournemouth where Hampshire were beaten thanks to major contributions from both the Watts brothers, Jim making his highest first-class score of 145, and Peter taking 13 wickets for 140 with his leg-breaks and googlies. David, exceptionally, was promoted to number eight in the batting order and justified this meteoric rise by scoring 20.

Reflecting on the season, David had every reason to be satisfied. He had captured 100 wickets for the first time (and would have had several more if he had not missed six matches through the intercostals injury), he had won his first England cap and taken nine Pakistani wickets in doing so, and on top of all that had been picked to tour Australia and New Zealand in the quest for the Ashes. The county, having narrowly escaped from bottom place in the championship the year before, had done well with their young side to finish in eighth place.

The team had become settled, and with a happy camaraderie engendered by their popular captain Keith Andrew they were improving year by year. The eleven, supported by the ex-Somerset off-spinner Sully, Brian Crump's young Staffordshire cousin David Steele and the recently qualified Donald Ramsamooj, had begun an upward trajectory – seventh in 1963, third in 1964, and top at the end of July 1965.

David, playing in 20 of the 30 matches, again topped the county's bowling averages, with 84 wickets at 18.92 from 690 overs. He was seventh in the national bowling averages following Sydenham, Loader, Trueman, Coldwell and Wheatley, with 101 wickets at 19 each, from 815 overs, and a strike rate of 48. His 13 innings, aided by five not outs and by his career highest score of 51 not out produced, for him, the sky-high batting average of 15.75.

The Cricketer's season summary noted that '*David Larter established himself as one of the fastest bowlers in the country and was chosen for the Australian tour. Compared with the previous season Larter obviously gained in strength and accuracy.*'

David's 22nd birthday had fallen one week before the season had started. He was thus 21 years younger than the County Cricketers Association's choice as their cricketer of the year. Bill Alley, the Australian-born long-time resident of Somerset, was 43. With 1,915 runs and 112 wickets age did not weary him. David regarded him with awe:

> One of the game's legends. A great all-rounder and as tough a competitor as you could meet. He later became an umpire and remained just as scary.

9

62–63 ASHES TOUR

The average UK house price was £2,670 and average yearly pay £800.

The thrill of getting fitted out with tour kit, cap, blazer, and sweaters made the immediate post county season a special time. Saying goodbye to his family and friends, David joined the other 16 playing members of the tour party at Heathrow on September 27. The 22-year-old from Suffolk was rubbing shoulders with some of the greats of the English game – Sheppard, Dexter, Cowdrey, Barrington, Graveney, Trueman and Statham. The party, including the manager, Bernard Duke of Norfolk, and the assistant manager Alec Bedser, departed for Aden, where air travel gave way to sea transport on board the Canberra. They reached Fremantle on October 9.

> The trip out was memorable. We were the last touring party to travel by ship, the Canberra, and even so we flew halfway, from Heathrow to Aden to board the ship there.
>
> Once on board it was time to look round and we could see a flotilla of local traders' boats bobbing about the ship's side. A system of baskets on long ropes was used to offer goods to the passengers. Brian Johnston – 'Jonners' - spent about half an hour trying to buy a single brogue shoe from one

Knight, Alan Smith, Coldwell, Barrington, BOAC Staff, Trueman, Pullar.

unfortunate shoe seller, who became more and more frustrated with this barmy Englishman who clearly had two feet but only wanted one shoe. To be fair to Jonners, after the laughing stopped he sent down enough money for the pair and some extra.

I have never eaten like it before or since. We travelled first class (dinner jackets – most strange!) and that put us among what seemed like a geriatric gathering of millionaires who existed on salads and special diets. The stewards loved having us on board as most of us were cajoled into trying everything on offer. We then staggered off after dinner to the lower decks where the real people and proper beer were to be found.

Ted Dexter encountered Gordon Pirie, the British long-distance runner on board, and asked him to run exercise sessions on deck for the players. These were rigorous and some of the older hands were not impressed. Fred Trueman for one refused on the basis that he needed a rest after bowling more than a thousand overs in each of the last three county seasons. Over his career he bowled more than 700 overs a summer on eight occasions. By comparison with modern-day bowlers, Steve Harmison only

TOP: Coldwell, Knight, JDFL, His Grace, and Fred Trueman trying to kill Gordon Pirie with the medicine ball.
BELOW LEFT: AC Smith, Parfitt, Dexter. BELOW RIGHT: JT Murray, Pirie, David Allen.

twice bowled more than 500 overs in a season, and no pace bowler since Andy Caddick in 1999 has bowled more than 700. Pirie made some rather ill-chosen remarks about overweight professional cricketers which gave the press something to write about.

> We broke the journey in Colombo to play a one-day exhibition game against Ceylon. After Len Coldwell's opening over Ted Dexter handed me the ball and I marked out my run. I ran in steadily, arrived at the delivery stride and fell flat on my face! I trudged back and came in again and fell flat on my face again. I had to be taken off and I think it was Barry Knight who finished the over. We had only done 5 or 6 days on board, but I had lost my land-legs, which I was not allowed to forget for some time afterwards.

Alan Ross, in *Australia 63*, living up to the sobriquet given him by Gideon Haigh – *'the Patrick Leigh Fermor of cricket – incapable of an infelicitous phrase'*, gave his view of the selection: *'By reasons of current form and future promise, there was little alternative to Coldwell and Larter to support Trueman and Statham. Coldwell, at something under Bedser's pace, had nearly bowled Worcestershire to the championship, and though his dependence on pronounced in-swing and some help from the wicket might make him seem a bowler unsuited for export, he had at least the necessary accuracy and stamina. Larter, a tall 6 foot seven, had youth, height, and physique to set against obvious lack of experience and control. He could be expected to get plenty of bounce on Australian pitches and with Tyson in mind – though Larter had nothing of his dynamism or speed – was as justifiable a gamble as any.'*

David was not only inexperienced; he was in some doubt as to what his role would be:

> Nobody sat me down to say as much but I concluded that I was meant to learn as much as possible from Fred Trueman and Brian Statham. The popular press did not take this view and promoted me as the destroyer of the Aussies and the quickest thing since Frank Tyson – an image I could not hope to fulfil.
>
> Upon arrival in Freemantle (Perth) our boots were cleaned for free. Customs knew we had trodden the Sri Lankan soil, and this was part of the Australian disease prevention programme.
>
> The stay in Perth was three weeks (three matches included) and gave us a good look at our host country. These days, it's a couple of days off the plane and you are into the cricket.

All Ashes series are followed closely by the press corps. In the early 60s there was an understanding between the press and the players as to what was printable and what not. The players made themselves available, and the journalists and broadcasters did not breach confidences.

> I met Brian Johnston several times, also Peter West, John Arlott, and others. Jonners was obviously the life and soul of any party. In those days we trusted all these fellows implicitly. I recall a lunch back home in Gloucester – on a Sunday day off – with John Arlott and three or four of us, and he gave a lengthy analysis of the benefits of red wine coupled with several sampling sessions as lunch progressed. We managed to play the next day, but there were some sore heads!

On the Canberra voyage from Aden to Perth Ian Wooldridge, covering the tour for the *Daily Mail*, approached David and his cabin sharer Len Coldwell for help.

> Ian was a sports journalist turning his attention to cricket. He wanted to know more about the technicalities of the game. He spent about 4 or 5 hours (precious drinking time!) over two or three sessions getting us to explain the finer points of short square leg, silly mid-on and even bowling maidens! He took copious notes and was a quick learner, and I hope our help gave him a bit of a grounding for his subsequent reporting success. He made it, so good luck to him.

Particular press attention to David was inevitable, as the young giant and a hope for the future. Denys Rowbotham was quick off the mark with comment from the first net session at Perth, noting that from a much shortened run David achieved a pace

Ken Barrington, Fred Titmus, Barry Knight, John Murray, Peter Parfitt;
W Watkins (scorer), Alan Smith, Geoff Pullar, Tom Graveney, JDFL, Len Coldwell,
Ray Illingworth, David Allen, Sam Cowan (masseur);
Alec Bedser, Fred Trueman, Colin Cowdrey, Ted Dexter, Brian Statham,
David Sheppard, His Grace.

markedly faster than normally he did in England, and from barely short of a length, a nasty steep lift. He felt that if David could gain accuracy and perhaps trim his run as Tyson did eight years before, he could become formidable.

Wooldridge was also at the nets: *'October 11: Larter ends his ten-day worry. He flings down his first ball on Australian soil – pitched on a length it lifted viciously and cleared off stump by a foot. He had brooded about this moment throughout the ten-day journey here. Tonight, at the Government House reception he looked happier than I had previously seen: "I'm no longer worried about whether I shall be able to bounce the ball", he said.'*

David was picked for the first match, a two-day affair against a Western Australia Country XI, opening opposite Fred Trueman, and he retained his place for the first state match, against Western Australia, opening this time with Brian Statham. The

'He and Statham blew the opposition away for 77...'

wicket undoubtedly helped him, more so than would be the case when the tour moved east, but he provoked concern amongst the home batsmen by the bounce he achieved from bowling on a strict length and swinging the ball away.

He and Statham blew the opposition away for 77, Statham with 3 for 21 and David with 4 for 25. MCC cruised to a ten-wicket win.

Ray Robinson was impressed: *'This penetrating pair dismissing Western Australia for 77, gave the most devastating start I have seen in the opening first-class match of a tour…. The way the Northants' giant bowled in his first four overs compelled batsmen to play at balls that lifted and cut away….Larter's 14 overs [in the second innings] have gone a long way towards settling doubts as to whether he will stand up to the stress of the tour. His only complaint was a blistered toe.'*

Perth was the world's fastest and bouncy wicket, in keeper Alan Smith's view: *I was standing at least a full pitch-length back to David, and to Brian Statham. David bowled well and was quick, at that stage close to the pace of Trueman and Statham. In the east we found that the Australian pitches did not have their usual bounce, and Sydney in particular was a poor pitch.*

Ray Illingworth particularly remembers that match: *As I recall, Larter had made his debut in the summer of 1962 against Pakistan and had had an excellent game. He was therefore regarded as a possible opening bowler for the Test series against Australia and did himself no harm with a seriously impressive display against Western Australia, which took place before the first Test match. If I remember he took four wickets in the first innings for next to nothing. During the match, a furious Fred Trueman was seen cursing to himself in the dressing room. When we asked what was wrong, he complained that Larter was "bowling so bloody well, it's the end of my Test career." That wasn't the case, of course, and Fred went on to become the first bowler ever to get 300 Test wickets. Larter, meanwhile, didn't play in any of the Australian Tests and only played in New Zealand because Brian Statham went home injured.*

All-rounder Barry Knight, who sat out that match, agreed that David looked very threatening with pace and bounce – *on a wicket which had good carry, the western grounds being rock hard, as would be Brisbane later and to some extent Adelaide. Sydney was unlikely to suit him.* Rowbotham stuck his neck right out in saying *'unless Trueman and Coldwell perform great deeds in the next match, Larter should have established himself as Statham's likeliest opening partner for the Tests… not merely a remarkable achievement but one beyond the rosiest prediction.'*

David was very surprised at Illingworth's story of Fred Trueman fretting in the Perth dressing room about his Test match place:

> Ray's story of Fred Trueman is great! True or not, it never occurred to me that Fred ever thought like that. We chatted and bowled together but I never had an inkling that he saw me as genuine competition. If Brian Statham had said anything along those lines, I would have taken it as a compliment and possibly mentally nodded in agreement, but Fred was, and still is, the best fast bowler I ever saw. Many people would not know how much thought he put into his bowling. A good few batsmen were psyched out by his reputation.

The last Perth-based match, on October 26, was against a Combined XI, which with Lawry, Simpson and O'Neill added to the Western Australia line-up, inflicted the first defeat any MCC side had ever suffered in Perth. Trueman and Len Coldwell formed the attack this time, as Alan Ross saw it *'making much less impression than Statham and Larter.'*

> I roomed with Len around Australia and New Zealand. A very skilful in-swing bowler, very well suited to English conditions, but he found the lack of swing in Australia hard work.

As the youngest of the party, and with a natural reserve, David was not part of the forefront of the social life to which all touring teams are subject, but he mixed in well. Others were more active:

Barry Knight lived up to his name and enjoyed everything on offer after hours. One morning in Perth around 7 am Barry was approaching the team hotel on his way back in when Alec Bedser came walking out. Alec was Assistant Manager (basically to keep the cricket in order while the Duke did the handshaking etc) and he was a strait-laced, rather old-fashioned type. He enjoyed an early morning walk before breakfast.

Barry thought quickly. He was dressed in shorts and casual shirt, so he started to breathe heavily and broke into a trot and ran towards Alec to be greeted with 'well done Knighty. Good to see you keeping fit.'

David was unaccustomed to the demands of young cricket fans but happily participated in occasional impromptu coaching.

Impromptu coaching

From Perth the tour moved east to Adelaide, where David and Knight were picked in support of Statham. As Alan Ross pointed out, the initial success of the fast bowlers at Perth had, predictably enough, not been maintained. *'Trueman had bowled scarcely at all; Larter, on the flawless Adelaide pitch, had come to realise that all was not honey and roses, Coldwell had been unfit, and Knight looked short of pace and accuracy.'*

Over 1,000 runs were scored in the four-day game against South Australia cut short by rain, David for the first time bowling against Garry Sobers who scored 42 and a marvellous 99 before running himself out. David's 32 eight ball overs in the match brought him two wickets for 132 runs. Statham had good figures and took seven wickets.

Adelaide is a beautiful city, but David had one bad memory of it.

> It was at Adelaide that I had the fright of my life. From our hotel outside the town we could walk out onto a beautiful beach. The beach had a very shallow fall and one could walk or swim some 50 to 60 feet in as the depth only increased by a foot or so. It was hot with the sun up high and a group of us were throwing a tennis ball about in the shallows. Some clown purposely threw it way over my head and into deeper water. I turned and swam after it, quickly getting to it and reaching to grab it. As I got it and turned to swim back, so a long black shape underneath me did exactly the same. I must have broken all records racing back, looking anxiously underneath me as I reached the shallows. Only then did I realise I saw my own shadow!

The party had a three-day break before moving on to Melbourne where on November 9 a perfect batting wicket produced over 1,300 runs, 219 of them going to Ken Barrington, and centuries for Dexter and Titmus in a total of 633 for seven declared. The weather was very warm. From Barrington: *'Bloody hot, Fred, we'll cut out the short singles. From Titmus: 'we'll cut out yours.'*

The Australian XI responded with 451, Simpson and Barry Shepherd scoring centuries. Phil Tressider for the *Guardian* observed that all-rounder Barry Knight would contribute more as a batsman than a bowler *'in a country where there is neither help from the wickets nor the encouragement of atmosphere to assist seam and swing appreciably.'* Having said that he noted that *'for the last 20 minutes of the second day Simpson and Thomas had to face the hostility of Trueman and Larter, the openers groping like blind men in the murk.'*

After four first-class games, Rowbotham's view of the fast bowling attack was now more balanced: *'neither Larter nor Trueman has yet clinched his Test place. Trueman* bowled too short and too wide. Larter's arm looked low and he delivered so wide of the stumps as to threaten to cut the return crease. Yet he bowled straighter and to a better length than Trueman and the five Australian XI wickets he took rewarded these virtues.'

From Melbourne the tourists moved further east to Sydney. There they ran into a very strong New South Wales state side for whom Simpson and O'Neill scored centuries, Neil Harvey and Alan Davidson 50s and Richie Benaud produced a wonderful spell of leg-spin bowling. He took seven for 18 as MCC were bowled out in their second innings in only three hours for 104, to lose the match by an innings and 80 runs with a day to spare.

> It was clear that we were going to be up against some fine opponents. Norman O'Neill, always built up by the Aussie press, did not let them down. A powerful back foot player he could take an attack apart in no time. He possessed one of the best throws in 1960s cricket, flat and accurate from nearly anywhere, having learnt how to throw as a baseball pitcher in his youth. Alan Davidson was a fine left-arm quick bowler but also a very good middle order batsman. Time and again Richie Benaud was able to whistle up big Alan to sort out problems – the 'go to' man and he usually delivered. Benaud himself was the cricket lovers' captain, possessing very good cricket judgement and the ability to manipulate a game to suit Australia. He was an excellent leg-spinner and an attacking batsman. He was to meet his second wife on the tour – Daphne Surfleet who was working for the MCC and assisting the Duke with tour admin.

David remembers Graham Hill turning up in the dressing room at this game:

> He was mad about cricket. Noddy Pullar, who owned a Triumph TR3, hogged his attention, but he proved a lively larger-than-life character, despite his small stature – an advantage for a racing driver.

MCC's tour selection committee was now closing in on the selection for the first Test starting on November 30. Trueman and Statham having played in the NSW match, Coldwell and David were paired for the next, at Brisbane against Queensland. There was now some concern over Trueman's fitness as he had to leave the field in Sydney because of a back problem. There was equal concern over the performance of Coldwell and David on a Brisbane pitch even too slow for Wes Hall, the West Indian fast bowler who was playing for Queensland. The home state scored 433 for 7 on the first day, Ross noting that Dexter, 'as sometimes happens on these occasions, alienating himself from the action altogether, and the bowlers were left to their own largely arbitrary, devices.'

Dexter was as a man full of theories, in Barry Knight's view, *and was easily bored. Even as a scratch golfer he would change his grip frequently. There was one occasion when Ted announced to the team that following a dinner conversation he had had with EW Swanton, the fielding positions would be 'in echelon'. Most of the team did not know what this meant but when Brian Statham, preparing to open the bowling, saw the odd positions being taken up by the fielders he threw the ball back to Ted, telling him to bowl himself as he, Brian, could not bowl to such a field.*

Ted Dexter was an exceptional batsman in Eric Russell's eyes. *Umpires at the bowler's end would always move back a yard when Ted came to the wicket, but slightly aloof and sometimes strange as a captain. In my debut Test, at Lahore, against Pakistan on the 1961/2 tour of the subcontinent, Ted had tried his five bowlers when he threw the ball to me. I was not a bowler. He must have seen me bowling's medium-pace stuff in the nets before the game. Anyway, I got over the shock and bowled 19 overs for only 25 runs, without taking a wicket.*

Sussex's John Snow had as much experience of Dexter as anyone. He was later to write: '*Some people found him aloof. There was one member of the Sussex side who swore that Ted never spoke to him apart from giving him directions on the field. I am sure this was not deliberate. Ted was a man of moods, often caught up in theories, keen when the action was hot, uninterested when the game was dull.*' Alan Ross put the same point this way: '*Dexter as a captain under pressure, or when bored by adversity or lack of success, was inclined to dissociate himself from the whole proceeding. He is a temperamental cricketer and temperamental cricketers depend on the stars being right for them. His choice as captain of the tour was something of a gamble.*'

Simon Wilde in *England – the Biography* viewed the early 1960s as a time when English cricket faced a crisis of confidence, its mindset having become less sure and more defensive. He considered that Cowdrey and Dexter, who captained England for most of the three years after Peter May's 1961 retirement, were unadventurous and temperamentally unsuited to the captaincy role.

It had been feared that Coldwell would suffer on Australian wickets from his lack of pace. That began to be realised as the party reached the good pitches in the east. As Barry Knight (who emigrated to Australia to begin a coaching career in 1970) recently put it, *Australians did not believe that off-spinners or medium pacers - such as Len Coldwell and myself - were of any use on Australian pitches. They would have picked David Larter, with pace and bounce, before picking Coldwell or me.*

David however was having trouble with his delivery, being repeatedly no-balled for dragging, with a resultant loss of rhythm and accuracy. He tried to overcome this by experimenting with a straighter run and a lower arm action designed to bring him closer to the stumps at delivery, but he was still finding himself bowling from wide of the stumps and was beginning to lose confidence.

> I developed trouble with my approach and started shying away from the stumps and bowling from too wide. It wasn't anything to do with the feet, and I gradually ironed it out by myself.

The first Test, traditionally played at Brisbane, untraditionally ended in a high-scoring draw with 1,400 runs scored. The selectors chose Trueman and Statham to open the bowling, supported by Knight and Dexter, Titmus as the main spin bowler, supported by Barrington. Alan Ross in the *Guardian* felt that England's bowling would be strengthened by the inclusion of Allen and David, but Allen had been unaccountably massacred at Melbourne and Sydney, and David, *'while a gamble as a bowler, was not in Barry Knight's class as a batsman and fielder.'* Trueman needed painkilling injections to get through the Test, his back problem having been diagnosed as a displaced bone in the spine, but he played through the pain.

There were two state matches between the first and second Tests, against Victoria at Melbourne on December 14 and South Australia at Adelaide over Christmas (with a break for Christmas Day and Boxing Day). Statham, Coldwell, and Knight formed the opening attack in the first and Coldwell, David and Dexter in the second. Victoria, apart from Lawry and West, were weak opposition. In their first innings Statham got close to full pace, whilst Coldwell and Knight were predictably docile. The second innings was a different matter: Coldwell got a wicket with his first ball, and then another, and in damp and overcast conditions, doing just a little off the pitch, he ended with six for 49 – a fine performance which was to prove, from David's perspective, very significant. Victoria's 175 left MCC to score 180 in four hours, which they did by five wickets with 40 minutes to spare.

At Adelaide it was David's turn to seek to impress the selectors. Conditions could not have been more different to those at Melbourne, 100-degree heat and a good wicket producing a run-feast. MCC scored 586 for 5 wickets declared, with 307 from Cowdrey, 122 from Graveney and 81 from Sheppard. South Australia responded with 450 with Les Favell scoring 120, and Garry Sobers, demonstrating why writer Duncan Hamilton described him as *'a genius, unique and separate'*, making a sublime 89 followed by a fiercely struck 75 not out in the second innings until rain prevented what might have been a close finish.

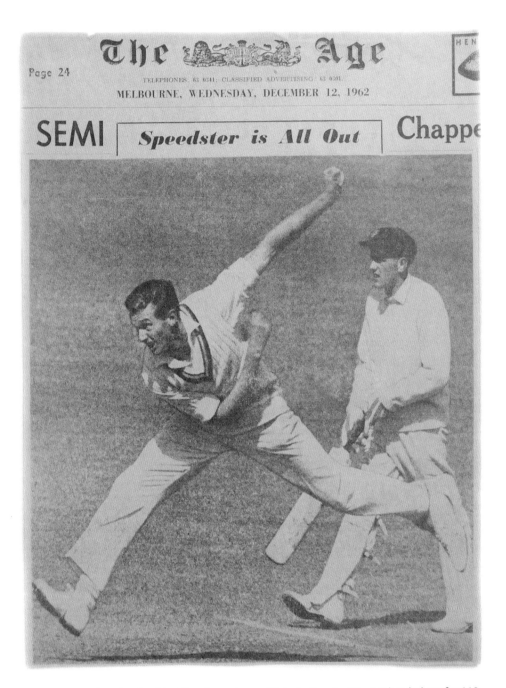

David Larter takes four for 31 at Bendigo, where a Victoria Country XI were bowled out for 110.

I enjoyed bowling to Garfield Sobers, in my view the best cricketer I ever met, and no doubt the best all-round cricketer ever. I watched him bowl quick left-arm over the wicket swingers, orthodox left-arm spin, left-arm chinamen and googlies, catch absolute blinders, and then caress the ball all round the park. You did not mind if he beat you, it was worth it to be part of it.

In this game I felt I had bowled a pretty good over and tried a yorker for my last ball. This was whipped through mid-wicket before anybody moved, and my abiding memory is this flashing toothy smile and a growl of 'well bowled'.

Denys Rowbotham expressed some optimism about David's improvement from his recent difficulties:

'He is beginning to win the lift from just short of a length that his height ought to give him, and when confidence in his changed method brings him greater control over length and particularly direction, he may prove a formidable proposition. On Monday, his direction was so awry that 10 overs cost him 73 runs. Today with better direction another 11 overs cost only 40 runs. It was perhaps unlucky for Larter that in this period of important transition he should have to challenge Les Favell in his most brilliant form on a mercilessly true though fast wicket….Dexter had to give Larter a good trial, whilst exercising both his off-spinners…and exercise himself for the job of supporting pace bowler.'

With the second Test starting in Melbourne in only two days' time on December 29 it was late in the day for Dexter's trial of David. As one of the tour selectors, David Sheppard, later wrote, England felt they needed another frontline bowler to support Trueman and Statham, 'and Coldwell's excellent bowling against Victoria put him in prime position to take Knight's place. We hoped he might be rather like Alec Bedser.'

Coldwell was duly chosen for the second Test and he played his part in a fine seven-wicket victory for England. It was their first win in Australia since the 1954/55 tour. Watched by over 247,000 spectators and in great heat MCC's bowlers restricted Australia to 316 and 248 in their two innings, thanks to eight wickets from Trueman – described by David Sheppard as the finest sustained and accurate fast bowling he had ever seen. Five wickets from Titmus, three from Statham and Coldwell's important wickets of Simpson and Harvey supported Trueman well. As Alan Ross identified, 'it was only the lack of final nip which Bedser possessed which prevented Coldwell from being even more troublesome.' In Barry Knight's opinion, it was also notable that Coldwell bowled in-swing only, whereas someone like Tom Cartwright at a similar speed could move it both ways. The batting of Cowdrey, Sheppard and Dexter saw England home.

David Frith later offered a tip for subsequent MCC batsmen playing at Melbourne: *'David Sheppard, Colin Cowdrey, and Brian Booth of Australia, all read lessons at a church in Melbourne before making hundreds in the Test there. Indeed, Sheppard spent most Sundays during the tour preaching. As Swanton observed: 'the presence in the pulpit of David Sheppard, the centurion of Melbourne, has filled the Anglican cathedral of every state capital from Perth to Brisbane.'*

Cowdrey was one of several tourists whom David felt he got to know a little on the trip.

> I found Colin Cowdrey a lovely gentle man and a very good player. He seemed to have more time than mere mortals, a bit like Tom Graveney. To see him catching in the slips was an education in effortless skill and coordination.
>
> I seemed to hit it off with Peter Parfitt and became good friends. That could have been due to the East Anglian connection – he was a good old Norfolk boy. A more than useful left-hander he knew how to make a lot of runs, not just a flashy 50 or so. He was of course a good chum of Middlesex colleague John Murray, 'JT', an urbane Londoner with a great sense of humour who, later in the tour, was to inveigle me into a contest with our hosts over a yard of ale.

He was also fascinated to meet cricketers whom he had only known as heroic names from the past.

> I was proud to shake hands with Harold Larwood, already blind 30 years after his Bodyline tour triumph. I had also had the privilege of being introduced to Sir Donald Bradman, who was still very involved in Australian cricket, during the Adelaide Test and we chatted briefly.

David put the memory of Favell and Sobers behind him and bowled impressively in the match against a Combined XI at Launceston in Tasmania on January 4. The local team was boosted by the addition of mainlanders Lawry, Booth, O'Neill, and Barry Shepherd, but to no avail. Trueman took 4 for 13 and David 4 for 24 as the opposition was shot out for 77 in just over two hours.

Rowbotham in the *Guardian* observed that these two gave 4,500 spectators some idea of what fast bowling is like: *'Finally Dexter has the possibility of a new force should he and his selectors think that they need it. This is the bowling of Larter. Not only is his slightly shortened run now smooth and rhythmical but his action is if anything higher than it seemed over Christmas at Adelaide. There, the mechanics seemed ordered but control of length and direction, though improving, still eluded him. Yesterday at fast medium-pace, he found the control and at once his lift again provided a formidable weapon.'*

It was the first high point of David's tour since Perth. Would it persuade the selectors to pick him for the third Test, starting on January 11? Rowbotham was doubtful: *'When England's selectors meet after breakfast on Thursday, it is unlikely that they will decide that Larter is yet ripe for the third Test, but in the event that lift and maximum accuracy should elude Statham, and should Coldwell if picked not rise above steadiness, Larter's recent advances will be of crucial importance.'*

For the Sydney Test the tour party's hotel was on the corner of King's Cross, in those days an area of some notoriety. Barry Knight tells the story: *The Duke of Norfolk was not a good sleeper, and could only catch about one hour a night by taking a large sleeping pill, which he was happy to offer to any member of the team unable to get good rest. This meant that the Duke was often wandering about in the early hours, which was occasionally embarrassing for those players returning from dining out. It also meant that when the Duke went for a walk from the King's Cross hotel, he was greeted by some of the local ladies. The next day all players received under their door a note from assistant manager Alec Bedser advising that the party was moving to the Travelodge.*

England stuck with the same bowling attack, with Coldwell as the main support for Trueman and Statham. Dexter did not use himself as a bowler. Australia won by eight wickets thanks to centuries from Harvey and O'Neill and nine wickets from left-arm pace bowler Alan Davidson. Records were broken – Titmus's seven for 79 was the best by an England spinner in Australia since 1929, the first day's attendance of over 54,000 was the highest on the ground since 1928, total receipts for the match were a record and finally, Benaud's two wickets took him past Ray Lindwall's Australian record of 228 Test wickets.

> I think it was during this Test that a classic Fred Trueman story occurred. Overseas tours used a postal system which managed to keep up with the travels, but even so it could take time for letters to arrive, and then usually only at the major venues. At Sydney one morning a telegram from his wife Enid was delivered to Fred and it immediately produced enough oaths to heighten the colour of the Rev. David Sheppard. When he was calm enough to speak Fred said 'She's sold the bloody house! My house! She's sold it!' This was followed by more oaths. The rest of us could only marvel at how this partnership worked. Sadly, it did not, and the inevitable split up occurred. She was certainly a match for Fred.

Trueman later felt Dexter cost England the Test. He had advised Dexter to pick two spinners on the dry surface, but Dexter maintained the three-man pace attack which had done well in Melbourne. In the event the pacemen managed only four wickets between them against Titmus's seven. Trueman felt Dexter compounded this error in the next Test at Adelaide by dropping Coldwell and bringing in Ray Illingworth on a pitch that Trueman thought was better suited to pace bowling. Trueman had little belief in Dexter's tactical ability. Statham wrote that he never understood Dexter as a captain and didn't think anyone in the dressing room did either, as he did things at times that were difficult to understand, making moves and bowling changes completely out of keeping with the run of the game. Barry Knight is of the opinion that both Trueman and Statham wanted pace and bounce in the matches at Brisbane and Adelaide, and thus would have welcomed David in support.

Peter Parfitt, whilst no great believer in Dexter's captaincy skills, had a lot of time for him as a batting partner: *Some of the great batsmen, and the great bowlers, could tend to selfishness. Take Kenny Barrington for example. If he did not fancy it, he would stay at the bowler's end. If he did fancy it, he would always take a run off the last ball of the over. Graveney was another one. If he fancied it, you never got a look in. For me Dexter was the most unselfish of them all. He would come up to me at the end of an over and say 'if you don't fancy so and so I will happily take him on. Just call clearly and early and I will respond.' There was no side to him at all.*

Rowbotham was concerned that Coldwell was still achieving *'little more than steadiness. The obvious answer seems to be to try Larter, particularly if he can repeat his Launceston performance these next days at Newcastle.'* The Newcastle fixture, a non first-class three-day game against a New South Wales Country XI, was unfortunately for David the only game for the touring team between the third and fourth Tests. Both he and Coldwell played in a match won easily thanks to David Allen's eight wickets. David took the first wicket to fall but thereafter made little impact and Dexter gave Graveney and Pullar, occasional bowlers, more overs than David, taking six wickets between them.

Selection for the fourth Test at Adelaide on January 25 was later much analysed. For *Wisden*, the Test provided the first real disappointment of the tour. '*The selection of the two sides and the manner of their play suggested that they were a little afraid of each other and both seemed content to settle for a draw, leaving everything to the final match at Sydney.*' It would have been a bold decision to pick David, but boldness was not a feature of selection.

Benaud set England an impossible target of 356 to win at 89 runs an hour, and the match was drawn, with England on 223 for four wickets. Illingworth, brought in to replace Coldwell, took one for 108. Dexter had a good game with the ball, taking three wickets in each innings, supporting Trueman's five wickets and Statham's six. Neil Harvey in his penultimate Test made 154 in the first innings having been dropped on several occasions, one in particular by the Rev David Sheppard causing Trueman, so it is said, to chide him with *'the only time your hands are together is on Sundays'*. This in turn gave rise to the tall story that a couple in Australia had asked Mrs Sheppard if the Reverend could christen their baby, but she advised them not to as he was bound to drop it.

The fixture schedule was again not in David's favour, with only one first-class game between Tests four and five - a four-day game against Victoria at Melbourne starting on February 4. Trueman and Statham were rested, and David opened the bowling with Coldwell after an elegant 185 from Tom Graveney had put the tourists into a strong position. Dexter gave David 29 overs, in which he again dismissed the opener Bill Lawry, caught behind from a good ball moving away from him, as one of four wickets in the first innings. In the second innings David experimented with some success, bowling one over before lunch and two afterwards from his shorter run, successfully achieving control of length and direction before turning to his long run in his fourth over. He then began striving for maximum pace without loss of the control he had achieved, ending with three for 45 in 14 overs.

Rowbotham noted that the lift he extracted *'was not merely startling but tested reflexes to the utmost. Even from his short run Larter can achieve something near his top pace, and it was the surprise of a much faster ball, 10 minutes after lunch, which completely undermined Test batsman Redpath's forward shot. Coldwell's best was only an innocuous steadiness which played Stackpole and Cowper into form. Dexter's strange field placing and bowling changes meant the match was drawn rather than won.'*

'Larter toiled away with great heart but painfully little luck', reported the *Irish Times: 'He suffered from two mistakes in the slips, both bad ones. He has been the fastest bowler in the match if not the straightest. Perhaps there is a chance yet that his power will one day be harnessed.'*

The Victoria game was followed by a one-day festival match at Canberra on February 6, arranged by Robert Menzies, the Australian Prime Minister and a dedicated cricket fan, as an annual event against the touring party. Menzies had persuaded 54-year-old Sir Donald Bradman to emerge from his 14-year cricket retirement, with the plan that when he came out to bat, he would receive the bowling of one of his great adversaries of other days, Alec Bedser. But it was not to be; he faced some leg-breaks from Tom Graveney and then a gentle over from Brian Statham. David was a spectator, but Barry Knight was in the field as Bradman cracked a square cut to the boundary. *The next ball was edged onto his pad and then very slowly rolled into the stumps: I recall Dexter telling Bradman that he should continue batting, but Bradman was, as always, prompt in leaving the crease before the umpire could give a late call for no-ball.* The Don did not play again.

The final Test, at Melbourne starting on February 15, four months after the first game of the tour, was played by both sides in an even more defensive frame of mind than they had the fourth. England's attack was in the hands of Trueman and Statham, supported by Dexter, and no less than three off-spinners. Harvey in his last Test equalled a Test record by holding six catches, whilst both Trueman and Benaud equalled Bedser's 236 Test wickets, with only Statham now just ahead of them. A great deal of barracking and slow hand-clapping accompanied a dull and lifeless game which in *Wisden's* words did immense harm to cricket, particularly in Australia. A dead pitch was partly to blame, but defensive thinking more so.

The niggardly spirit shown by both captains in the fourth and fifth Tests was highlighted by EM Wellings in *Dexter v Benaud*, his tour account. Sparing no blushes, he wrote: *'the spirit of adventure which Walter Robins, chairman of the selectors, and others had tried hard to foster before the team left home was allowed to die on the tour. Had this side been well led, England would I believe have gone on from the triumph of the second Test to win the series before reaching Sydney for the final Test. Dexter must take the blame for these failings.'*

Cantankerous as ever, Wellings was also critical of the choice of manager – the Duke of Norfolk's relationship with Dexter *'was as monarch to prime minister'* and his lack of business and cricket experience meant that too heavy a burden was cast upon Bedser; this in turn meant *'that David Larter for instance was not given all the coaching he needed to fulfil his promise.'*

Indeed, neither David nor Barry Knight saw much of Alec as a coach. Knight recalls Bedser's famous lament along the lines of:

'I don't know what my role is – I'm supposed to be on a missionary hunt with David Sheppard and Colin Cowdrey preaching every Sunday, then I'm assisting a modelling tour (Ted Dexter's wife came out on a modelling assignment) and now with the arrival of the Duke's three daughters I've got the Norfolk Broads to look after.'

The tour, including the New Zealand leg, encompassed no less than 32 matches and took more than six months. Apart from the 19 first-class games there were 12 up-country fixtures, which was far too many given the poor attendances they

David, Jim Parks and wife, Ken Barrington.

attracted. Ian Wooldridge was critical of the schedule: '*as one example, we all travelled on a Sunday rest day between two sparsely attended minor matches, 1,600 miles, making eight take-offs and landings, and hitched the last leg by motor coach.*'

The schedule did permit the inevitable photo shoots and receptions – at which the Duke always spoke well – as well as visits to schools, talks and coaching. Importantly there was also time for relaxation in a hot Australian summer – a happy escape from the UK's worst winter for years where snow and ice persisted through till March 1963. David spent some time in the company of Ken Barrington.

> The Colonel was a great bloke who seemed to take to me on the tour. The 'Colonel' bit refers to his habit of marching out to bat in charity matches with his trousers pulled up over his tummy, using an MCC tie as a belt and a cap which I think was I Zingari. He would then belt the ball to all parts in complete contrast to his everyday professional behaviour, which was as solid as you could get. A Barrington hundred was never hurried, but there were no chances either.

David would have hoped to spend some time with his captain on a trip of six months duration. He felt it a great pity that Dexter shared so little time with any of his team off the field. As Alan Ross noted, he was not alone in this: Jardine, Hammond, Hutton were equally remote characters, and to some extent also Peter May. '*Social responsiveness, affability, evenness of mood are not noticeably part of Dexter's personality, though he is consistent to the extent that he would unconcernedly cut the Duke of Norfolk or the chairman of the selectors as he would look through a plain hostess at a cocktail party. Where he failed in in his relations with his team was that he left them over-much to their own devices often without guidance or direction when both would be appreciated.*'

> My overall impression of Ted Dexter mirrors that of many others. He was a remote and distant character who hardly said a word to me. I was still only 22 and learning much about life as well as cricket, and to be honest I did not learn much about either from him. As I was to learn later this was also reflected in the 'management' of Test and MCC cricket. There was very much an elite group (Gubby Allen, Freddie Brown and RWV Robins among others) who ran everything like a private club. Their influence lasted longer than my career.

David's concern about that triumvirate was widely shared. Simon Wilde in *England – the Biography*, noting the considerable undue influence on selection wielded by them, also recorded their unpopularity with the rank and file of England players. The MCC hierarchy's influence extended as far as sitting in on selection meetings to ensure those selected were of 'good character'. Trueman was one who failed this test in his youth.

Peter Parfitt, when asked whether David could have expected Dexter to put a proverbial arm around his shoulders, shook his head: *Edward was not that sort of person. He certainly never spoke to me. I think he was too young when he was first made captain but got better with age – as was the case with Brearley, much better once he had some experience. Illingworth was by far the best in my view.*

With only one Test match behind him before the tour, David had been the new boy learning the ropes, happy quietly to observe the dressing room interaction of his fellow tourists. There was much to observe, as Ray Illingworth recounts:

There were quite a few characters in England's dressing room in that series, notably Fred, of course. Cowdrey had a lot to say and those Middlesex chums, Parfitt, Titmus and JT Murray, were chatting non-stop. The Rev David Sheppard was never short of a few words, either, and nor was 'Lord' Ted Dexter. David kept himself to himself and he was a good team man.

In those days there was quite a big rift between the amateurs and the professionals and that played a major part in the dynamics of the dressing room. It did not do much for team spirit. David did not take sides – he did not mind which camp he was in. He just saw himself as a cricketer. Whilst he was a shy and modest man and as a quick bowler, at times very quick, he did not have that instinctive aggression that many fast bowlers had – I am thinking of Fred Trueman of course or John Snow. Yes, maybe David was too gentle…

David responded to Ray Illingworth's comments:

I always thought of Ray as a thoughtful student of the game and a very good tactician. He is around 10 years my senior and in your early 20s, as I was on the Ashes trip, that is a big gap. We talked, and of course, played on many occasions together and I have to say I agree with his assessment of my character. He was not the only one to try to find the aggressive mean streak in me. In a way I am quietly happy that I did not, and still do not seem to possess such a trait. I have seen a few barmy people along the way, and it seems to me that all people remember is the ugly side.

' … not the only one to try to find the agressive streak in me.'

Eric Russell regarded Ray Illingworth as a great character, outspoken, and not a great fan of amateurs. Huw Turbervill interviewed Ray for his book, *The Toughest Tour*: '*Ray did not feel at ease on the tour: the amateurs never invited the professionals to dinner, the amateurs nabbed the four cars given for the use of the party, and Illingworth having been ill for a week was obliged to field for Colin Cowdrey because he wanted to take his wife to the cinema.*' In Eric's view Cowdrey was something of a bête noire for Ray, but was a pleasant enough man, passionate about beating the old foe: '*For an English cricketer there is still something special about playing against Australia. The sight of the green cap of our oldest enemy does something to me.*'

The irony of the references by Peter Parfitt and Ray Illingworth to the amateur/professional divide is that the tectonic plates of that age-old social class distinction had shifted during the tour. Four days before the first Test at the Gabba, on 26 November, the MCC Advisory committee recommended the abolition of the distinction, so that all cricketers would be players. No one from London appeared to have told the Duke or Ted Dexter, and the press had fun with the topic in Australia.

No longer would spectators be advised, as they had been on May 3 1950 at Lord's, of the need for a correction to their scorecards: 'for FJ Titmus read Titmus FJ', amateurs carrying the distinction of their initials before their name rather than after it for the professionals. On January 31 1963, the Advisory committee's recommendation was formally accepted by MCC, as guardians of the laws of the game. From that moment, Illingworth and Larter became socially the cricketing equals of Dexter and Cowdrey.

MCC was slow to bring its own club rules up to the new norm. It was not until 1968 that it permitted professional cricketers, even those who had played for the club, to become members.

Wisden's take on David's tour was that whilst he did not come up to the high hopes which had been held of him, '*he did occasionally look good enough to take over from either Statham or Trueman but too often lacked accuracy in length and direction. For a long time, he had trouble with his approach to the wicket and was repeatedly no-balled, but later managed to iron this out. For all that, he was potentially the most likely wicket taker, after Trueman, and if he develops consistency, to become a leading Test bowler.*'

Johnny Moyes, Australia's senior cricket commentator, felt that although David did not come up to expectations, he improved in the later stages of the tour and ought to be kept in mind, especially on grassy English pitches; he believed Coldwell, although influential in the Melbourne Test victory, was thereafter ineffective on pitches too slow for him; and that whilst Trueman exceeded expectations by bowling as well as ever, Statham had lost some of the zip which made him previously so dangerous, a phrase repeated by Leslie Smith in *Wisden's* tour summary.

Statham's record in the five Tests was 13 wickets at 44 apiece, Coldwell's in his two Tests three wickets at 53 – in stark comparison with Trueman's 20 wickets at 26. Statham's marvellous career was to end after only three more Tests, as was Coldwell's. Neither Knight nor Coldwell were thought by *Wisden* to be fast enough or to do sufficient with the ball to worry good batsmen.

David Sheppard in *Parson's Pitch* admitted, as a member of the tour selection team (the others being Dexter, Cowdrey, Statham and Bedser) that in his opinion two mistakes in selection were made during the series as a result of *'not believing our eyes when we looked at the wickets for the third and fourth Tests. At Sydney we picked Len Coldwell, who had done well at Melbourne, when we would have been glad to have another spinner. At Adelaide, the wicket appeared to have more grass on it than we had ever seen there before…and we should probably have done better to have another quick bowler instead of Illingworth there.'*

That other quick bowler could only have been Len Coldwell or David.

> Once the State games started to roll by, I was optimistic about my chances of making the Test side. However, the selection committee (mostly Dexter) did not see it that way. Barry Knight played one Test and Len Coldwell two, as third seamer alongside Fred and Brian, taking three wickets each, but there was no room for me. As I finished the Australian part of the trip second in the first-class averages and did well on the New Zealand leg, it was depressing to see some of the popular press writing me off as a failure.

David certainly deserved his selection for the tour in Alan Smith's view, but was up against stiff competition to force his way into the Test side:

I would have thought David would not have expected to get in the Test side, if Trueman and Statham kept fit throughout the series. When Statham left for the UK at the end of the Australian leg of the tour, David had his opportunity and took it very well, being picked for all three New Zealand Tests and taking some wickets. With both Trueman and Statham playing there was no room for David in the Australian Tests. Dexter could fulfil the supporting role pretty well, Barry Knight similarly with his all-round ability and Coldwell was given a chance with his different pace. In the fourth Test, at Adelaide, Ray Illingworth bowled seamers and some swing. David was a number eleven batsman, and with his great height not in Trueman and

Statham's class as a fielder.'

He really was a gentle giant, lacking any nastiness or aggression often found in fast bowlers, and perhaps wanting some of the – what is the right word? – determination or resolve of Trueman and Statham. In my view he would have come through to play more Tests if his career had not been cut short. One might say he was almost too tall, his height being on the one hand a wonderful weapon in achieving his bounce but on the other causing niggling injuries. I played of course a lot with Bob Willis, almost as tall as David, and his body just did not stand up to the stress he put into it. Bob did not in fact bowl a lot for Warwickshire as a result.

Peter Parfitt shared Alan Smith's view that with Trueman and Statham keeping fit there was not much room for David: Barry Knight could score a century from number eight, and Coldwell did get some wickets at Melbourne. That might have given rise to the old amateur approach of 'we can't drop him – he got wickets in the last game'. On reflection I think David was unlucky not to get a Test on that tour.

Even with occasional problems with his action, David had some great moments: he and Statham were too good for Western Australia; at Launceston, against a Combined XI including a number of Australian Test players, he and Trueman demolished some quality opponents for 77, and at Melbourne his seven wickets in the match drove MCC close to a win over Victoria.

David, looking back nearly 60 years later:

> My problem on that first major tour was not with Fred or Brian, it was Ted Dexter and the selectors. I suppose they just did not like what they regarded as a non-batting slow fielder. I agree about the batting – as they say, a natural number eleven – but the fielding: I had a better throw than most of the Aussies and my long legs could cover the ground.
>
> It was clear that neither Ted Dexter nor Alec Bedser would contemplate playing three quick bowlers – Fred, Brian, and me – and as Fred was still very much worth his place it was me or Brian. Neither Len Coldwell nor Barry Knight were in the quick category and found it hard to make much impression.
>
> I was a little embarrassed that Richie Benaud and Neil Harvey, on separate occasions, buttonholed me and wanted to know who I had upset, as they were both aware of how awkward I was to face on hard Aussie wickets.

David as photographer: I had a decent camera with a telephoto lens and took a good few shots of Fred in action, including some in the Melbourne Test in front of 65,000 spectators.

10

NEW ZEALAND FEBRUARY 1963

The Big Freeze hits Britain on Boxing Day, temperatures dropping to minus 22C, and continues until March with snow drifts up to 6m deep.

As soon as the fifth Test in Sydney ended on February 20, Allen, Graveney, Pullar and (importantly for David) Statham all returned to England, missing out the New Zealand leg. David, frustrated by not getting a Test chance against the Australians, now saw there was a real chance of playing in at least some of the three New Zealand Tests and hopefully showing that he could perform on the biggest stage.

This leg of the tour would only last one month and just four matches – the three four-day Tests plus a three-day contest with an Otago Invitation side. The first Test, in Auckland, began only two days after the end of the drawn Sydney Test. David's prayers were answered as he won his second Test cap. England's batsmen put together the highest total ever made against New Zealand, 562 for seven declared, with centuries from Barrington, Parfitt and Knight, and 86 from Cowdrey.

David opened the bowling opposite Len Coldwell, Fred Trueman being rested to recover from a leg strain. With his fifth ball David had Playle caught by Dexter at backward short leg, and in his third over Barton caught by David Sheppard at forward short leg. Coldwell castled Dowling and the hosts were seven for three. John Reid then steadied the ship with 59, though he struggled against David's lift. Ted Dexter remembers Reid saying to him *"this chap keeps hitting the splice"*. When David had Sparling caught by JT Murray it was his 300th first-class wicket; a career milestone, but a small one when compared with that of 1,650 reached by Fred Trueman during the next match.

New Zealand were all out for 258, with David taking three for 51. Following on 304 behind, the host country's batting collapsed from 42 for one to 89 all out, with captain Reid stranded on 21 not out. David bowled Sinclair and removed three other lower order batsmen as he took four for 26, sharing the honours with Ray Illingworth's four for 34.

> This seven-wicket haul in Auckland, straight after the disappointments in Australia, gave me a quiet satisfaction – to make the point that I could do it when given the chance.

Trueman resumed his place for the second Test, at Wellington, with Coldwell, whose style would, it might be thought, have been better suited to New Zealand conditions than Australian ones, being dropped. England's batting emphasised the considerable gulf between the two sides as they scored 428 for 8 declared, with centurion Cowdrey and wicket-keeper AC Smith setting a new ninth wicket world record of 163. England won again by an innings, David going wicketless this time as Trueman, Knight and the spinners swept New Zealand aside by the evening of the third of the four allocated days.

MCC enjoyed a three-day break before the match against an Otago Invitation XI which included New Zealand's foremost post-war batsman Bert Sutcliffe and former West Indian Test player Bruce Pairaudeau. The latter had earned a place in Test oddities history when in the 1957 Edgbaston Test, having been dismissed for a duck, he acted as a runner for Walcott for over three hours and then for Worrell for five hours – as Andrew Samson in *The Cricketer* wrote: 'Weekes only made nine , so Pairaudeau was denied the chance of collecting all the Three Ws in the same innings.' Coldwell took David's place and took four wickets in the match, which combined with Trueman's eleven gave MCC a win by an innings and 10 runs.

The last match of the tour was the third and final Test at Christchurch. England won by seven wickets, though New Zealand were much more competitive, even taking a first innings lead. It was David Sheppard's last Test match. Here is how he looked back at it in *Parson's Pitch*:

> 'My last Test match was played against New Zealand in 1963 and a fine tussle it was on

*the fine ground at Christchurch...
When New Zealand batted for
the second time, they led by 13.
Our bowling gave nothing away,
but John Reid hung on,
occasionally flashing out a
powerful square cut which left
third man standing... he went on
to fight his way to exactly 100.'*

What happened next was
quoted by Sheppard as a good
example of where Dexter's

David and the Colonel on a rare cold evening.

decision-making, *'based on his intuition as a natural cricketer,'* could pay off:

'Freddie Trueman had bowled them out first time, but we could not expect him to do it every time. At lunch Colin Cowdrey tried to persuade Ted that we should need Ray Illingworth, who was off the field with a slight ailment, to bowl some overs for us to get us through the day. "I don't agree" said Ted. "The fast bowlers will bowl them out." My mind was working the same way as Colin's, and I was wondering what we should do if, as seemed likely to me, the fast bowlers didn't bowl them out. So I tried a few minutes later, feeling it was important that Freddie Titmus should have the choice of which end to bowl; I said to Ted, "I think Freddie Titmus is going to be your most useful bowler." "I don't agree." he said. "I think the fast bowlers will bowl them out." There was a lot to be said for our point of view, but he was right and David Larter, who had bowled poorly in the first innings, came good and the fast bowlers did break through.'

Trueman's nine wickets in the match took him to a world record 250 Test wickets, overtaking his friend Statham's figure of 242. In the second innings Dexter gave David more overs than the others, and on a slow pitch his 23 accurate overs yielded three for 32, including the wickets of Dowling and Sinclair at the top of the order. The *Guardian* noted that it was David *'who, with every justification, was pushed forward to prominence by his captain Dexter as the team left the field at the end of the innings.'* A nice touch by the skipper.

Ted Dexter says he was impressed by David's bowling on this leg of the tour: *In Australia David had injuries and niggles and did not make the Test team, but he did well in New Zealand, Auckland being his finest hour. He was a shy man, a quiet chap and a good fellow to have around. He was a good bowler – his final Test record of 37 Test wickets at 25 each proves that.*

Graham Dowling opened the batting for New Zealand in each of the three Tests and was one of David's three victims in the second innings of the third match, caught behind by AC Smith from a ball that left him. He had first come up against David when MCC toured New Zealand in December 1960:

I had then just made selection for NZ but had not yet toured overseas. My scores in that first season were rather meagre but enough for my selection for our tour later in the year to Southern Rhodesia and South Africa (5 Tests) with State games in Australia on the way, and again in Oz on the way home. We shared the series 2-2 [NZ's first Test victories over South Africa, and only the third and fourth in all NZ Tests] and I guess I booked an opening berth role for the next decade. I recall many duels with England bowlers, but I did have trouble facing David Larter when MCC toured New Zealand at the end of the Ashes series in 1962/63. His height, genuine pace, and ability to gain bounce made him unique. Having Fred Trueman at the other end must have helped him enormously.

At the New Zealand Cricket Council's dinner for the tourists after the last Test, Trueman was presented with the ball with which he broke the world record, mounted on a stand. Perhaps feeling his age, he said afterwards he thought he had about five more years of cricket in him *'if I bowl mainly from my shorter run!'*

One of the best aspects of the tour for David was the opportunity to watch Fred bowling, close up; the unity of rhythm and power. It takes John Arlott to paint that particular picture in the brightest colours:

'He was a cocked trigger, left arm pointed high, head steady, eyes glaring at the batsman as that great stride widened: the arm slashed down and as the ball was fired down the pitch, his body was thrown hungrily after it, the right toe raking the ground closely beside the wicket as he swept on.'

So ended the Antipodean tour, after a long five months. David finished third in the bowling averages for all first-class matches in Australia and New Zealand, with 39 wickets at 24, behind Trueman whose 55 wickets were taken at 18 each, and David Allen, 20 at 23. Statham's tour wickets cost 31 apiece, Knight's 34, and Coldwell's 39. Fred Titmus, who starred as the leading spin bowler, took 49 wickets at 28. Barrington held the batting together, failing by only 19 runs to break Denis Compton's record for an overseas tour aggregate. His 1,763 runs in only 27 first-class innings compared with Compton's 1,781 runs in South Africa in 1948/9 in 26 innings.

The party did not return to the UK until March 21. This gave the players six weeks to recover and to prepare themselves for the May 1 start of the new county season.

1963 HOME SEASON

Martin Luther King delivers his 'I have a dream' speech on August 28 at the Lincoln Memorial, Washington DC.

1963 was potentially a crucial season. Alan Ross in the *Guardian* felt that although the winter tour had been a qualified success, the general impression in the country had been that the Tests were '*a fiasco*', an opinion he saw as strongly influenced by the fifth Test. '*Whatever Dexter's social shortcomings or strategic eccentricities he more than held his own. England still has the basis of a powerful side though with certain missing pieces that will be hard to find. Trueman may need a new partner. Statham now bowls rather from memory than with anticipation. White, his run and weight drastically reduced by request of his captain and committee, should jostle Larter and Coldwell for the chance of opening with Trueman.*'

As it turned out, Ross was wrong on the question of Trueman's partner. Nor could he have guessed that the season was to be one of the most momentous in cricket's long history. The series of Test matches against West Indies produced not only the most absorbing cricket one could hope to see, but enormous crowds, enhanced by the large numbers of West Indians resident in England. In addition to the Tests, great interest was stimulated by the inauguration of a limited overs knock-out county cup competition – the Gillette Cup.

Arlott's prediction was more accurate. He felt that Northants were strong outsiders for the title, with a young side of immense gifts. The county did perform well as the rebuilding of the side bore fruit. At the end of July, lying third in the table only 13 points behind the leaders, the sunny uplands were in view. But that vision was to fade.

David's season started on a highly worrying note, lasting several weeks, of adjustment to the new no-ball law. The experimental change, which applied in the championship but not in the Tests, was significant, particularly for a fast bowler and especially one of great height. David had been brought up since childhood to make sure his back (right) foot landed behind the bowling crease. Now it did not matter where the back foot landed, as the law now required that his front foot landed, at least in part, behind the popping crease.

The picturesque Arundel Castle ground, built by the 16th Duke of Norfolk in 1895, was the setting for David's first game of the season. The date was April 27 and the game was the traditional fixture between the Duke's XI and the touring side. The home team was more powerful than usual, drawn entirely from the recent MCC Ashes touring party. Set to score 204 in 170 minutes, the West Indies won by three wickets in a thrilling finale, with skipper Frank Worrell hitting the winning run from the last ball of the match.

> I was pleased to be included in this match – unfortunately it did not lead to further more serious encounters with the West Indians. One highlight however was the opportunity it gave to meet Denis Compton for the first of several occasions. In the course of a good chat I learned what a very shrewd cricket brain he had. He was indeed the lovely sociable man described by all those who knew him.

In his first outing on his home Wantage Road pitch David started strongly, dismissing six of Yorkshire's finest for 61 in a Yorkshire total of 339 which contained a maiden first-class century from Fred Trueman and an aggressive innings from new captain Brian Close. Close scored 161, attacking all the bowlers, towards the end of his innings even moving down the wicket to take on David, a tactic which David had not previously encountered in any opposing batsman. Milburn cudgelled a violent 123 in under two hours as Northants followed on. In Yorkshire's second innings David bowled Padgett with a beauty, pitching on middle and hitting off, but it was a rare success as Yorkshire quickly knocked off the target of 105 to win by seven wickets, Close repeating his assault with two successive sixes as he struck David for 17 runs in one over:

> You knew you were in for a battle when playing against Brian. I watched him take a battering in the Lord's Test from the West Indies quicks later in the season. I actually thought he was mad to let them hit him, but I don't think anything or anybody ever put the wind up Brian.

Close was embarking upon the best season of his career, ending with his selection as one of *Wisden's* five Cricketers of the Year. Made captain of Yorkshire, he inspired the county to the championship; a true Captain Courageous, he led from the front and was as tough as teak. He regained his position in the England team and showed at the age of 32 an all-round maturity previously undisclosed. A true all-rounder, as a footballer he had played professionally with both Leeds United and Arsenal, and as a golfer he was a single handicapper, whether playing left or right-handed. As a cricketer he had been picked by England in his first season with Yorkshire, becoming at 18 years of age the youngest English Test player. It took him a long time to overcome that accolade. As he was to write in his autobiography *'well, for 28 years I have been saddled with the title of England's youngest Test player.'*

Milburn followed his century, which included seven sixes and 14 fours, with a storming 83 against Sussex in the next match, putting him into contention for higher honours. That Worthing match on May 10 was also remarkable for David and for wicket-keeper Laurie Johnson. In David's case it was a game of highs and lows. The low was the no-balling seven times for overstepping the crease in the first innings and the high came in the second innings, despite a further seven no-balls.

Jim Watts smiles as he recalls Ted Dexter's decision, following heavy overnight rain, to reverse his batting order to save his better batsmen for what he assumed would be better batting conditions later on: *David had the first three back in the pavilion with the total at 14, and when the effects of the roller wore off after lunch he ran through the rest of them.*

Tony Winlaw in the *Telegraph* thought that David, *'at this pace certainly presented an unattractive prospect for any batsman'* as he recorded career best figures of eight for 41, including Oakman and Parks, Langridge, Suttle and, satisfyingly, Ted Dexter, caught behind from a ball that left him. Sussex, seeking 293 to win, were crushed for 117.

Laurie Johnson, deputising for Keith Andrew as Northants' wicket-keeper, took 10 catches in the match, equalling the record of two Gloucestershire players, wicket-keeper Andy Wilson who in 1953 had 10 victims at Portsmouth, and Wally Hammond whose 10 catches against Surrey at Cheltenham in 1928 were, astonishingly, achieved as a fielder. Johnson would have broken the record had he managed to hold on to a skier from Sussex tail-ender Don Bates which moved disconcertingly in the wind. Johnson with all his delightful modesty recalled *When I dropped it, all of us, me included, roared with laughter.*

His career had been an uphill struggle all the way: *I played my first 2nd XI match for Surrey in 1953, alongside Stewart, Barrington and Loader. I was 16 years old. I was understudy to Arthur McIntyre, a great keeper who would have played many more times for England if his career had not coincided with that of Godfrey Evans. In 1957 he announced that he would retire after the 1958 season, which would give me my chance. However, Surrey then signed Roy Swetman, who developed into a good keeper and went on to play for England. So I moved to Northants in '58, where Keith Andrew was talking of retiring, but he then changed his mind and thus again I spent my time as an understudy. The irony was that Swetman retired from Surrey in '61 to go into antiques.*

It was a mark of the high value which Northants put upon Laurie, whom some rated better than Swetman, that the county gave him the rare honour of a cap in 1960, even though when he was playing mainly for the county 2nd XI.

I loved keeping. I looked after the hands – putting plasticine into the gloves in the event of bruising - and I never broke a finger. It was always interesting keeping to David Larter as he was different from other quick bowlers in that he could extract bounce from a length. He was a great trier and, on his day, when everything clicked and conditions were in his favour, he could be as quick as Tyson (for whom I used to stand back the full length of the wicket). David swung it away from the bat, but also back in. He didn't bowl many bouncers – he didn't need to. I don't think he had a reputation for breaking down – and if he did have such a reputation it was probably because people expected it, with his physique, but all fast bowlers miss matches each season.

He and I were good friends. He was a lovely gentle chap, a good team man quietly in the background but good fun socially. For 10 shillings we would occasionally go out to Bernie's steakhouse. David would usually go up for seconds. We played in a benefit match at Castle Ashby, the Earl of Northampton's country estate, and afterwards he and I were drinking Guinness until someone challenged him to stand on a table and drink a yard of ale. He just tipped it straight down – hollow legs! But I never saw him drunk.

The eternal truth that cricket can make one a king one day and a knave the next was proved in David's next match, at Dartford against Kent, when he was no-balled on 18 occasions for overstepping. The umpire was Arthur Jepson.

The fearsome prospect for Kent's batsmen at Dartford on Saturday when Larter, of Northamptonshire, bowled. He is finding difficulty in adapting his delivery action to the new front-foot rule and was no-balled five times

He called me for a record number of front foot no-balls – soon to be bettered by Butch White.

David was despondent, telling the press:

The new front foot rule has ruined me. I have completely lost my rhythm and also my accuracy. I do not know what I can do about it.

It was little comfort to him that five other Northants bowlers were also no-balled, though there was some consolation in his ending the day with a fine spell, taking the wickets of Cowdrey, Catt and Dixon. The match was otherwise notable for the Kent debut of Derek Underwood, who was to become one of the discoveries of the season, at the age of 17 taking 101 wickets and topping Kent's averages.

David got letters from all over Britain, and a telegram from Scotland, with assorted but well-meaning advice as to how he should approach the problem of this major change to his delivery stride. Keith Miller, writing in the *Daily Express*, sympathised: *'Larter is not a severe dragger. His confidence has been shattered. It is a great pity because he is a much better pace man than most, and was heir apparent to Brian Statham who must soon reach the end of his Test career. This no-balling business could ruin his Test chances at least for this season.'*

Richie Benaud, in England for the *Daily Express* to report on the Test series, was also supportive: *'having been unable to conform to the requirements of keeping his front foot behind the line on Wednesday, on Friday Larter used a drying wicket to perfection as he ripped through the Sussex batting line-up. He will I believe in the future be a regular bowler for England, but this season his main chance of prolonged success seems to be to get into the Test matches against the West Indies – for they are not playing the new no-ball rule in those games.'*

The first Test was due to start at Old Trafford in three weeks' time. Alan Ross's pre-season question as to who would partner Trueman was the popular debating point in the sporting press. Would it be Larter, Rhodes or the long-standing incumbent Brian Statham?

Harold Rhodes, now 26, had partnered Trueman in two Tests against India in 1959, but had been discarded when later called for throwing by umpire Paul Gibb. There was no technology to assess the legitimacy of his action - no slow-motion cameras or studies by sports bio-mechanical experts – and he was instead put through the humiliation of a trial at the Nursery ground at Lord's before a jury of MCC notables. Mike Selvey talked to Rhodes recently, now both presidents of their counties, and Rhodes explained that his only sin was to have been born with a hyper-extensive elbow. That condition is nowadays accepted – a recent example being the Indian fast bowler Jasprit Bumrah. Although Rhodes was eventually cleared of cheating, as Selvey says, the stigma remained, and he never played for England again. David felt for Rhodes:

> Harold was as quick as anybody in England and with Les Jackson at the other end there was no let up against Derby. In my view, and in the view of a lot of other cricketers, umpires. Gibb and Buller had a lot to answer for by calling him for throwing. Harold was not a thrower. Geoff Griffin, Charlie Griffith and Ian Meckiff were. Meckiff was an affable chap who had the bad luck to be at the centre of the Australian throwing controversy. He really troubled the batsmen and took regular wickets. I faced him for a few balls in Australia and never saw any of them. When the ball is coming from behind the chap's ear instead of over the top it does make it difficult.

MCC picked Rhodes rather than David to open the bowling alongside Barry Knight in the traditional early season match at Lord's between MCC and the champion county, Surrey. The early appointment of Dexter as England's captain for the first Test meant that he would be consulted by the selectors as to the make-up of the team. David was not overjoyed at this news given the difficulty he had experienced of establishing a rapport with Dexter on the winter Ashes tour, notwithstanding David's good bowling on the New Zealand leg. David would have to redouble his efforts to get selected.

Northants against Lancashire at Rushden on May 18 was a match of interest to the Test selectors, pitting David, his no-ball trouble now under control, against Statham, head to head. Rushden was one of the out-grounds the county relied upon to spread the load from Wantage Road's cricket square, and to attract different spectators. A town on the A6 between Bedford and Kettering, it had been as famous as any other town in the county for its boot and shoe-making. In the mid-1900s there were well over 100 boot and shoe factories in Rushden – today there are only four.

The out-ground strategy carried risks, as other counties also experienced, the main one of which was whether the pitch at Rushden cricket club was good enough. Whilst some magnificent match bowling figures were achieved, David taking 11 for 131 from 55 overs and Brian Statham 10 for 68 from 41 overs, the pitch played its part with the ball keeping low at times and spitting at others. One such delivery caused Northants' Albert Lightfoot to be carried from the field after being struck in the face by a lifting ball from Statham. The *Guardian* reporter accepted that Statham in particular had bowled Lancashire to victory with undoubted skill, *'but he was greatly helped by the pitch, which in many people's opinion was not fit for first-class cricket.'* Rushden, with its Victorian pavilion and its rusty tin fence, had hosted its last county game.

A fine match, with fine competition between the bowling champions on each side. In the personal battle Statham shaded a narrow win, but David had impressed and was pleased to have run the long-standing champion close:

> For me Brian Statham was the absolute epitome of a northern professional cricketer; always trying like hell and always at the batsman. If there was anything in the wicket at all you could foresee him getting six or seven. I loved to watch him from the old sideways viewpoint at Old Trafford.

David's admiration was shared by Eric Russell: *Brian was a terrific chap. He bowled what I regard as fast off-breaks always on a length, so that I had to play forward all the time. The old phrase which people use to sum up Brian's philosophy was true: 'if you miss, I hit.' What a pair he and Fred Trueman made. I never played well against Fred.*

The county lost for the fourth time when heavily beaten by Middlesex at Lord's on May 31, two days before the selectors picked their side for the first Test. David did his best with the ball getting the wickets of Russell and two tail-enders, Price and Moss, but had unusual success with the bat. In the first innings total of 163 David struck 16 not out and in the second, with Northants only seven runs ahead with nine wickets down, he threw caution to the winds in the face of defeat and made 30 out of 36 in a hectic 20 minutes for the last wicket. Ian Wooldridge commented: *'Larter was uncivil enough to strike Titmus for two sixes in three balls, the first into the red and gold ties in front of the Long Room windows, and the second on to the awning halfway up the Tavern wall. Like all last men who have just made 30, Larter thereupon decided that batting was kids' stuff, and was caught next ball.'* This was the first time David had scored double figures in both innings of a first-class match.

David continued his (relatively) good run with the bat in the next match against Leicestershire, scoring 10 in the first innings in a last wicket stand with his captain Keith Andrew, who then promoted him to number six in the second innings when quick runs were needed for victory. He was caught by Dickie Bird for five, but thanks to Milburn's 41 from 51 in 27 minutes the match was won with three minutes to spare.

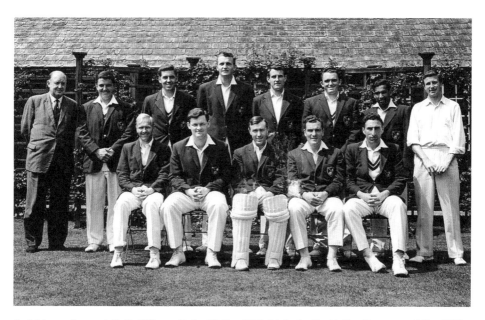

Jack Mercer (scorer), Colin Milburn, Peter Watts, JDFL, Malcolm Scott, Don Ramsamooj, Roy Wills;
Maurice Norman, Roger Prideaux, Keith Andrew, Brian Reynolds, Albert Lightfoot.
At Lords v Middlesex May 29-31 1963

The Test selectors were not however going to pick David on the basis of his batting. David's bowling figures did however make a strong case for his inclusion. In the national averages he lay fourth after Trueman, Ken Palmer and Loader, with 40 wickets at minimal cost – 14.2 apiece.

But it was not enough. For the first Test, at Old Trafford starting on June 6, the selectors opted, in Wooldridge's phrase, for *'an ageing Statham rather than a youthful but erratic Larter'.* Alan Ross in the *Guardian* wrote that *'on how Statham bears up in the forthcoming Test will depend Larter's chances of selection later in the series.'* The prediction was again incorrect!

A number of the Ashes tour party were rejected, including Pullar, Graveney, AC Smith, Coldwell and Knight, as well as David Sheppard, who had now returned to his church duties, his cricket sabbatical ended. Deprived of the services of the injured Tony Lock , the selectors decided to exclude strong contenders in Barber, Sharpe and Murray who had been members of the MCC side defeated by the tourists at Lord's in the May 'Test trial'.

It was an odd-looking Test team: no less than five county captains and no less than eight men over the age of 32. Test debutant John Edrich was the youngest at

25, and there was a popular recall for Keith Andrew whose one previous cap had been nine years earlier. The selectors kept to the familiar bowling attack of Trueman and Statham with Dexter as the third seamer, plus two spinners. For the tourists, the advent of the four-man fast attack was still fifteen years in the future. In the 1963 five-Test series they relied throughout on Hall, Griffith and Sobers as quicks, Worrell as an occasional seamer and Gibbs and Sobers to provide the spin.

At Old Trafford the visitors, under the leadership of Worrell, bested England in all facets of the game in four days, running out winners by 10 wickets, with off-spinner Lance Gibbs claiming eleven scalps. It was their first ever victory at the famous ground. Although Trueman bowled with his usual fire, Statham was not penetrative and went wicketless, adding to the speculation about his selection for the second Test at Lord's.

Benaud wrote in his newspaper column: *'I wouldn't be surprised to see Larter given a belated chance to play for England (Australian players would have given him three Tests in Australia last year) and sadly the man to go may be that great cricketer Brian Statham.'* The *Daily Mail* concurred: *'for all his erratic shortcomings, Larter should be given a chance. He is now strong and experienced enough to prove a shock weapon against batsmen who apart from Sobers in Australia, have never faced him.'*

Swanton put forward a number of alternatives to Statham: Larter, White or Rhodes, or perhaps *'the finest medium-pace length bowler in England – Shackleton?'* So far as Shackleton was concerned, Yorkshire-born journalist Jack Barker, a long-time resident in Trinidad, in *Summer Spectacular*, his record of the 1963 tour, wrote: *'Shackleton had Statham's accuracy without his pace, whilst Larter had his pace without his accuracy.'*

In the light of this speculation, the cricketing gods appeared to have smiled on David by giving him the country's greatest stage to show his skills. On June 12, two days after the Old Trafford Test defeat, he was at Lord's with Northants for the second round of the 65-over knockout competition. The novelty of the tournament meant that the cricketing press was well represented at the home of cricket, and David did not let his supporters down. He effectively won the match in the first half hour, in a dramatic opening spell taking four wickets for eight runs in his first three overs. The *Guardian* described how Middlesex were wrecked by Larter's pace. *'In a thunderous opening spell – taking the wickets of Drybrough, Parfitt first ball, Gale and Bob White in three overs – Larter decapitated Middlesex. This must have improved Larter's chances of a place in the next England team. Drybrough promoted himself to open the innings. Even in this type of cricket liberties become risks – especially if a side contains a Larter...'*

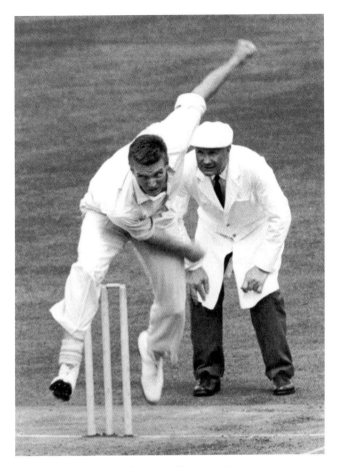

Lord's June 12 1963. John Langridge umpiring.

The *Telegraph's* Ron Roberts was there, observing David *'bowling very well, rhythm and control nicely harnessed as though he had never in his life had to worry about the position of the front foot. His figures were 11-4-22-4, finishing his spell perhaps a shade early, short of the 15 over limitation.'*

The birth of official one-day cricket in England had taken place early in May, with the opening salvoes of the Gillette-sponsored knockout cup springing from the loins of the previous year's successful Midlands trial tournament, the final of which David had dramatically foreshortened by removing both Leicestershire's openers with only 17 on the board.

Northants' victory over Middlesex had propelled them into the Gillette semi-final at Wantage Road against Sussex on July 10 before probably the largest crowd since 1953. Sussex ran out clear winners thanks to a masterly century from Dexter. Whilst David suffered a recurrence of his no-ball problem, being called five times by umpire Buller, there was some compensation in his ending the Sussex innings with a hat-trick, the only one of his career. He bowled Cooper and Pountain with the last two balls of his 13th over and Buss with the first ball of his next. This was the first hat-trick in the knockout competition, and the last for Northants until John Emburey, late of Middlesex, achieved the feat 33 years later.

David's hat-trick ball.

The final took place at Lord's on September 7. The football season was in full swing but the novelty of a cricket cup final and of a top-class match finishing in one day attracted 25,000 spectators. By 21st century standards it was a low scoring contest, with Sussex scoring 168 and Worcestershire falling 14 runs short, strangled by Dexter's tactic of placing every fielder on the boundary. It was not long before the administrators introduced restrictions on such field-placing in the one-day game.

Sussex received £1,889 as winners, whilst their players were given a bonus of £25, some of which they spent that evening at the Victoria Palace theatre watching the Black and White Minstrel Show.

For the nine days between the end of the first Test and the beginning of the second at Lord's on June 20, the selectors Walter Robins, Alec Bedser, Doug Insole, Willie Watson and Ted Dexter struggled with the task of selecting a side to compete with the rampant West Indians.

Benaud felt that *'the West Indies strength lies in their deep batting. To counter this the England selectors will have to give a lot of thought to the bowling strength of the team.… If Dexter is not going to do a full stint as third seamer then they must bring in David Larter.*

Australian cricketers often take a different view to their English counterparts, and last season [the 62/3 Ashes Tour] there were many in our side, myself included, who would have made far more use of Larter. I saw him bowl twice during the tour, in Perth during the first game, and against Queensland just before the first Test. On both occasions his direction was wayward and he bowled no-balls. But he also had penetration, lift and hostility and he took wickets. He is young and enthusiastic and the recent front foot worries that have beset him will not apply against the West Indies. I'd pick him immediately for he is England's best bet for the fast bowling future.… With one loss under his belt, Ted Dexter must know that it is no use his team trying to out-weight the West Indian fast bowlers. The only way to get them on the defensive and on the way to defeat is to attack.'

On Sunday June 16 the selectors announced their chosen twelve. Both Benaud and Swanton could make a good claim for prescience, as both David (23 years old) *'in case the pitch came up green'* according to the selectors, and Derek Shackleton (38) were included. Statham was dropped after 68 Tests as was David's county captain Keith Andrew, after only one Test, in favour of Jim Parks, a better batsman. Swanton commented *'like most fast bowlers Larter has returned from Australia stronger than when he went, and he certainly deserves to be on the list.'*

On that Sunday Northants were at Bristol, the match against Gloucestershire having started the previous day. To show how David, and many of his fellow cricketers, were happy to play on their rest days and particularly, as in this case, to support a fellow professional's benefit, he, Brian Close, David Allen, Fred Trueman and Colin Milburn were all playing in a six-a-side tournament for the benefit of Gloucestershire's Martin Young. Speaking from there on hearing the news of his selection for Lord's, David said:

I have had to adjust my whole approach to having been no-balled about 40 times in the process. Now I have mastered it at last. I took three for 33 in 19 overs in the championship match against Gloucester yesterday without being faulted once.

He had been promoted to number eight in that game as Northants sought quick runs before declaring, but with Gloucestershire's off-spinner John Mortimore (who had fallen lbw to David on 99) and his fellow spinners David Allen and Sam Cook running through the Northants second innings batting, a completely different role was called for in the second innings when David and Malcolm Scott, the last pair, came together with the score at 77 for nine. In the words of the *Daily Telegraph* '*they proved equal, albeit narrowly and ungraciously, to the occasion, by batting out time with nine wickets down.*'

David was to tour with Mortimore in the winter of 1964 to India and with Allen to Australia in 65/6. He rated them highly:

> Both of them were bowlers of the highest class and in tandem were easily the most respected pair of off-spinners in the game.

Who would be stood down out of the Lord's 12? Shackleton, with his tireless medium-pace, was Mr Reliable. He was one of the top three wicket takers in England in each season from 1961 to 1965. In his career he was to take over 2,857 wickets at a miserly average of 18 per wicket, conceding only two runs per over. He had a very good record at Lord's. If he won precedence over David it would be on the basis of safety first rather than attack with some risk. As Swanton put it, this would deprive the attack of the most effective counter to the speed and physical threat of Hall and Griffith. David's statistics did not suggest his lack of Shackletonian accuracy would make him an unaffordable expense: his 50 wickets at 16.20 put him second only to Trueman amongst the season's English fast bowlers.

Thursday June 20 was a chilly day with grey skies, a heavy atmosphere and a well-grassed pitch. '*Notwithstanding the made-to-order seamers' surface*, Jack Barker wrote, *Larter was omitted and the two off-spinners picked. This was undoubtedly an England error... Only Shackleton's inability to command the extra yard of pace to convert his phenomenal accuracy from threatening to lethal enabled West Indies to reach their total of 301.*'

Dexter's bowling choices were odd, given the presence of the additional spinner. Titmus was not bowled at all until the second innings, and Allen bowled only 10 overs, while the seamers Trueman, Shackleton, Dexter and Close bowled 98 between them.

Dexter, the England captain (LEFT), briefs the towering Larter, who at 23 is the youngest of England's 12 for to-day's Second Test at Lord's. Shackleton (CENTRE) is the oldest, 38. Also taking a breather during practice at Lord's yesterday are Stewart and Parks (RIGHT).

There was no doubt that Shackleton bowled immaculately in his style, maintaining accuracy with some seam movement, and his figures were remarkable: 84 overs in the match with seven wickets for 165. But JL Manning in the *Daily Mail* looked at it a different way: *'to play Shackleton, a container instead of a fast bowler to strike hard with Trueman, on a wicket where fast bowlers have always done well, is a severe handicap to any captain. And Dexter made it look that way. Whose idea was it? The difference was caused by a lack of aggression the other end to Trueman, and not to give Titmus a single over all day was bizarre.'*

Manning's point about aggression can be read against some statistics for the 1963 season. The strike rate in first-class cricket achieved by David that season was one wicket every 6.78 overs, and by Shackleton one wicket every 9.5 overs. They were equally economic, David's 121 wickets costing 16.76 apiece (from 821 overs) and Shackleton's 146 costing 16.75 apiece (from 1,387 overs).

Some 125,000 spectators, including 31,000 on the second day, enjoyed one of the most dramatic Test matches ever to be played in England, with a thrilling innings of 70 from 73 balls in 80 minutes by Dexter against the high pace of Hall and Griffith, an innings *'shot through with imperial majesty'* in Jack Barker's phrase. AA Thomson wrote *'in spite of my life-long privileges I still count it among the very greatest. It was art. It was drama. It was elegance. The glory of that innings is like the glory of Kipling's garden: it shall never pass away.'* [This author remembers observing, with a Tavern pint in his hand, the rifle crack of Dexter's bat on ball followed in seconds by the similar sound of ball on boundary boards at extra cover].

Then came a brilliant century from Butcher for the West Indies, and a final over to the match from which any one of the four possible results could have occurred. With nine wickets down Cowdrey, with an arm broken earlier in the match, was the non-striker as David Allen played out the last two balls with England six runs short.

It is interesting to speculate what might have happened to David if he had played. Would it have been him rather than Shackleton batting against Wes Hall in that tense last over which started with England needing eight runs to win with two wickets in hand? After three balls England's target was 6 to win. Shackleton was run out off the fourth ball leaving David Allen to decide that the better part of valour was to draw rather than risk a loss.

The performances of Wes Hall and Griffith were extraordinary. Griffith bowled all but five overs from one end on the rain-affected last day whilst Hall bowled unchanged – three hours and 20 minutes – maintaining high speed throughout, ending with four for 93 from 40 overs. He was to say much later that this spell was his best in Tests. He thereby bowled the final over in two of the finest of Test matches – the other being the historic tied Test in Australia in December 1960, when Australia lost their last wicket to a run out off the last ball, having started the over needing only four runs to win and with three wickets in hand.

David thought Wes Hall was special:

> He was the most magnificent sight in 60s cricket: a superb athlete and probably the quickest of the period. In complete contrast to big Charlie Griffith, Wes was fluid poetry in motion, except when he lost his run – which he did regularly. I faced one ball from him at Lord's in a Rest of the World match. One was enough as I tried to hit him over the pavilion and failed.

Hall was frightening to face but a popular man with cricketers. Geoff Smith of Essex played for Gilligan's X1 against the tourists in the Hastings Festival at the end of August that year. To set the West Indies a target he and Mick Norman, in true festival style, put on 108 together in 43 minutes. Hall joined in the spirit by bowling off-spin. Geoff remembers it well: *I took advantage and struck him for six, provoking Wes to warn me with a smile that if I did that again he would revert to his long run. I took the hint and was out stumped the next ball.*

David was released from Lord's after the first day of the Test, twelfth man duties as usual being taken over by a groundstaff junior. This meant David did not get to meet the Queen, having instead the slightly lesser thrill of a night in a Peterborough hotel; for the return fixture against Middlesex. This game petered out into a rain-affected draw, but not before David let fly, no doubt releasing some of his pent-up frustration. The *Daily Telegraph's* John Thicknesse was watching: '*Larter put in an extremely hostile spell this evening and thanks to him they are much better off than they might be. He bowled faster than I've seen him this evening and both Russells were beaten for pace by deliveries which trimmed their bails on their way to the boundary.*'

In his next county match, bowling on a drying wicket in difficult light, David broke the back of Glamorgan's innings at Cardiff. On a sluggish pitch which made a draw inevitable David nevertheless produced plenty of lift and fire, his five wickets including that of future England captain Tony Lewis. In a team including two Joneses, two Lewises, a Rees and an Evans, only Bernard Hedges, with 60 out of 150 showed much of the traditional hwyl.

Sticking to his pro-David stance, Benaud proposed that for the third Test at Edgbaston starting on July 4 the selectors should pick David in preference to one of the off-spinners; '*I mentioned earlier that I would have played him in three Tests in Australia, and I would play him at Birmingham to add dash to an attack that will certainly be minus Dexter as a bowler.*'

David was again included in the twelve but on the morning of the match Dexter chose to exclude him, preferring Trueman, Shackleton and himself as the seamers and two spinners, Titmus and Lock. With a victory over West Indies by over 200 runs it would have been churlish for the press to criticise that choice. There was however justification for puzzlement. Jack Barker reported to West Indian readers that he could not understand England's strategy: '*Dexter came in for immediate criticism. Having decided to leave out Larter in favour of his spinners, he won the toss and elected to bat. Both, according to certain experts, were tactical errors. The pitch was green and soft. Larter should have played, they said, and West Indies should have been sent in. This wasn't the only time Dexter was taken to task during the match.*'

David was disappointed:

> Team selection around the West Indies UK tour was strange. Nobody in the game could quite believe Derek Shackleton's repeated selection. It was hard to see what the selectors wanted. They said they could not play three quick bowlers but the West Indies soon demolished that policy. Fred Trueman had already made it plain in dressing room chat at Lords that I was his choice of partner, and when the same thing happened – passed over for Derek – he cornered me at the back of the Edgbaston dressing room and quietly (not Fred's usual style!) sympathised and expressed his disagreement with the selection. Whilst the official announcement was that Tony Lock was preferred to me, Fred knew that the real choice had been between Derek and me. (Tony bowled only two overs in the Test). I had got to know Fred fairly well by this time and I appreciated his wanting to let me know how he personally felt.

Swanton expressed sympathy for David: *'Dexter left out poor Larter for the second time running (and though he is bowling with much success) and got so near and yet so far.'* He thought that *'as things turned out Larter's pace would not have given any cutting-edge on this wicket.'* A moot point given that the match was won by a magnificent performance from fast bowler Trueman whose match analysis of 12 for 119 was the best by any bowler in an Edgbaston Test. Shackleton took three for 97 in the match. Not only did Lock bowl only two overs but Titmus was given none in either innings. Dexter bowled 23 overs of seam and did well with five wickets.

The dominance of the English seam and swing bowlers gave rise to calls for one spinner only in the next Test to permit the inclusion of another quicker bowler to take advantage of the very English conditions that had prevailed thus far during the series. Conditions lent themselves to seam bowling: David should have been in his element.

JL Manning argued that Trueman's performance was all the more remarkable as since the first Test he had had no fast bowler to support him. *'No Voce to his Larwood, no Miller to his Lindwall, and no Statham. But I bet he will have a Larter subsidy next time out.'*

David was at Lord's on July 17 playing for the MCC Touring Team – those who had been on the winter's Ashes tour – against The Rest, a somewhat meaningless match designed to fill the gap in the calendar left by the loss of the annual Gentlemen v Players fixture. He thus missed Northants' match against Surrey at the Oval but the county did not miss him, Northants maintaining their extraordinary record at the Oval where only once in the past nine years had Surrey managed to gain any points from them. Northants' seamers Brian Crump with 10 for 73 and Jim Watts eight for 70 dismissed Surrey for 89 and 122 to give Northants a decisive ten wicket victory.

At Lord's, bowling opposite Brian Statham on an over-grassed slow pitch, David was wicketless in his 17 first innings overs but second time around the two of them rattled the Rest's batsmen as they lost eight wickets en route to their easy victory target of 177, a target set by Dexter's curious decision to declare at 72 for seven with Graveney still at the crease. David dismissed Micky Stewart, Milburn and Mortimore within six balls. Ken Palmer, the Somerset opening bowler, took advantage of the conditions to take eight wickets in the match, Shackleton, accuracy personified, took seven and Statham bowled well for his six.

Barry Knight did his best to force himself into the next Test team with a fine innings of 81 and six for 35 in the first innings. Wooldridge's wry comment was that *'like Larter, with 70 wickets at fewer than 17 apiece, he is unlikely to get the call.'*

David made his way back home for the next day's fixture against Essex; another draw, David capturing seven wickets in the match, including his 'rabbit' Geoff Smith for 11, Trevor Bailey for three and 19 year old Keith Fletcher, immediately after completing his one thousandth run of the season in his first championship season.

Fletcher had learned from listening to the chat amongst the older batsmen in the side that Larter was someone to watch out for – *a pretty quick bowler who could get bounce from short of a length from his great height.* He recalls that David did not swing the ball much on that occasion, but moved it off the seam, particularly in to the bat, eventually getting him caught in the leg trap, undone by the bounce, for a hard-fought 60. Fletcher, who went on to captain and then manage England, had a high opinion of David:

He could have been one of England's top fast bowlers if he had not suffered from injuries which prevented him from reaching his full potential. If he had been playing in the 21st century he would have been carefully nursed. But back in the 1960s fast bowlers had very little time off. The worst time I remember was once in the 1970s playing 29 days on the trot. David would also have thrived in the one-day game, which was to become so important later. Like two other 6'7" fast men, Chris Tremlett in the 1990s and Steven Finn recently, Larter's proneness to injury would have been a problem but it would have been managed. Mark Wood currently is an even better example of what modern medicine can achieve.

Tremlett managed 12 Tests, taking 53 wickets at 27 with a strike rate of 54. Finn in 36 Tests captured 125 wickets at 39 and a strike rate of 51, but sadly then lost that form. In Michael Henderson's words *'A knee injury has not helped… He has just floated away before our eyes… Not everybody can fly like an eagle. Even Frank Tyson bowled flat out for only a couple of years.'*

Wood's 16 Tests so far have produced 50 wickets at 32 and a strike rate of 59. All three played in the era of covered wickets when the pitches gave the bowler less help.

The pitch for the fourth Test, at Headingley, six days after the Lord's MCC Touring party match, was another well-grassed wicket, *'as green as an emerald'* in Jack Barker's words. The England selectors dropped David from the squad and replaced him with Ken Palmer. Wooldridge had sympathy for David: *'Palmer is principally called up to spare Larter the feeling that he has become the permanent bridesmaid of English cricket. He has been 12th man at Brisbane, Adelaide, Melbourne, Sydney, Manchester, Lord's, then Edgbaston, within the last eight months.'*

Selector Alec Bedser, seeking to fend off press comment, said *'we've proved in the past in those conditions that a man of Palmer's pace would be more useful than faster bowlers like Larter.'* In the event Palmer, like David in the previous two Tests, did not make the final XI, so that England's opening attack again consisted of Trueman and Shackleton with support from Dexter, with Titmus and Lock as the two spinners taking nine wickets between them. The West Indies, dominant in all aspects, won for the first time ever at Headingley by 221 runs, in four days, to go to 2-1 up in the series. *'England disappointed,'* in *Wisden's* words, *'in batting and lacked penetration in attack.'* Shackleton bowled as he always did – with metronomical accuracy – ending with four for 151 in 63 overs. Although green, the wicket had been the batsmen's friend against this bowling. Oh, for some bounce and verve!

David's omission from the Test squad enabled him to play in his skipper Keith Andrew's benefit match at Northampton on July 27, where a suitably emphatic victory by an innings in two days celebrated the popular skipper's big day. David put victory in the sights with five wickets in the first innings, only a couple of the Derby batsmen facing his speed with any confidence, and two more early in the second, including opener Charlie Lee, who had been David's debut dismissal three years before. Fittingly Keith Andrew took four catches behind the wicket in the second innings.

The county now occupied third place in the championship table after a wonderful twelve-match unbeaten run. There were seven championship games to come before the season's end on 30 August.

But the magic dust evaporated as unexpectedly as it had arrived, with August bringing losses to Leicestershire away; Glamorgan at Wantage Road, where David, watched by selector Alec Bedser, managed seven wickets in the match (off his short run); Worcestershire at home, where David returned eight for 88 from 44 overs in the match; and the return fixture against Hampshire at Southampton. As Engel and Radd point out in their *History of Northamptonshire CCC*, the now retired Northants spinners Tribe and Manning would have been unplayable on many of those August pitches. Jock Livingston's search for their equivalent had been unsuccessful.

Occasional shafts of light did shine through the August darkness. A victory over Hampshire on August 13 on a helpful pitch at Wellingborough was memorable for David as he, Brian Crump and Jim Watts bowled out Roy Marshall's team for 83 and 68. David's seven for 37 from 21 overs, including Marshall twice,

> *'David's seven for 37 from 21 overs... took him to the prized 100 wickets in a season.'*

took him to the prized 100 wickets in a season. This was the first time he had done it and the first time any Northamptonshire fast bowler, including Tyson, had done it since EW 'Nobby' Clark in 1929.

The county almost defeated the West Indies side at Wantage Road on August 14. Northants led by 350 with only four second innings wickets down at the end of the second day. Two brilliant innings by Milburn of 100 and 88 and good seam bowling from Crump, David and Kettle bowling the tourists out for 107 had put the county into a winning position. It was not to be as rain washed out the last day, depriving David of the hope of showing the English selectors what they had been missing.

David again put his best foot forward in the next match – against Worcestershire at home. Norman Gifford had good reason to remember it. On a rain-affected pitch he took seven for 37, bowling Northants out for a miserable 78. David responded with five for 46 as Worcestershire crumbled to 105 all out. Worcestershire needed 143 to win and made it despite losing their first five wickets for 64, three of them to David.

My captain at Worcestershire, said Gifford, *opening batsman Don Kenyon, used to enjoy taking on fast bowlers – he didn't mind at all it coming at him round the ears, claiming that a bouncer was to him just like a half volley. In the game at Wantage Road I got seven wickets and David, in reply, got some real steam up. Don came back into the pavilion after being dismissed by David in the second innings, not saying very much at all, other than 'this man's got a bit of pace' – high praise from Don.*

Don was a brilliant captain. Of the captains I played under for England I would rate Ray Illingworth as tactically the best, and also a good man manager - see the way he could handle John Snow when no one else could.

I have no doubt that David would have played many more Test matches if he had not been injured. After Worcestershire I went to Warwickshire and so got to know Bob Willis and David Brown. Browny was a tremendous trier, but not as quick as David. Bob was, like David, very tall and susceptible to injuries. At 6 foot five he bowled brilliantly for England, but crippled himself in the process, with the result he just couldn't do it physically, week in week out, in the championship.

For Ian Wooldridge there was one obvious change to be made to the England side for the fifth Test at the Oval on August 22 – Larter for Shackleton. *'It may seem shabby treatment for a veteran who has slogged his heart out for England in three Tests, but the truth is that Shackleton was brought in to fill a special role at Lord's but by Leeds was helping West Indies batsmen to play themselves in. Trueman has been left without real attacking support, and Larter, for all his unpredictability, is at least a man who takes the battle to the batsmen's toe caps.'*

Two-one down in the series going into the last Test, it was reasonable to assume that the selectors might be bold, but no; they brought back Statham as Trueman's partner and retained the steady Shackleton, thus for the first time playing three seamers and one spinner instead of the usual two seam bowlers plus Dexter and two spinners.

'I still think Richie Benaud's XI made more sense than any other or, for that matter, the one selected,' wrote Jack Barker. *'Richie chose Dexter, Richardson, Graveney, Barrington, Close, Sharpe, Parks, Lock, Trueman, Statham and Larter. Larter, for Richie, was a must and Richie observed with gentle irony that the giant David was being protected out of Test cricket, adding, "if it is any consolation to Larter the Australians would have picked him in three of the Tests against our country [in the 1962/63 Ashes tour]." There is no shrewder brain in cricket than the great Australian skipper's and he declared flatly that he would have had Larter playing in every Test [against the West Indies] against a team whose very brilliance brings frailty against the excessively bouncing ball. I can vouch for it that Larter was the one man West Indies didn't want selected.'*

West Indies won the Wisden Trophy by defeating England by eight wickets, to give them a 3-1 series win. Statham, playing what was to prove his last Test, took three wickets of the twelve to fall and Shackleton one for 105. It was to be his last Test too.

Trueman established a new record for England-West Indies matches by taking 34 wickets in the series, and would no doubt have had more if he had not suffered from a damaged left heel which prevented him bowling more than one over in the West Indies second innings. JM Kilburn paid lyrical tribute to the ending of the Trueman/Statham pair's 104 appearances for England between them: *'Their fires are dying now but the flames they kindled during the years of their mastery leave a glow across the cricketing sky to warm the heart in gratitude.'*

The bond between the pair went deep. Late in life Statham fell on hard times. Chris Waters in his biography of Trueman recounts how Trueman personally organised a tribute dinner to raise funds for Statham and also bought him a car.

David's view that Fred Trueman was the best fast bowler he played with or against was shared by many, including Keith Fletcher for whom *the top three were Trueman, Malcolm Marshall and Lillee,* and by MJK Smith who thought that Trueman was the best English quickie ever, *he could get them out bowling at only 90% of his speed.*

That opinion would no doubt have been endorsed by the fourteen men who saw him in close-up - those with whom he opened the bowling for England in his 67 Tests – Statham 35 times, Bedser and Loader five, Tyson, Moss, Coldwell and Shackleton three times, Bailey, Rumsey and David twice and Rhodes, Jackson, Flavell and Price once.

It may have been the cramped coach journey to Southampton on August 20, taking Northants to the return fixture with Hampshire, which exacerbated a weakness, but David strained a groin muscle early on the first day and could bowl no further in the match, and the match was narrowly lost. Brian Crump remembers this match in the context of David's batting:

David was never a batsman. This did not matter in those days when 9, 10 and Jack were not expected to score runs. I can remember the game against Hampshire at Southampton where David and I batted together. We were both carrying injuries and each of us had a runner. Total chaos ensued!

He was certainly not much of a fielder either, having such a long way to bend to get down to the ball, and he surprisingly did not seem to have an understanding of the need, when fielding in his usual position of fine leg or square leg, to take account of the sideways spin which the ball would follow when swept to leg by the batsman. I would often shout to David 'watch out it's going to turn to the right', but in vain as it went over the boundary. I still smile at the recollection of David forlornly standing at third man at a Wantage Road match, soaked to the skin by rain in his corner of the field, whilst the rest of us basked in sunshine covering the rest of the ground.

The groin injury meant that David missed the last two matches of the season – a ten wicket victory over Sussex at Wantage Road and a battling draw at Edgbaston with Warwickshire, ending on August 30. So ended a 'nearly but not quite' season for Northants. Only 13 points behind the championship leaders at the end of July the poor results in August meant the final position was seventh. Good for the small county - but it could have been so much better.

The progress made in developing the side was heartening, with Norman, Reynolds, Prideaux and Milburn all making over 1000 runs. The high point was the joint success of the opening attack, with both David and Brian Crump taking 100 wickets in all first-class matches, the first time in the county's history that two seamers had achieved that mark. Not even Frank Tyson had managed that feat, operating on the placid Northampton wicket.

The Atomic Pill (as he was christened by the Essex players), 5'4 tall Brian Crump, was generous when asked about his 6'7" opening partner. No one could bear more closely observed witness to David's abilities:

As a bowler he was brilliant for me: bowling fast on a good line of middle and off with a bit of outswing and seam movement taking the ball towards the slips, he created trouble for all batsmen. This meant that when I bowled in tandem with him, as I often did, the batsmen would endeavour to loosen the tight grip David had created by having a go at my bowling at the other end, with the result that I got a lot of wickets through the pressure he had created. He was polite enough to qualify this by saying how he owed many of the wickets he took to the fact that I managed some tight control at my end.

He was accurate – I can really never recall him bowling badly - and he certainly did not spray it around like some fast bowlers – bowlers like Steve Harmison for example. David's great ability was the way he could get bounce out of even the least responsive pitches, frustrating batsmen with line, length and bounce. Very few other bowlers could achieve this balance – I recall Norman Graham of Kent was one who could, but of course he was at much less pace. It was remarkable that David could achieve this on the very slow Wantage Road track. The wickets there were traditionally slow, and they were doctored to give every help to our spinners, George Tribe and his successors, by shaving off the grass, so that the wicket would take spin on the first day. David sadly missed out on the faster wickets which resulted from the relaying of the square in 1966.

In terms of speed he was of course not as fast as Tyson - nobody was - he was the same speed as John Price and Jeff Jones, but not I think as quick as John Snow when John was in the mood. And I faced David a lot in the nets, and also Frank Tyson, whom my dad, playing in the Staffordshire league, had persuaded to move to the county from the Central Lancashire League. David had a really good action, a nice curving run-up in the Fred Trueman mode and a high delivery. The problem was that he was injury prone and seemed to have difficulty in playing through the pain of injury, as some of us could do.

If newspaper reports described him as inconsistent, in my view this was not a comment on the control of his bowling, but more a comment about his difficulty in avoiding the niggles which would prevent him from bowling consistently at his top speed. One can imagine the frustration the team felt when we were hoping to defeat Worcestershire in the penultimate match of the 1965 season, and thereby hopefully win the title, when David pulled a hamstring and could only bowl off a few paces, without much effect. He was the leader of our bowling attack and without him, with no other fast bowlers around, our championship chances were much reduced.

I don't recall much of the final years of David's career, after the ankle injury he sustained in Australia in 1965, when he played a few one-day games and a handful of championship matches. He was however still able to bowl well but only in very short spells.

Recovered from the groin injury, David was invited to play in the season-ending MCC against Yorkshire game at the Festival at Scarborough. England and Glamorgan's Tony Lewis has written:

'A call to the Festival is one rarely turned down by a county player. It holds out the promise after the toils of the championship season of first-class cricket without the tensions and dreads of failure. It offers heaven-sent hours of play 11.30 to 6 pm, a round of evening social functions which leave the less hardy performers rather flat-footed during the day, and all to the accompaniment of the Scarborough Brass Band which blows quietly away in the far corner of the ground.'

David loved the atmosphere:

> A lovely town ground, not too small, in a true oval shape with banked terraces. The ground is surrounded by seaside lodgings and, during the Festival, the boundary at the lower end of the slope is populated by tents and marquees, a flagpole and the band stand. Only 100 yards from the sea, play was sometimes interrupted by sea fret.

Milburn, born to be a Festival star, clubbed a quick 87 and David ended with five good wickets in the match. He also played in the second Festival match, this time for England against Young England. Trueman, recovered from his ankle injury in the final Test, hit six sixes in a century in 67 minutes. David then opened the bowling, clean bowling Somerset's Graham Atkinson with four runs on the board. This brought Milburn to the crease.

> I thought to liven it up a bit and I had a word with Colin between overs suggesting that I bowl a bouncer second ball of the next over, to which he agreed. Although I say it myself it was a useful delivery, quick and about head height. He hooked the ruddy thing out of the ground! He was an amazing cricketer and had the cricket world enthralled. It took a little time, but he did learn to build an innings, based on a very sound technique.

Milburn's first innings 26 was just a warm-up for a second innings assault of 52 out of 62 in 31 minutes, containing four sixes and five fours. David did not bowl in that innings having strained his back, an injury which prevented him playing in the final match of the festival, for TN Pearce's XI against the tourists.

Trueman's 1963 season was magnificent, even by his high standards: 129 wickets at 15 apiece, leading Yorkshire to their fourth championship in five years, topping the Test averages and scoring his maiden first-class century at Northampton. Off the field of play he continued to provoke stories to make young colleagues' hair stand on end. Don Wilson was brought up with Fred: *'He wanted to get everyone out. Marvellous self-confidence. He would come in after getting nought for 85 and say, "no bloody luck at all – should have had eight for 20 – buggers played and missed all day." And he'd believe it.'*

David was friendly with Don Wilson – they toured together to New Zealand and India – and David recalls Don's account of 'a gem of a Fred story':

> Fred was always known as fiery Fred, not by cricketers but by the popular press, because he always seemed to be on the wrong side of somebody, be it the MCC, Yorkshire, the press themselves or his first wife Enid. She was the daughter of the Mayor of Scarborough and had something of a reputation.
>
> Yorkshire were at Scarborough where the dressing rooms are at ground level in the grand old pavilion, and the team had come off the field at close of play and were changing out of their whites, when the door burst open and in walked Enid wanting to know Fred's whereabouts. The language was short and to the point.
>
> According to Don most of the team were only half dressed and Brian Close was stark naked. Someone pointed towards the showers at the back of the dressing room into which she charged. Someone, I think Doug Padgett, came

hurtling out very red in the face, and the mother and father of all rows then started up. Within a couple of minutes, she came charging back and out through the door. Don assured me that Fred never said a word when he eventually emerged.

The statistics of the Test series lend support to Benaud's views on selection – the fast bowlers dominated: Griffith took his 32 wickets at 16 apiece, Trueman his 34 at 17, and Sobers, bowling mostly fast-medium, took 20 wickets at 28. Shackleton, who bowled more overs than any other English bowler, took 15 wickets at 34 each. It is difficult to find justification in these figures for Bedser's stated reason for David not getting a game – that a bowler of Palmer's pace (or presumably Shackleton's) would be more useful than faster bowlers like Larter.

From a young age David had built himself up to be a fast bowler. Right from the start of their relationship Alec Bedser had sought to model David on his, Bedser's, style, cutting down his run, cutting down his speed, and getting him to focus on medium-fast in-swing, hopefully also with a leg cutter. David had the highest regard for the way Bedser, bowling in that mode, had dominated his era. He was in David's opinion the best English bowler of that style since S.F.Barnes.

> I had great admiration for him, but he gave up on me when he found that I did not want to be AVB Mark 2. I fear that my desire to bowl fast meant he lost faith in me.

With 121 wickets from 821 overs, at an average per wicket of 16.76, the eighth best average in the country, it had been David's best season. Not to have been recognised by the selectors was frustrating. But there was joy in matters of the heart:

> Again I was side-lined, but did crack 100 wickets for the season. The best thing that happened was that I met a Miss Thelma Hawkins, a Sister at Northampton General Hospital. She was to become my wife some three years later.

EAST AFRICA TOUR OCTOBER 1963

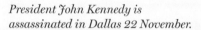

David's break from cricket lasted for one month only. On October 2 he was to be found in Nairobi, pounding in to bowl on the matting wicket of Nairobi Cricket Club. MCC had chosen him as a member of their 12-man touring party to East Africa.

David had already participated in MCC's programme of encouraging cricket in different parts of the globe when he was part of the 1960/61 MCC tour to New Zealand. The following autumn, in another example of that programme, MCC organised a four-week tour to East Africa, under the leadership of FR Brown of Northants. Two years later in the autumn of 1963 a further East African tour was arranged, this time under MJK Smith, with Willie Watson as player manager. The 12 players included three from Northants – apart from David, wicket-keeper Laurie Johnson and Colin Milburn. David and Jeff Jones of Glamorgan were the two fast bowlers, with Tom Cartwright bowling seam, and two spinners, Robin Hobbs of Essex as the leg-spinner and John Mortimore of Gloucestershire to bowl off-spin.

There was just one disappointment for David: back in July when the plan for the tour had been released by MCC, it had been announced that Denis Compton would be one of 13 players in the party. Sadly, his plans changed, and he was not one of the party which assembled on September 29 at Heathrow. The first stop of the five-week tour was Nairobi. There Willie Watson gave his first press conference, pointing out that apart from the benefits he hoped local East African cricket would derive from it, the tour *'represented a big chance for players like Milburn, Hobbs, Langridge, Jones, and Larter, who are on the fringe of Test places.'*

I got to know David well on this trip recalls Jeff Jones. *We sat next to each other on the plane into Nairobi. We were served tomato soup. David, who could only just fit into the seat, adjusted his knees and the soup went all over me. I had to go and change. Fortunately, I had a spare pair of trousers in my bag. That got us off to a good start.*

It was a good tour in the company of some very good players. I got on very well with Colin Milburn, who was the life and soul of the party, and was always playing pranks on us. One day we decided to get our own back. We were in the swimming pool and when we saw Colin arriving, we all went to the shallow end, with our knees on the bottom so that it looked like we were in the deep end. As Colin leapt to jump in, we all stood up. Colin had to go to hospital with quite bad bruising. With him, Hobbs and others around the social side of the tour was excellent, aided by a lack of formality at social functions. David although generally quiet, was a good mixer and after a few drinks…

Jeff had a high regard for Milburn as a cricketer: *People remember his size and weight, but he was very agile close to the wicket, taking all sorts of catches, and was a very good medium pace bowler – bowling Glamorgan out at Swansea once I remember. In his Test career he was unlucky – on an important tour to the West Indies he got, as a batsman, a number of bad lbw decisions.*

Eleven matches were played, all on matting, mostly jute and some coir. Jeff remembers the concern he and David had about the run-ups: *We couldn't wear spikes, which would tear the matting, and had to wear rubber-soled shoes, which meant we did not feel secure running up. We both were draggers and I think David and I both went through eight pairs. We certainly frightened a few of the batsmen. I remember even Tom Cartwright, with his beautiful action, couldn't prevent the ball bouncing over the stumps.*

> Tom was what one could describe as an old school medium-pacer, and a more than useful bat. He would bowl all day and still have a smile on his face. I got the impression that he never wanted to do anything else but play cricket.

The Kenyan and Ugandan opponents did not greatly extend MCC, but they did prevent them from winning all their matches, four ending in draws. The toughest opposition was expected to be from the East African Invitation XI in the tour's final match at Kampala, but despite a useful 50 from John Solanky, later to play for Worcestershire and Glamorgan, MCC won by an innings. The most spirited opposition came from the Kenya Kongonis, whose final pair of Giles and Shuttleworth added 83 to get within 11 runs of victory before losing. Shuttleworth's leg-spin bowling had earlier been treated irreverently by Milburn who struck his only over in the second innings for 30 runs, the first five balls out of the ground for six and caught on the boundary from the sixth. The local player who most impressed the tourists was the Kenyan Basharat Hassan, who was to go on to a successful career with Nottinghamshire.

Laurie Johnson was outstanding behind the stumps, particularly keeping to leggie Robin Hobbs for whom he took a number of stumpings. The high bounce of the ball from all bowlers, including Hobbs and Cartwright, meant that the local batsmen left the ball a lot, making Laurie's job no easier: *I loved standing up to the wicket, something I learned from Herbert Strudwick, the old England keeper when he was the scorer at Surrey. I would stand up to Brian Crump's seam bowling at Northants, even though Keith Andrew (the best keeper in England and only prevented from playing for England many times by the fact that Jim Parks was a better batsman) preferred to stand back to him.*

Parfitt was the most prolific of the batsmen, with two centuries, whilst Milburn, MJK and Micky Stewart excelled with the bat. Hobbs was the outstanding bowler with 46 wickets in the 11 matches, followed by Cartwright and by David, whose best bowling efforts were four wickets against Kenya, five for 14 against a Jinja Invitation XI and four for 32 in the final match against the East African Invitation XI, whose batsmen found his pace particularly difficult to cope with. Parfitt recalls David being *pretty lethal* on the matting.

Although this was David's second trip to Eastern Africa, the first - the February 1962 Commonwealth tour organised by Ron Roberts - had been short and sweet, involving only four matches. Taking part in this five-week trip to Kenya and Uganda provided another wonderful learning experience for David. Culturally and socially there was much to absorb and new friends to make. The presence of two of David's Northants colleagues meant he was not going to feel lonely, even if he was, at 23, the baby of the party.

The trip was interesting, not least because Colin Milburn and Laurie Johnson were there too. As neither had toured before I was a sort of guide to them. We tended to stick together when off the field, but it was a very good touring group, with a number of strong characters who contributed to the happy atmosphere. One of these was Robin Hobbs, whose cheerful personality, always ready for a laugh, made him an important member of the team off the field. On the field he was such an asset as a bowler. I think he bamboozled most of the opposition, but more importantly gave us hardworking bowlers a rest from the midday sun. Much of his success (and for the rest of us) came from the fact that a lot of the cricket was played on matting, which for Robin was wonderful. Bounce and turn were all he needed, and he used them well.

The cricket was generally a bit more serious than my previous Commonwealth tour to Rhodesia had been. Most of the opposition was made up of Asian sides and they were determined to put up a good show. However, the considerable bounce off the matting meant that Jonesy and I were dangerous at times and had to tone it down on occasions. Being a friendly sort, this resulted in a lot of half volleys and yorkers, as short of a length could have killed someone. This did not stop them trying to bowl bouncers at us, but Colin Milburn just smacked them out of the park, so they soon got the message.

Jeff Jones, Robin Hobbs, Richard Langridge, JDFL, Tom Cartwright, Colin Milburn, Laurie Johnson; John Mortimore, Willie Watson, Mike Smith, Micky Stewart, Peter Parfitt.

With only 12 players in the party there was always a worry about the possibility of injuries preventing a full team turnout, but there also considerable benefits: everyone was involved in every match, and thus team spirit built very quickly, hugely helped by the leadership of Watson and Smith. As Robin Hobbs put it: *Willie*

Watson was a joy to be with for six weeks, very kind and full of lovely stories, and we had one good thing or bad thing in common – we were both smokers.

Robin had played against David a few times in county games, but the two did not get to chat much on those occasions, as Robin tended to be grabbed by Northants leg-spinner Peter Watts wanting to share thoughts and techniques on the dark art of googlies and so on. *I did get to know David a little better on the East African tour. He was a good team man, but not one of those who sought the limelight, being quiet by nature; he was a gentle giant off the field, and on it a bowler who could generate pace and lift sufficient to worry all opposing batsmen. He turned in some good performances, with four wickets in an innings twice and five wickets once. The matches were played on matting and the pitches were very quick and very dangerous when David was at full pace. I remember very well a small left-handed batsman who opened against us on several occasions being hit on the head several times, and we feared for him. Both David and Jeff Jones had to slacken off the speed in such situations to avoid hitting the batsmen.*

The matting was wonderful for my bowling: I could always turn the ball, but in East Africa the added bounce gave me huge help, and I managed 46 wickets in the 11 matches, many of them stumped by Laurie Johnson. Outstanding throughout the tour, he was known as one of the finest wicketkeepers of his time, a good man, happy to be understudy all his career to Keith Andrew at Northants.

David was as quick as any other bowler in county cricket – so that when Essex went up to Northampton we would be delighted if we heard he was not playing for whatever reason. Perhaps I am influenced too much by my experience of watching David bowl in East Africa, but when thinking of him I think also of Steve Finn, of Middlesex and England. Both tall men and rather ungainly fielders with their great long legs, and both perhaps lacking some of the killer instinct in that they did not want to hurt anybody when they bowled.

The question of killer instinct often comes up in discussion about David. Fast bowlers each have their own views as to what is acceptable fast short bowling and what crosses the line into dangerous and intimidating deliveries. In those days it was the unwritten rule that one did not bowl bouncers at number eleven batsmen who were less capable of defending themselves. But it is always difficult to lay down any hard and fast rule. Even those who believed in the concept might occasionally cross the line. Mike Brearley, himself an opening batsman, captaining England against Pakistan at Edgbaston in 1978, was asked to justify Bob Willis's short-pitched bowling at Pakistan's night-watchman who required stitches after being hit in the mouth. Brearley had to admit *'we had tried everything, and he had batted for over an hour.'*

David could never have brought himself to say, as John Snow wrote in 1968: *I'm not ashamed of leaving a trail of fractures among the opposition – a finger, a thumb, a whole right hand and one foot on the latest count. After all, that's what I'm there for. Not to inflict deliberate injury of course but to rough up a batsman, make them apprehensive and destroy their confidence.'*

Nor think what Dennis Lillee thought in 1974: *'I wanted to hurt so much that the batsman won't want to face me anymore. I bowl bouncers for one reason – that is to hit the batsman thus intimidate him. Not many batsmen recover from a really good bouncer.'*

David was different from them. He didn't bowl many bouncers but when he did it had a single purpose – to get the batsman out. Different characters, different motivation. Gentle Brian Crump no doubt got it right: *each fast bowler has his own personality and a way of doing things.* Jim Watts is another who doesn't subscribe to the theory that a successful fast bowler must possess an aggressive character: *I don't think David's reserved personality meant that he was less successful as a bowler than if he had had more devil or aggressiveness about him. He was one of the quickest bowlers on the circuit and he could be very hostile.* A glance at some of the photographs of David's follow-through show just that.

Engel and Radd saw him this way: '*Off the field, Larter was far from the snarling fire breather. Team-mates remember his fondness for a nap in the dressing room. He was a gentle man who had to manufacture the fast bowler's aggression.*'

Tony Lewis, recalling some of the Northants personalities for the 1978 Northants centenary publication, saw David's on-field demeanour in more flamboyant terms: '*Memories over those years will cover many players... many will recall the cool benign Keith Andrew, calming the snorting thigh-slapping Larter.*'

On the East African tour, the players could play hard but also have fun, a result of the team spirit engendered by the Smith/Watson leadership. David enjoyed playing under Mike Smith:

> A very good, strong batsman, despite the ever-present spectacles. He could read a game and his bowling changes were always sensible. When bowling at Mike I was always trying to york him, but he must have had the best spectacles ever, because I never got through! Of the few England captains I played for, Mike was the pick.

Jeff Jones shared that view: *Mike was a lovely man, charismatic. Perhaps not a brilliant tactician on the cricket field. I got on well with him through a mutual interest in rugby – he got an England cap at outside half, and I was a Welshman.* As did Robin Hobbs: *MJK was a fantastic leader – most of the players would have walked on water for him, and I was lucky to go to South Africa with him again a couple of years later.*

David recalls happy times:

> On an afternoon off in Mombasa, a group of us played football on the beach. It was really hot and hazy. Laurie decided not to play and instead stretched out on the beach on his back and went to sleep. Big mistake! That night we had a reception to attend which was suddenly interrupted by Laurie doing a dying swan act in the middle of the group; sunstroke through closed eyes, which the locals told us was quite common. Laurie was carted off to hospital but made a quick and complete recovery.
>
> Laurie and I shared billets in the different locations. It seemed as if everybody smoked in those days, and Rothmans were handing out cartons of 200 cigarettes to the party all the time. Laurie opened a new carton, taking out a single pack of 24 for the day, leaving the almost full carton on the dressing table in our digs. Two days later, wanting a replenishment, we found that the carton was now short of number of packs, with the local

newspaper stuffed in to disguise the shortage. Lesson learned, but we decided not to tell our hosts – there would have been big trouble for the housemaid.

Everything seemed bigger and more numerous in Africa. For example, the moths at night – huge things big as butterflies. Guess which 18 stone batsman was terrified of moths? Colin! It was a fun trip.

In summing up the tour Watson praised his bowlers and the fielding – which he described as the highlight of the tour. The one area in which the tour did not succeed was financial. Attendances, particularly in Nairobi, were sadly below expectation. The tourists were treated very well by their hosts and in turn were worthy ambassadors.

Reporting from England, Swanton damned Hobbs with faint praise: 'Hobbs seems to have had a promising first trip.' He continued: 'Larter and Jones, who would be forming the spearhead of England's attack in India after Christmas, should come back from East Africa wiser and better bowlers.'

The wisdom that Jeff and David picked up was sadly to prove of precious little value on the totally different pitch conditions of India.

13

INDIA TOUR 1964

Mary Quant, fashion designer, inventor of the miniskirt and hot pants, named Woman of the Year.

On his return to Suffolk in early November David resumed winter work for his father – but not for long. Six weeks after returning from East Africa he was back at Heathrow, joining the MCC main winter tour to India.

The last MCC tour to the sub-continent had taken place only two years earlier. It had been criticised as too long, covering as it did not only India but Pakistan and Ceylon. England lost 2-0 in the five Tests against India but beat Pakistan 1-0 from three. Eric Russell had been on that trip (and spent two or three days there in hospital): *it was a very tough tour, taking five months. There will never be a tour like that again.*

Determined to avoid that mistake, MCC went to the other extreme for the 1964 tour, cramming five five-day Tests and five three-day first-class matches into an eight-week span. It didn't work: the view of the players was that the demanding nature of all sub-continental tours was increased rather than diminished by making them shorter, given the significant amount of time taken up in travelling and the consequent reduction in sleeping hours. This time MCC paid particular attention to alleviating the typical dietary issues on Indian tours by taking tinned food from England for use in those cricketing centres with little familiarity with European cooking. This was of some value, but did not impress some of their hosts. Nor did it stop the tour becoming notorious for MCC having only ten players fit enough to play in the second Test, stomach illness confining all others to bed or bathroom.

Although the trip was short and did not start until after Christmas, Trueman, Statham, Graveney and Lock all declared themselves unavailable, withdrawals which presented opportunities for England's young bowlers, including David, to make a name for themselves. As Dexter, who had led the 1961/62 tour, was on the hustings in Cardiff preparing, unsuccessfully, to stand for election to Parliament for the seat there held by Jim Callaghan, Cowdrey was chosen to lead the party. He then withdrew due to illness, Micky Stewart taking his batting place with the captaincy passing to MJK Smith. The party of 15 included three pace bowlers, David, Jeff Jones and John Price from Middlesex, plus pace bowling all-rounder Barry Knight, two off-spinners, Titmus and Mortimore, and slow left-armer Don Wilson. Price expressed himself pleasantly surprised to be selected for the tour, having only become a first-team Middlesex regular the previous summer, 25 years of age and still uncapped. He was to prove the best of the fast bowlers.

For Indians the tour was of huge interest. *The Times of India* in December 1963 assured its readers that this was a big event: *'Under pressure from India MCC has decided to consider the tour an official one.'* The writer set the country three tasks – to

John Edrich, Phil Sharpe, Don Wilson, JDFL, Jeff Jones, John Price, Jimmy Binks, Brian Bolus;
Peter Parfitt, Jim Parks, Fred Titmus, MJK Smith, Manager David Clark, Colin Cowdrey,
Ken Barrington, John Mortimore, Barry Knight.

provide hard fast wickets for entertaining cricket, to pay attention to the visitors' gastronomic needs, and lastly *'to make every possible effort to provide an outsize bed so David Larter may be able to rest his 6 foot 7 ½ inch frame, after a tiring day in the field. Otherwise Larter, as he himself has mentioned, will have to make do "with a bed with no rails at the bottom".'*

The *Indian Cricket Field Annual*, in those days the nearest approximation to an Indian *Wisden*, presented pen pictures of the MCC touring party, written by Ron Roberts: *'Larter was selected for the 1962/63 MCC tour of Australia and New Zealand but did not play in a Test match in Australia which Australian captain Richie Benaud, for one, found difficult to understand. He did quite well in New Zealand, but again was bypassed in favour of senior players against West Indies. Now, however, England must look to younger men for the bowling future, and Larter obviously features prominently in the team building plans.'*

Pleas from various local sources for the authorities to prepare faster wickets sadly were ignored. MCC found virtually every pitch on which they played to be uniformly true but exceptionally slow. The quicker bowlers had great difficulty in creating any pace off the pitch and the spin bowlers – other than those imparting leg-spin – could only achieve slow turn; the batsmen could only score heavily by exercising great patience.

It was no surprise therefore that of the ten matches played on the tour, nine were drawn, including all five Test matches. MCC won just the one match, and that ironically by an innings. For the *Daily Mail's* Ian Wooldridge, accompanying the tour party, it was all too predictable, as forecast in one of his early dispatches: *'I am here less to report a Test series than witness five draws of fixed odds, India having packed their side with batsmen. England will be confronted with wickets that threaten to be about as lively as a fireside rug.'*

That did not put off the spectators, inured to such conditions and fanatically supportive of their cricketing heroes against the old colonial power. One million of them filled the stadia over the ten matches, ensuring that the tour was a great success from a financial point of view.

Bangalore was the venue for the first match of the tour, starting on January 3 against a President's XI. MCC captain Mike Smith did his best to achieve a result with a challenging declaration, but the challenge was declined, the home side happy to play for the draw. A clear portent. The second match took place at Hyderabad against South Zone and it gave David a limited claim to success as the only match of the tour to be won. MCC batted in great style, scoring 480 at more than four runs an

Clean Bowled

Belliappa, who scored a splendid century for South Zone against M.C.C. on Wednesday in a gallant but vain attempt to foil the tourists' bid for victory, is here seen being clean bowled by Larter.

over with Yorkshire spinner Don Wilson, who went in on the first evening as night-watchman, staying until after lunch the next day and making his first century in first-class cricket. MCC hit seven sixes, including one from last man David. In the second innings, at a cost of five runs an over, David removed both openers, one of them before a run had been scored and the other the important one of Beliappa, bowled for 102. The spinners Titmus, Wilson and Barrington, with 14 wickets between them, sealed the victory.

That was an early indication of the importance spin would have. Both John Price and David suffered from front foot trouble, David with three no-balls and Price with four. For David and his new ball colleagues the maintenance of hope and spirit was going to be important in the long hard struggle ahead.

At Hyderabad there was some spare time in a very crowded travel schedule.

We were spending a day or two at a large and decrepit country club, left over from the Raj. At that time, it was difficult to drink and you certainly did not chase the girls, so we made up our own fun with card games etc. Ken Barrington and I had become good mates and we wandered round the grounds, coming across a weed-encrusted full-sized swimming pool. We found a pumphouse and venturing inside saw a big single pot diesel engine standing there covered in cobwebs.

Ken was a qualified car mechanic, and I was used to father's lorries, so we had a poke around the engine not really knowing what it did. Anyway, there was diesel in the tank and after a bit of bleeding and cleaning, along with some hefty swings on the huge starting handle we got it thumping away. Feeling pleased with ourselves we went outside to find a billowing cloud of black smoke making its way upwards and an artificial wave mechanism in the pool thrashing about, sending water everywhere. This was soon accompanied by a throng of very excited Indians, who did not seem too pleased with our efforts. Apparently, the thing had not worked for years!

The party moved south to Madras where the first Test was to begin on January 10. Bowling selection for the Test was straightforward: all three spinners, Titmus, Wilson and Mortimer, supplemented by Barrington's leg-spin, played. With only two opening bowlers to play, David was chosen to offer such pace and bounce as he could muster, sharing the new ball with the medium-fast pace of Barry Knight, whose batting gave him a second suit over Jones and Price.

Henry Blofeld, reporting for the *Guardian*, saw David bowl the first ball of the match just short of a length to Mehra: *'It came through at lower than waist height. To all intents and purposes Larter was banging his head against a brick wall and his length and direction did not serve to contain either batsmen.'* The nearest David got to taking a wicket was when he had opener Kunderam, who scored 192, dropped by Bolus at long leg on 80. India batted at what was in local terms a helter-skelter rate of three runs an over to make 277 for 2 wickets by the end of the first day.

On the second day sub-continental stomach illness visited the tourists. Both Stewart and Parks were confined to bed, and Titmus and Knight felt distinctly unwell. The party seemed to be short of medical experts. Wooldridge again: *'Only Mad Dogs and Englishmen could have attempted ten matches, a full Test series and 20,000 miles of travel in eight weeks without a full-time medical and hygiene supervisor. England have only just avoided the ultimate disaster of having no fit batsman to go in next.'*

Backs to the wall, facing an Indian total of 457, England's ambition was to avoid losing wickets at all cost. Bolus, with 88 in seven hours, and Barrington with 80 in five hours, achieved just that with a gallant, devastatingly dull stand. They thereby provided sufficient recovery time for the other invalids – who now included David – all of whom were back on their feet by the third day. A mere 27 runs were scored between lunch and tea that day as England reached 317. Micky Stewart, the most seriously ill with a temperature of 102°, unable to eat anything solid for three days, left his sick bed to bat at number ten with a runner (no pun intended), with 21 needed to save the follow on. Save it he did, with Titmus, keeping going for 85 minutes before going back to bed. Bapu Nadkarni bowling slow left-arm orthodox, barely discernible, spin, came on towards the end of the second day, bowled throughout the third day, and continued into the fourth, ending with an analysis of 32-27-5-0, the most economical spell of 60 or more deliveries in Test cricket history. He conceded his first run with the final ball of his 22nd over.

Tiger Pataudi was not, in the early days of his captaincy, likely to risk a loss to the English tourists by making anything approaching a generous declaration. He set England a target of 293 in 4½ hours, never remotely achievable on such a slow wicket. England did well to end only 52 runs short at 241 for five.

Wicketless in the match, David did, in the second innings, dismiss, involuntarily, Manjrekar, the first innings centurion, by running him out for a duck in a manner described by Michael Melford as unique in his experience. Pataudi pushed a gentle defensive shot back to David who, weary in 85° of heat, tried to flick the ball up into his hands with his toe cap. Making a mess of this old professional trick, the ball instead flicked over his shoulder, whence it rolled gently up the pitch with no one paying any attention, including the non-striker Manjrekar, until it disturbed the stumps behind the bowler. Of England's bowlers Titmus took the honours with nine for 162 from a mammoth 70 overs. The spinners got through 157 overs in the match against the 64 of David and Knight.

Summing up the match, and the likely trajectory of the series, Ian Wooldridge was in scornful mode. Under the subtle headline: *'England curried Madras style'* he wrote: *'Farcical Indian wickets are devaluing the international currency of cricket. Deliveries did not deviate one fraction of an inch.'* The pitches were even deader than the English fast bowlers had been warned about. Jeff Jones had been told by Ken Barrington *'there was no good trying to get them out by speed, one has to swing it as the pitches are made for the batsmen.'* Sadly, swing also proved elusive.

Travel formed a substantial part of the tour itinerary. For David the difficulty of squeezing into aircraft seats designed for smaller Indian frames was a constant issue. Fortunately, aircraft malfunctions were less frequent. On January 16, the day after the Madras Test, the tour party transited Bombay en route to Ahmedabad. After some 40 apprehensive minutes for the passengers, the pilot of the Fokker Friendship aircraft turned the craft back towards Bombay for repairs.

It was thus a somewhat weary David who opened the bowling in the fourth match of the tour, at Ahmedabad against West Zone, against India's former captain Nari Contractor. He had only recently returned to cricket after his skull was fractured two years earlier by a short ball from Charlie Griffith on India's tour of the West Indies. He had recovered thanks to blood transfusions, one of them promptly supplied by his

West Indies opposite number Frank Worrell, and by the insertion of a four-inch metal plate in his head. It was not until 1965 that Dexter, Benaud, O'Neill and Barrington publicly voiced the widely-held conviction that Griffith threw some of his deliveries.

A frustrated David had one catch dropped and finished the match with three for 81 from 30 hard overs. He, Jones and Price found that whilst they could contain the batsmen, it was very hard to force a dismissal with no help from the pitch. The lack of penetration was evident from their tour figures after four matches: David 5-288, Price 4-189 and Jones 3-151.

Comparing the three, Michael Melford noted that *'the word has gone around India that Larter is not as fearsome as his six and a half feet suggest, and though he had some ill luck, he was generally played with time to spare today.'* He thought Jones had the initial virtue of being different, a left-armer, and he was decently accurate. *'Price seems occasionally faster than either and certainly moves the ball more, but his lack of direction raises doubts.'* He concluded that if, as was sometimes the case, the Bombay pitch for the second Test was to be lively on the first morning, David's extra bounce and variation could be useful. Wooldridge felt that with David, evidently demoralised by the no-ball happy Indian umpires, suffering with his direction, *'Jones, willing and cheerful, could well replace Larter in the second Test.'*

Jeff Jones, like the others, was quite unaccustomed to the local culinary delights. *David and I went out for a meal in Bombay, looking for a change from the provisions which we had brought out with us from England – which consisted mainly of corned beef and whisky (which didn't endear us to our hosts). We saw a restaurant advertising fish and chips. We went in and sat down. David then pointed out the presence of a rat, big enough to put a saddle on, and that rather lost us our appetites.*

There was a string of bad news as the Second Test at Bombay approached. Barrington had broken a finger whilst attempting a slip catch in the West Zone game. As a precaution Peter Parfitt of Middlesex was called up as a replacement, flying direct to Bombay in the hope of being available for the second Test, but he did not arrive in time for selection. Stomach illness and flu now laid low Edrich, Sharpe and Mortimer, which, with Stewart barely fit, left England with only two specialist batsmen, Bolus and captain Mike Smith, available for the Test.

With only ten of the 15 tourists fit there was some debate about the *Guardian's* Henry Blofeld being drafted to make up the number. On the day, the valiant Stewart volunteered, but was then not well enough to bat in either innings. On January 21 the ten men standing represented a strange mixture of a team: the two specialist batsmen, the reserve wicket-keeper Binks making his debut and – a new experience

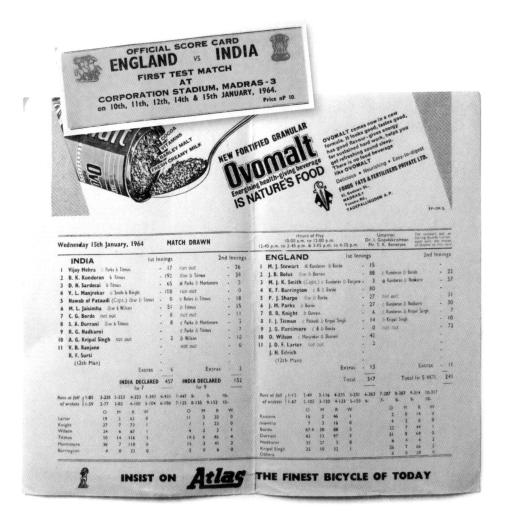

for him – opening the batting, the principal wicket-keeper Parks playing instead as a specialist batsman, two spinners, Titmus and Wilson (Mortimore being bed-bound), and all four faster bowlers David and Knight plus Price and Jones, both on debut. *'The oddest England side ever to have played in an official Test match'* wrote John Woodcock in *The Times*. Quite a contrast to the Indian attack of four spin bowlers and two medium pace seamers.

John Price had assumed that having been left out of the first Test he was unlikely to feature in the second. Interviewed recently by *The Cricketer* he explained: *'By the eve of the second Test in Bombay four players had gone down with stomach complaints so I reckoned that I should turn up to nets next day as I might be in with a chance. As one of only eleven tourists eventually fit to play, they had no choice but to give me a Test debut. Four of the eleven were seamers, so I came on second change and took three first innings wickets. By tea on that first day another player had been hospitalised, so we played the rest of the Test with 10 men. Although all the Tests were drawn on very slow pitches, playing in front of massive Indian crowds was amazing – even though they would often try to put us off by shining mirrors or catapulting fruit on to the field in our direction.*

Played out in front of 40,000 people crammed into Bombay's Brabourne Stadium, the Test was to take its place in history as something akin to the cricketing equivalent of the Warwickshire Regiment's defence of Rorke's Drift in the Zulu war in 1879. In the heat of January 21, batting first, India's defensive timidity produced a slow total of 300 - a failure to take advantage of the absence from the field of Stewart and Parks, and of Titmus and Knight being far from well. India had to lend England a substitute fielder. Micky Stewart had to be led from the field after he had thrown up on the pitch after diving forward from short leg on to the pitch for a catching chance. Jeff Jones remembers bowling with Jim Parks fielding in the covers, looking awful but saying *'I'm all right - I will carry on,'* and Jeff, having reached his bowling mark, turning to run in saw *Parks was no longer present, having made a very fast departure from the field.*

In both innings Price ran in with great energy and alone extracted life from a sluggish pitch. Although lacking the fire achieved by Price, David to his credit disposed of the Indian numbers 10 and 11 in consecutive deliveries on the second day.

With five of the six batsmen waiting to bat in bed at the hotel, David spent the day padded up ready to bat at number six. The stuff of nightmares! England, and David, were saved by a magnificent innings over five hours by Titmus who made his highest Test score of 84 not out, and by Price's 32 – his highest first-class score. Their stand gave recovery time for the bedridden, so that David ultimately batted at number nine, ahead of Micky Stewart who was in hospital and Jeff Jones (*'to go in lower than Larter, a batsmen's reputation must be modest indeed'* in Melford's words). David was given out for a duck, caught at short leg from a ball he had hit hard straight into the ground.

This dismissal, following other incidents, raised scorn in the press: Ian Wooldridge wrote that *'this constant criticism of Indian umpires must sound churlish, but the result of this match might yet prove to have turned on [Larter's] decision.'* Fortunately it did not, as Jones, belying his status as last man, stayed at the crease for 85 minutes whilst adding 48 runs with Titmus. India, leading by 67, again failed to press home their advantage by batting defensively. Faced with an impossible target of 317 in four hours, Binks, the emergency opener, batted for three and a half hours making

See Page 9 | the Uganda Rifles stationed at camp

Lanky Larter is caught by Borde off Durrani before he had opened his account.

55, putting on 125 with Bolus, thus ensuring the draw.

A four-hour flight from Bombay to Calcutta for the back-to-back third Test did little for the recovery of MCC's invalids. England now had the luxury of a choice from 12 fit, or relatively fit, men, thanks to the arrival of reinforcements from London in the form of Parfitt and of Cowdrey, replacing Stewart who had returned to England for medical treatment. Cowdrey had not played cricket since his arm had been broken by a ball from Wes Hall in the Lord's Test against the West Indies the previous June. Who would open the bowling alongside Price? Blofeld thought that although David's length and direction had been awry he could be hostile on a sympathetic wicket. The selectors agreed, opting for David over Jones, relying on the Calcutta track's reputation for some early life and swing in humid atmosphere.

The pitch lived up to, and even exceeded, its reputation, being quicker than any yet met on the tour. Blofeld noted that for the first time a fast bowler had the greatest influence on the day's events: *'Price took his chance well at Bombay but today he seemed an even better bowler. Larter bowled with more purpose than hitherto and was also a little unlucky.'* Price took five for 44, whilst David and Knight, struggling for accuracy, took one wicket each, David's being the important one of top scorer Sardesai for 54, to one of five catches behind the wicket by Binks. It was now England's turn to fail to press home an advantage by batting too cautiously, Cowdrey taking more than six hours to make 107. Not helped by a bizarre umpiring decision that the ground was unfit when only one millimetre of rain fell on the third day, taking two hours out of the match, England's lead of 26 was not achieved until the fourth day. India batted England out of the game in their second innings, declaring on 300 for 7 wickets. David was the only one of the fast bowlers to take wickets, having both Pataudi and Durani caught close to the wicket in his eight overs. Only 19 of 120 overs came from England's three fast men. MJK Smith played attractively for 75 not out as another desultory draw was played out. 38,000 spectators at Eden Gardens however seemed happy.

With Price rested after his labours, David and Jeff Jones opened the bowling in the only first-class match played between the third and fourth Tests, against East and Central Zones at Nagpur on February 4, 5 and 6. David took two wickets in the first innings but found the pitch even slower than those which had drained him of hope earlier, with many of the bumpers he bowled bouncing twice before reaching wicket-keeper Parks. David's great asset was his ability to hurry the batsman's shot by getting the ball to lift from a good length. If the pitch prevented that, David was Samson shorn of his locks.

To add to his frustration, he bowled only one over in the second innings having strained a thigh muscle. The home team sadly adopted a completely negative approach to their run-scoring efforts. *'Another match best forgotten,'* in the words of *Wisden*. It did however provide one memorable event, regrettable for David but for Michael Melford *'the best moment of a pleasant warm sleepy day:*

Just before lunch a heavyweight bee penetrated up David Larter's trouser leg. The offender was caught but not before it had stung six times and not before Larter had surely earned a niche in cricket history by being debagged on the field of play.' The MCC team, conscious of the need to protect

'... a heavyweight bee penetrated up David Larter's trouser leg.'

David's modesty, immediately gathered round him while he lowered his trousers. He went off for a few minutes to be replaced by Barry Knight, *'seen to be wearing his trousers tucked into his socks.'*

> I felt a sting or two around my knee during an over, and a quick shout round the field soon had the lads gathered round me and off came the trousers! A flying red ant was the culprit – they were all over the place. At least it provided some comedy for the sizeable crowd...

...and for the MCC team, as evidenced by Jeff Jones's recollection: *David was fielding at deep mid-wicket right in front of the ladies' stand. Suddenly he started dancing about and dropped his trousers in front of the ladies. Did we laugh!*

There was one rest day before the fourth Test at New Delhi, where the pitch was described by Melford as *'a grey slab of clay unworried by grass, save for a few bristles at one end and rolled so that footsteps ring out on it as on a pavement. The rough brown outfield is speckled by the odd patch of clover.'* The England selectors now finally adopted India's approach to the choice of opening bowlers – using a medium pacer to bowl for 4 or 5 overs until the shine wore off the new ball, when he would hand over to one of the spinners. Barry Knight partnered John Price with the new ball whilst John Mortimer, recovered from the illness which kept him out of the second and third Tests, replaced David, joining Titmus and Wilson in a three-spinner attack.

The pitch proved to be the deadest yet encountered. England took a first innings lead of 100 runs, but again squandered the advantage, Cowdrey's second six-hour century making a draw inevitable. Hanumant Singh on Test debut scored a fine century and his skipper Pataudi a double century, India's first ever against England. Price and Knight did their best, getting through 51 overs between them in the match, whilst the spinners wheeled away for 224, taking nine of the 14 wickets to fall.

The fifth Test at Kanpur followed two days later, back-to-back Tests for the second time in the series. *Wisden* was blunt: *'the same groundsman who had produced the drugged Delhi pitch was responsible for another defunct strip of turf, which ensured that the dull sequence of draws should be continued to the end.'* Blofeld was appalled: *'The series ended on the note of frustration which has accompanied it throughout. In this final Test England came nearer to victory than in any of the other four. Not one ball turned all day.'*

England declared on 559, their highest ever total in India, Knight and Parfitt both making centuries. India stuck to their plan, going into the match without a single bowler quicker than slow medium. Titmus put in another remarkable shift of 60 overs, taking six for 73. Price, effectively England's only pace bowler, Knight bowling only three overs in the match, finished with two for 32. The 106 overs bowled by the spinners Mortimer, Wilson and Parfitt produced two wickets for 147 runs. India, following on, killed the contest with further cautious batting, the spinner Bapu Nadkarni, promoted to number three, scoring his only Test century. The closing overs of a long-dead match were delivered by non-bowlers Edrich, Bolus, Cowdrey and keeper Parks (who took his first Test wicket). Only captain Smith did not bowl.

Against North Zone at Amritsar in the last tour match the two captains Smith and Pataudi did at least try to get a result with three declarations. England's batsmen batted aggressively, hitting six sixes, enabling Smith to declare at 299 for 3 at tea on the first day. David, recovered from the thigh strain he suffered against Central and East Zones, removed Vijay Mehra, a Test opener, with the first ball of North Zone's innings. Two wickets for 22 gave him some brief satisfaction as the trip ended on February 24, entirely appropriately, in a draw.

None of the bowlers came out of the tour with anything like a normal analysis for the ten fixtures. Titmus was the best with 36 wickets at 27 apiece, followed by Price with 17 at 33, David with 14 at 34 and Mortimore 16 at 37. Barry Knight's efforts yielded 11 wickets at 44 each and Jeff Jones nine at 46. David's figures for his three Tests reflected the disappointment he felt - five wickets at an average of 46 per wicket from 71 overs.

Henry Blofeld's tour summary in the *Guardian* observed that it would have been surprising if even the absent Trueman and Statham had had much success on the lifeless Indian pitches. *'Price at 26 could become a regular member of the full England side. Larter has not been successful and Jones is not yet up to this class of cricket.'*

David was far from being the last bowler to suffer on moribund Indian tracks. The Australian Rodney Hogg took 41 wickets at 12 apiece in his first six home Tests in 1978/9, but managed only a demoralised 11 at 53 each in the six Tests in India one year later.

It was David's first trip to the subcontinent, save for his one match visit to Dacca in East Pakistan on the Commonwealth tour:

> The India tour was of course a vastly different experience to the East African trip, both in terms of the cricket and the country. We were generally criticised in the press for not getting on with it, but the whole pace of the game changes when you play on Indian terms. It is hot and its dry pitches are dead. This was a shame because the crowds were enormous, and they deserved better cricket.

His two tours that winter had given him a wonderful cultural and social experience. From a cricketing perspective the East Africa tour had provided little help in preparing him for the soulless grind of the Indian trip. In Africa the helpful pitches had meant that he had to throttle back on his speed and bounce. Indian pitches were the exact opposite, where every ounce of his energy was relentlessly drawn from him.

> I knew that my future Test career was now in the balance. I had tried my best but had not found a way of extracting life from the Indian tracks. The main weapon in my armoury – the ability to get a ball of good length to lift at pace –

being completely nullified, I was reduced to ordinariness. Never having experienced this before, my frustration led me to press too hard for pace, but this only caused loss of accuracy and length.

Not having spent time with MJK Smith before these trips, I was delighted to get to know him a little. Mike was such a good all-round bloke that I cannot think of anybody having a bad word to say. He commanded respect before you even met him, because of his sporting achievements, and when you met him the impression became even more favourable.

My problem with Mike's tenure as England captain was my performance. To try to explain that I can only say that the Indian trip was a huge disappointment to me. I was too thick to be able to work out the conditions and I don't think I bothered a single Indian batsman, as I became a straight up-and-down bowler.

Jeff Jones felt that his own Test career was possibly at an end. *David and I were both quick and were known for being able to achieve bounce and carry. But neither of us could get the ball above stump height. John Price and Barry Knight both bowled a fuller length and consequently did well. David and I persisted in banging it in shorter, trying to get the bounce which was second nature to us. We should have learned from Price and Knight.*

It was a fascinating if physically testing trip. When we got back to Heathrow my wife walked straight past me, not recognising me as I had lost so much weight. She told me I looked like Gandhi's ghost.

Tours to India continued thereafter to present interesting issues. One example was the 1976/77 MCC tour. The Indian Board of Control had decreed that cricket balls made in India would be used for the Tests. It was expected that England's swing and seam bowlers would have great difficulty in getting the balls to deviate. It was therefore something of a surprise when John Lever, Essex's left-arm seamer, making his debut in the Delhi Test, took ten wickets in the match at a very low cost. It was suggested that his unlikely success must have been due to his smearing Vaseline, ostensibly rubbed into his forehead to stop sweat running into his eyes, on to the ball. Ex-England captain Tony Lewis, who had in the previous decade faced David Larter on several occasions, wrote in the *Sunday Times*: '*Mind you, the talk about Vaseline and shining the ball illegally, is a mystery to all who have soldiered out there before. Ask Butch White, Alan Brown, Barry Knight, Jeff Jones, John Price or David Larter how they used to keep the shine on, and they would look at you with disbelief. Shine? If you coated it every 6 overs with gloss paint the ball would still feel like a rough coconut in your hand.*'

1964 HOME SEASON

Labour unseat the Tories'
13-year rule by capturing the
October election by 4 seats.

The season was a difficult one for David. Although Northants finished a highly creditable third in the table, with eight wins in the last 14 matches, his personal return, although on paper impressive, represented less than had been widely expected. He was second in the county averages, to the slow left-armer Malcolm Scott, both in terms of the overs bowled, 811 against 945, and wickets, 95 against 104. Wisden concluded that the county's excellent third place in the championship might have been even better *'had Larter and Crump, the opening pair for most of the time, reproduced their form of 1963… both were worried by injuries.'*

David had felt pretty low on his return from the unsatisfactory tour to India, but when the pre-season nets started he was as always enthused by the thought of playing the game he loved, bowling fast and, if things went well, perhaps extending his international career.

The season started on May 2 with the first round of the 65-over competition the

Gillette Cup, against Derbyshire. His batting form in the nets must have impressed captain Keith Andrew for David found himself batting earlier than usual. *'No matter'*, said Ron Roberts, *'Larter, used to heights, and although elevated to the dizzy position of number nine, responded with 27 runs.'* Jack Bailey in the *Daily Telegraph* also watched this innings: *'Larter is no stylist as a batsman – you could drive a minicar between bat and pad on occasions, but he has a good idea and today the saints were with him. His 27 included a straight six off Richardson which fairly soared to the sightscreen and was a large contributing factor to Northants being an even money bet when play resumes on Monday.'* Bailey's money was safe – the Monday saw Derbyshire crumble to a 35-run defeat.

No doubt as a repercussion from the India tour, David was not selected by the MCC for the season's pipe-opener at Lord's against Surrey. On May 7 he was raring to go for the first championship match, at Wantage Road against Sussex, for whom Dexter would be available until the end of August, the general election having been put off. Tony Winlaw of the *Telegraph* was interested to see if the home wicket was still of the quality which *'had in the past driven fast bowlers to despair.'* For David the pitch was lightning fast when compared with his recent Indian experience, as he and Jim Watts put Sussex on the rack chasing 253. Jim Parks saved them from a certain defeat with a fine innings of 97.

David's match figures of seven for 42, including a spell of three for five in 11 deliveries in the first innings, supported by excellent leg-spin from Peter Watts, broke the back of Somerset's resistance in a second consecutive home win in May. The county then went on their travels for seven matches, five of them in the championship. Draws ensued against Derbyshire, Surrey, Lancashire and Somerset. In the Surrey match David took six wickets, including Micky Stewart, and satisfyingly, given David's high opinion of his abilities, Ken Barrington twice.

Interest in the match at Old Trafford centred on the bowling of the West Indian spin bowler Sonny Ramadhin, specially registered for the season by Lancashire. He took six wickets in the match from 63 overs and troubled all the batsmen. David's haul of three wickets included that of England opener Geoff Pullar.

On May 27 in the second round of the Gillette Cup David and Mick Kettle demolished Leicestershire's batting on a green Grace Road pitch. Bowling, as the *Telegraph* reported it, *'with enormous fire'* David tore the heart out of the Leicester innings with a wicket in each of his first

'...David tore the heart out of the Leicester innings...'

two overs, and his figures of five for 24 made him an easy choice for the award of man of the match. *Larter and Kettle bowled so well – stronger sides might have fared just as badly at the start on the green wicket.'* Northants' batsmen had no difficulty in reaching the target of 57.

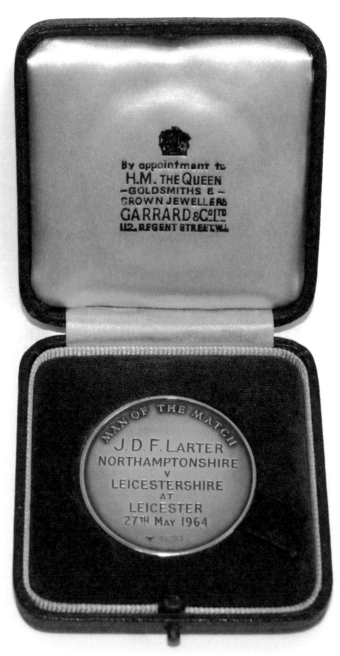

After his disappointing time in India, David was not given his customary boost from the cricketing press calling for him to be picked for England, and the selectors duly ignored him for the first Test against the visiting Australians, at Trent Bridge on June 4. Jeff Jones was also ignored. Following his difficult time on the Indian wickets, he had failed to regain form on his return to England. A nagging injury to his right ankle restricted him to less than half Glamorgan's matches, and he ended a frustrating season with a mere 18 wickets at 35 apiece.

John Price, of whom expectations for the domestic summer were high following his considerable success in India, also struggled to repeat that performance back home, ending the season with 76 wickets at an expensive 28 each. He too was ignored by the selectors until the fourth and fifth Test matches, where he found the Australian batting line-up unforgiving, managing only four wickets at 62 apiece. Shackleton, who had played in four of the five Tests against the West Indies the previous season was excluded, despite ending the season as the championship leading wicket taker, with 142 at 20 apiece. His Test career was over.

In this atmosphere of all change, the selectors, for the first Test, went for the first time for what David had long been wanting – a three-man pace attack – with the Worcestershire pair of Coldwell and Jack Flavell supporting Trueman, in addition to Dexter. The match was a draw, notable for the debut of Boycott, who made 48, and for an act of sportsmanship from Australian keeper Wally Grout, who declined to run out Titmus after he had been in collision with the bowler Hawke. This act reminded those present of the occasion in 1960 on the same ground when Statham had thrown down the wicket with South Africa's captain Jackie McGlew impeded and out of his ground. On that occasion the umpires refused to permit Cowdrey, the England captain, to withdraw the appeal that had already been made.

David was able to watch the Test on television, recovering from injury. He missed the county's first loss of the season, by seven wickets at Swansea to Glamorgan. It was a match which Northants' popular opening batsman Micky Norman would only ever remember with horror, dismissed by Ossie Wheatley twice in a day. The first time being to the first ball of the match and the second, in the afternoon of the same day, to the first ball of Northants' second innings.

Wheatley was a popular captain of Glamorgan and a character who lived life to the full. Some years later he sued the *Daily Sketch* for libel for accusing him of playing in a match after an all-night party. He succeeded and was awarded damages, thanks to his barrister Brian Neill QC, who somehow persuaded the jury to overlook the newspaper's crucial allegation that Wheatley had attended the toss at the start of the match still wearing his dinner jacket.

Mick Norman did not in fact dwell overlong on his disaster. He was a sensible, level-headed man who never wavered in support of the team. He was in many ways of similar mettle to David, of whom he was fond.

David was one of the nicest men you could meet. He was shy, and thus did not socialise greatly - he never lost his temper. He was a good team man. In the dressing room he would smoke and occasionally sleep. He was modest to a fault. I really liked him.

As a bowler he could generate huge pace and particularly a steep lift from the wicket from his good high action. His ability to do that on the dead Northampton pitches was remarkable. Frank Tyson, whom he succeeded in the team, used to say that he, Frank, might have been better off on those pitches as an off-spinner.

His gentle personality meant that he perhaps lacked a bit of spite as a fast bowler, but he took wickets with regularity on all pitches. Perhaps he needed more confidence. He was injured quite a lot and that was a problem for him. Although it was a good cricketing decision for me, my decision to move to Leicestershire at the end of the 1965 season, with Mushtaq Mohammad qualifying the next year, meant that I missed being with the Northants boys, including David.

Refreshed from his 10-day break David was fit again for the run of five consecutive home matches, three of which were in the championship, one in the Gillette Cup, and the last against the Australian tourists. In the return match with Glamorgan Jim Watts with six wickets was the architect of Glamorgan's dismissal for 61, and with two brilliant knocks from Colin Milburn of 111 and 55, Keith Andrew was able to declare to give Glamorgan 359 to win. David won his personal tussle with Jeff Jones with six for 107 against Jeff's three for 62, but thanks to Jim Pressdee's four-hour knock Glamorgan saw out a draw with eight wickets down.

At last, on June 23, Northants notched up their first win for five weeks, beating Surrey by six runs in a thrilling finish at Wantage Road. David's first innings five for 34 was his best performance of the season so far. The county lost their third round Gillette Cup match against Warwickshire. They inserted their opponents only to watch Bob Barber score a fine 114, with the bowlers powerless to stop the flow. Northants' batting let them down and the 65 over match was lost by 147 runs.

The Australian touring team visited Northampton on June 27 and gave the county a lesson in batting. David's only wicket was that of keeper Wally Grout as the tourists won by 10 wickets. There followed three away games. On July 1 at Southampton Derek Shackleton took 10 wickets in the match to give Hampshire victory. Northants were relieved to get back to winning ways with an eight-wicket victory over Leicestershire. In the first innings they were more than 80 behind with one wicket left when David joined Keith Andrew. The two added 55 important runs, David finally being out for 24, Andrew being 60 not out from 110 minutes. Milburn ended the match with a six.

> Milburn's explosive batting was a joy to watch, interspersed with getting out cheaply when trying to force the bowling, his natural instinct. Notwithstanding his size he was a brilliant fielder, fielding for me usually at forward short leg. I lost count of the catches he took merely by standing his ground and absorbing the ball somewhere about his ample frame. His reaction time was phenomenal and the equal of any of the other great close fielders of the time. He was also an amazingly strong man. One time, during a bit of dressing room messing about, Michael Dilley, our quick bowler said, or did, something jokingly to which Colin took exception. He grabbed Mike by the wrist and said something like 'get out of that'. I should say Mike was around 15 to 16 stone and built like a brick out-house. Short of hitting Colin with the bat, Mike tried everything possible to break Colin's grip while Colin pretended to read a newspaper. This went on for over 10 minutes, with Mike finishing up with bruises to prove it!

Milburn was also a very useful seam bowler. Engel and Radd shared with many others the joy of comparing Northants' bowling attack: 6'7" David Larter and 5'4" Brian Crump providing huge variety in size and lift, *'and when Milburn came on as first change seamer there was something of a freak show about Northants attack.'*

At Hastings in early July thirty wickets fell on the second day on a sticky wicket. David's five wickets in the match, including his England colleague Jim Parks again, and Malcolm Scott's 13 for 94 – for which he was awarded his county cap – were overshadowed by a career best six for 39 from Sussex paceman John Snow. Northants' batsmen then slid to defeat at the hands of Sussex spinners, 28 runs short with half an hour of the match left.

John Snow was a magnificent fast bowler who played far fewer Tests than he should have done, owing to what Gideon Haigh has described as *'a somewhat wintry personality… the authentic rebel soul, faithful only to itself.'* Of the 103 Tests played by England during his 1965/76 career he played in only 49, whilst taking 26% of the opponents' wickets. His difficulty in accepting officialdom, it has to be said in some cases with cause, saw him dropped for various misdemeanours, but when his personal sun was shining he was a top-class performer, with 202 Test wickets at 26 and 1,174 first-class wickets at 22. In Australia his 31 wickets in the 1970/71 series were crucial to Illingworth's team winning back the Ashes.

Home tracks proved more amenable for Northants, with innings victories first at Kettering over Notts and then at Wantage Road over Essex with Milburn scattering their bowlers to distant parts with a powerful 83, 68 of which were in boundaries, whilst Prideaux did his own thing with a stubborn effort of nearly five hours for his first century of the season. David went in at number six, following his recent batting triumph against Leicestershire, but was dismissed by off-spinner Paddy Phelan, caught by Wilcox for a duck. David made both Wilcox and Phelan pay for this affront when Essex batted by dismissing Wilcox in a hostile opening 11-over spell, and then bowling Phelan as he wrapped up the innings with four for 36, David Steele pouching two catches in the leg trap.

David Steele had joined the county in 1963 from Staffordshire where he had played for the minor county under the leadership of ex-England all-rounder Jack Ikin. His brother John chose to sign for Leicestershire but David was drawn to Northants, joining his cousin Brian Crump. He was to become a stalwart of the Northants side - and for a short period of England for whom he played eight Tests. Prematurely grey, bespectacled and nearly 34 years old, he was called up to face the rampant Lillee and Thomson in 1975, scoring 50 on debut, and averaging 60 in the series. The *Sun's* Clive Taylor famously christened him *'the bank clerk who went to war.'*

When he joined Northants Brian Crump asked Keith Andrew for his cousin to field at leg slip, and David made the position his own, not only for David Larter and Crump, but also for the spinners. He enjoyed his fielding: *It was uncovered wickets in those days, and the ball would come through at different speeds and heights depending upon the way the wicket responded to the weather. David Larter and Brian Crump were the perfect contrasting opening pair, the very tall David as quick as any of the fast bowlers in England at the time and creating an uncomfortable bounce for the batsmen, and Brian much shorter, skidding the ball through and seaming it off the wicket. I caught 546 catches in first-class cricket, 16 of them off David in that position, which often came at me like a shell from a gun, and 45 off Brian. It was a very professional Northants team, the fielders all knowing where to go for every situation without being told. Mind you, that was out of necessity, given how forgetful our great skipper Keith Andrew was.*

David was a very nice man, quite unlike many other fast bowlers in that he was quiet and reserved, preferring to sit in the corner of the dressing room, keeping out of the limelight. A very good team man. He frequently suffered from injuries but always gave his all. I remember he used to drive a Jaguar sport car and that his wife was a nurse. In my 20 years on the circuit I consider the two best opening bowling pairs for Northants were Larter and Crump, and Sarfraz and John Dye.

It looked as if the county would achieve an innings victory double over Notts at Trent Bridge when David and Peter Watts dismissed the home side for 159, and Jim Watts with 99 took Northants to a 146 run lead. But Notts resisted staunchly to end the match 55 runs ahead with only three wickets left.

Jim Watts had joined Northants in 1958 as an eighteen-year-old left-handed bat and a right-arm medium-pacer. Capped in 1962, he retired at the end of the 1966 season to become a teacher but was persuaded to return as captain on two occasions. The first was for the three seasons 1972 to 1974 when he led the county to fourth, third and third in the championship, and the second from 1978 to 1980 when he called it a day after the Benson and Hedges Cup was won at Lord's. On his 80th birthday in 2020 he was given the signal honour of induction into the county club's Hall of Fame.

David views him with affection:

> Jim Watts is the only bloke I know who could throw a cricket ball further than me. God knows why but we had a competition one day during training and he was better than me. He was (and is) a quiet chap who went on to schoolteaching. He did not drink but was good company. He had a determination about him. At Bournemouth one day we were all fed up with watching Derek Shackleton going for a measly one or two per over, when Jim declared to all that he was going to do something about it – and he did. As soon as he went in and as a long-reach leftie, he started swatting Derek all over the place, particularly over mid-wicket. I cannot remember if it resulted in a big score, but it certainly livened the game up.

Mike Selvey, England, Northants and Middlesex bowler and cricket writer regarded Jim as an underrated cricketer: *'a quiet but understated cajoling leader whose man-management skills enabled him to turn an under-achieving group of players into a whole which was considerably greater than the sum of the parts.'* He was invited by MCC to indicate his availability for the 1962/63 Ashes tour but did not make the cut. Laurie Johnson, who kept wicket to Jim on innumerable occasions, was in no doubt: *Jim Watts should have played for England.*

On August 5 Northants played Worcestershire at Worcester. For David this was not just another championship game - there was a bit of extra competition to it as he was playing against Len Coldwell and Jack Flavell, Worcestershire's opening bowlers both of whom had been picked twice by England that season. Neither Flavell, who broke down with injury in the third Test, nor Trueman had bowled well and had been replaced for the fourth Test by John Price and debutants Fred Rumsey and Tom Cartwright. The merry-go-round continued into the final Test, Cartwright losing out to Trueman, who in that match became the first bowler to take 300 Test wickets. Journalist JJ Warr had played in just two Tests, both on the unsuccessful 1950/51 Ashes tour, where he had bowled his heart out to take one wicket for 281. He now congratulated Trueman on his achievement, which meant, he wrote, that *'Fred could put his feet up after his monumental achievement; another 299 Test wickets and I could have done the same.'*

Flavell was a strong, quick bowler who had suffered more than his fair share of injuries. A back injury had terminated his playing days as a footballer at West Bromwich Albion, a similar injury had kept him out of cricket for almost two years and an Achilles tendon problem had put him out of action for the second half of the 1962 cricket season. He came back from his injury in the third Test as he had done for all previous setbacks. Now at the age of 35, he was to embark upon a purple patch of five county matches during which he took 46 wickets at an average of 11. This effort propelled Worcestershire to the championship and Jack Flavell to one of *Wisden's* five Cricketers of the Year.

The Test series had been won by Simpson's Australians, one nil. As the merry-go-round showed, England lacked a settled opening bowler partner for Trueman, Statham having been dropped. Coldwell, Flavell, Price and Cartwright each played twice, and Rumsey once. Simon Wilde in *England – the Biography*, describing the Australian side as unexceptional, viewed this series result as the finish of Dexter's captaincy.

Wisden attributed the loss of the series to not finding a settled team (20 players were used) and *'possibly in the choice of captain'*, quoting Dexter's decision-making in the defeat at Leeds: *'He prefers to act alone and is usually reluctant to take advice.'* Wilde's view was that two decisions Dexter made at Leeds left his reputation *'permanently scarred.'* The first was to take Titmus out of the attack when he had Australia on the rack with seven down for 178, preferring to take the new ball with which Trueman and Flavell conceded 211 for the last three wickets. The second was to refuse Trueman's request for a fielder out on the hook. From a position from which a victory was a strong possibility, England subsided to a major defeat by seven wickets with a day to spare. Dexter was to play nine more Tests but not as captain.

In the Worcester match David was to play a part in a major cricket milestone. He bowled the bouncer from which Worcestershire's Tom Graveney scored his 100th first-class century. It made him only the 15th player to record a century of centuries in first-class cricket – *'a glorious stroke-maker condemned to play in a dour age'* in the view of writer Scyld Berry. Tony Goodridge described the moment: *'Graveney hooked Larter off his forehead to pass 100, at the age of 37. The ease and grace of stroke makes him as good a model as any batsmen… Bradman in 1948, Ames in 1950, Hutton in 1951, and Compton in 1952 were the only previous post-war batsmen to reach this milestone, Graveney being the only one to score all his centuries since the war – 1948 to 1964.'*

> It was a somewhat dubious pleasure to have bowled the ball that gave Tom his 100th century at Worcester. I bowled a short delivery and he gloved/hooked it down to fine leg for four. He smiled, raised his bat to the crowd and accepted our congratulations and settled down for the next ball. So much better (and dignified) than all the leaping about and kissing of cap badges today.

Graveney was severe on most of Northants' bowlers and in particular on David who returned one for 69 from 17 overs. In a reminder of how transient and unpredictable is the game of cricket, the tables turned in the second innings when David had Graveney caught behind for two as he took five for 44 in 13 hostile overs, dismissing both Jack Flavell and Len Coldwell. Rain however turned out to be the winner in the end of this historic match.

Eric Russell opened the batting with Mike Brearley when Middlesex visited Wantage Road on August 12. Eric remembers it well: *Brearley hit the ball back at David and it bounced off his boot onto the stumps; I would have been run out but the umpire had turned away to avoid the shot and I carried on and scored 138. That was the day when some 20 minutes before play started our middle order batsman Mike Smith said to us in the dressing room 'there's nothing to worry about with Larter – I've been playing him all night in my sleep: he'll be worn out.'* Sure enough, Smith scored 64 not out and David, troubled by a stiff back, managed just one wicket in the match. The match was memorable for a hat-trick from Drybrough with David providing the crucial third leg of it. Northants went on to win by 10 wickets thanks to David Steele's four for 29 with his left-arm spin.

The return match with Kent took place within one week. 18 year old Alan Knott, who went on to play 89 Tests for England, was then in his first season for Kent, playing eight matches including both those against Northants. Knott remembers those encounters: *the matches at Wellingborough and Dover were both played on very slow wickets and David Larter's fitness was not at its best, with niggling injuries that hindered him, but he bowled with pace, was tall and got bounce. Perfect for the harder wickets of Australia. He got picked to go on the England winter tour there in 1965/66, but unfortunately for him and*

England injuries reoccurred, and he had to return home. A great shame.

David remembers the Dover game for a different reason:

> I was somewhat surprised to be invited to lunch by the doyen of cricket journalists, Jim Swanton, at his Kent home. Great food cooked and served by Mrs S. He did not want anything in particular, just seemed to want to get to know me. An unusual but happy interlude in my professional cricketer's routine.

Northants defeated Hampshire by 137 runs, and Leicestershire by an innings, Prideaux having made a chanceless 153. David collected four wickets for six runs in one blistering spell of 17 balls, finishing off the match by having Ray Julian caught close in by Brian Reynolds with the first ball of his second over, bowling Greensword with the first ball of his third over, getting Barratt caught by Jim Watts off the next and bowling Thompson with the fifth.

Northants' season ended with two away matches. The first was at Southend. David bowled fast, from a run of 34 paces, almost twice the limit which the county captains had tacitly agreed the previous winter of 20 yards or paces. Keith Andrew had no problem with this, explaining that Larter had three separate run-ups according to the speed he wanted to bowl. *'I have no objection, provided our over-rate is comparable to our opponents.'* Keith Fletcher scored 84 not out as Essex were beaten by 20 runs with 11 minutes to spare, David claiming three wickets. There was one incident which fortunately did not end in tears. Alex Bannister reported in the *Daily Mail* on David's unintentional beamer bowled at Trevor Bailey. *'As Larter delivered the ball his back foot ripped the nearest stump out of the ground, distracting enough for a batsman at any time, let alone with a beamer to follow. Bailey's dry comment was "a most devastating delivery".'*

With 61 matches for England in a career lasting from 1945 to 1967 Trevor Bailey had a reputation as a man for a batting crisis, with a stubborn refusal to give up his wicket cheaply. The most often quoted example was at Lord's in 1953, when he and Willie Watson staged a remarkable rear-guard action over four hours to deny Australia a win. That win would have almost certainly have prevented England regaining the Ashes after 19 years, which they did by winning the final Test at the Oval.

Barnacle Bailey had a less well-known lighter side to him. At Bradford Park Avenue in August 1951 Len Hutton was 70 or 80 not out at lunch (he made 99 eventually). The first ball after lunch Bailey bowled him an orange which Hutton gently played to the onside.

Cricket was taken a little less seriously in those days, although perhaps it was simply that certain personalities were more readily permitted to escape the disciplinary leash. Writer Christopher Sandford recalls the story of how, one night during the 1948 Oval Test against the all-conquering Australians, Godfrey Evans and Denis Compton returned Australia's fast bowler Keith Miller to the Australian's hotel in a wheelbarrow they had requisitioned from a market porter at Covent Garden. And Tom Graveney told of how in the 1954/55 Ashes series in Australia (Tyson's victorious series) Miller had helped him to a century in the Sydney Test. *'I hit three of his first six balls for four. The seventh [it being an eight ball over] was a slow long hop down the leg side and I missed it. He then bowled me another one. It was like that then.'*

The final match of the season for Northants was at Lord's against Middlesex:

> Lord's was always a fascinating place to visit. And there were always characters there, happy to chat to the cricketers. Somehow Trevor Bailey always managed to be there for important occasions! Film star Trevor Howard was an avid cricket fan, often to be found in the bar there after a game. Sometimes post-match conversations would transfer down the road into the Cricketers Club in Baker Street, where Denis Compton and sometimes Bill Edrich would hold court. A trip to London for some out of town county cricketers would not be complete without a visit to Raymond Revuebar in Soho. The general manager was a Lancastrian cricket nut – George Richardson. If you played first-class cricket you got a life membership card from George! Colin Milburn could not believe that George was responsible for interviewing all the girls and assessing their physical assets!
>
> All of these were fleeting events, and it seems a bit like name-dropping, but back in the 60s it just happened.

It was during this match that David encountered a legend of the game:

> I was delighted to meet Sir Len Hutton and pleased when he complimented me on my action and wished me luck.

Hutton was generally rated the finest English batsman of the 20th century, alongside Hobbs and Hammond. Paeans of praise for the elegance of his strokeplay abound. But not many poems. Harold Pinter, a cricket lover, wrote one in 1986. It was (typically) pithy, consisting of three lines only: *'I saw Len Hutton in his prime; another time; another time.'* He sent the poem to his friend Simon Gray, another cricket-loving dramatist, for his opinion. Gray, answering Pinter's phone call pressing for a response, apologised, *'Sorry Harold, I haven't finished reading it yet.'*

Middlesex batted first. John Thicknesse for the *Telegraph* gave the day's honours *'to the two bowlers whose efforts had done most to lift Northants to an unassailable third place in the championship – Larter and Crump. Larter bowled quick and mighty straight for his three wickets.'* In Middlesex's second innings David hurt his back having dismissed, for eight, opener Mike Brearley, voted by the Cricket Writers Club as the best young cricketer of the year. David was thereby unable to bowl more than nine overs - unfortunate in that he only needed four wickets for his 100 for the season. Eric Russell scored 70s in each innings for Middlesex; in Thicknesse's view one of the three best opening batsmen Northants had met that season. Set to make 287 to win Northants collapsed to Drybrough and Hooker and the game was lost by 145 runs.

It was September 1. Since the loss to Sussex at Hastings on July 10, Northants had been unbeaten in thirteen championship games, winning seven of them. They were in third place in the table. But they had been unable to touch Worcestershire, who had had a splendid season. On August 25, with three matches still to play, Worcestershire became champions as they clinched their sixteenth victory of the season. It was a wonderful way to celebrate the centenary of the club.

At the November celebration dinner, recalling the many years in which the two counties had rivalled each other for bottom position in the table, Worcestershire's president praised Northants for their effort in coming third in the championship

Jack Jennings (physio), Ray Bailey, Roy Wills, Jim Watts, JDFL, Peter Watts, Malcolm Scott, Colin Milburn, David Steele;
Albert Lightfoot, Roger Prideaux, Keith Andrew, Brian Reynolds, Brian Crump.

when they and Worcestershire had the two smallest populations of any of the counties in the competition: *'a mere one-tenth of either Lancashire or Yorkshire.'*

David had played in 27 of the 28 championship matches. Malcolm Scott took the most wickets for the county with 104 wickets at 18 each, followed by Brian Crump with 76 at 19, and David with 95 at 20. The Watts brothers both did well, Peter taking 59 wickets and Jim 58.   In the national averages David was 33rd with 96 wickets at 21.28, just ahead of Trueman and Snow.

For the first time since becoming a professional cricketer, David missed out on a winter tour, and to a country he had not visited: MCC's winter tour was to South Africa, led by MJK Smith in place of Dexter who was standing for Parliament in the autumn election. Smith was not given much chance of winning the series, with his bowling attack looking very limited against what was likely to be a strong South African batting side. Trueman had not been selected so John Price, David Brown, Tom Cartwright and surprise selection Sussex seamer Ian Thomson (MJK Smith having wanted a stock bowler for the tour and Tony Nicholson of Yorkshire having dropped out) formed the bowling attack in front of off-spinners Titmus and Allen. Brown suffered a number of injuries which prevented him playing in any of the Tests, where Price with eight wickets at 52 apiece and Thomson with nine at 63 struggled to make an impression, and it was the spinners who saw England through to a welcome if unexpected one-nil series victory. Titmus and Allen ended as the two leading wicket takers on the tour ahead of David Brown.

> I had hoped that my successes in the championship would have restored my reputation after the India tour, but although my improvement was recognised, it did not lead to selection for any of the Tests against Australia nor for the winter tour. That India tour was casting a long shadow.

In early September David was driving the flat Suffolk roads in a Jaguar XK150, a step up from his first 'serious' car, a Ford Zodiac, which he had purchased the year before using some of his 1962/3 winter tour earnings. The Jaguar bug was to be taken further in 1965 with the purchase of a Jaguar Mk11 3.8.

> I bought a lorry (a 13 tons gross, TS3 flatbed, for the technically minded) and joined my father, working on his licence for the winter. I actually made more money that winter than in the summer playing cricket. This spell of proper work started me thinking about what happens after cricket and my conclusion then was that the transport industry might well be for me.

1965 HOME SEASON

State Funeral of Sir Winston Churchill 30 January. Buried at Bladon, Oxfordshire.

It was Northamptonshire's Diamond Jubilee season. The county had never won the championship – a target for this auspicious birthday.

> I sold the Commer to father in the spring of 1965 and headed back to Northampton for the start of the home season. I thought that the season might be a repeat of the frustration of 1964, but Ted Dexter had retired (this may or may not have been significant) and I felt that if I continued to knock on the door there was still a chance it would open to me.

No one could have predicted after the first month of the season that the county would be leading the championship in July. On the last day of May the team was looking up at all the other counties from the bottom of the table, having not won in six matches. At that moment Northants' first win brought a dramatic change in fortunes, so that by the end of June four of their seven championship matches had been won and only one lost, putting them on the top of the championship table, level with Middlesex. The loss to Surrey by an innings and 134 runs on July 1 only served to renew focus and the team was spurred on to an eleven-match unbeaten run, including five successive victories in August.

In the early season knockout Gillette Cup, 'now in its third year', Northants beat Gloucester by two wickets in the last over, with Keith Andrew and David slowly piloting Northants to victory with four deliveries left. David's innings was described by John Reason in the *Daily Telegraph* as *'a sterling performance of one not out, as he flung his bat and struck the winning run.'* His four wickets for 38 made him a close but unsuccessful contender for the £50 man of the match award, granted to Gloucestershire's Arthur Milton. Northants were then demolished by Surrey, the competition's ultimate winners, in the next round, in effect the quarter-final, David contributing three for 50 from the maximum permitted 13 overs.

David, like the team as a whole, had started the season slowly. Short of significant successes in May he failed to make a sufficient case to be included in the England team for the first Test against New Zealand, at Edgbaston on May 27.

For that Test a strong candidate should have been John Price but he was unlucky with injury and was to play in less than half Middlesex's championship matches during the season. David having not been picked for the winter tour, was evidently not on the selectors' list of candidates. As the partner for Trueman they considered Butch White of Hampshire, Jack Flavell of Worcestershire who at 36 was embarking upon the best season of his life, and two uncapped fast bowlers, John Snow and David Brown. They plumped instead for Fred Rumsey, for whom life could begin again at 29, sacked by Worcestershire and dropped by England after a solitary Test the previous season. Tom Cartwright was third seamer and Titmus and Barber were the spinners. Under Mike Smith's captaincy England overwhelmed the visitors by nine wickets, Titmus and Barber taking six wickets each and Trueman four.

Northants' first victory on June 1 was created by Brian Crump and David taking eight Warwickshire wickets each on a helpful Peterborough track. The next match, against Sussex, was lost, with Milburn breaking a finger in two places, but success resumed in the return fixture with Warwickshire at Edgbaston when England captain MJK Smith got a close-up comparison of the two Davids, Brown and Larter. Larter and Crump out-bowled David Brown and Jack Bannister, Crump with six wickets in the match and David nine, including a spell of three for three in five overs. The identity of his victims was significant: current England players MJK Smith, Barber (in both innings, for one and nought) and Cartwright, plus Dennis Amiss and AC Smith. Laurie Johnson, standing in for the injured Andrew, took two stumpings and eight catches.

This performance came the day before the selectors met to choose the England team for the second Test, at Lord's. Melford thought David might get the pick as he was *'regularly removing the better batsmen and bowling better than before the last Australian tour.'* The selectors however opted to blood John Snow as third fast bowler in support of Trueman and Rumsey. Snow in his autobiography attributed his quick rise to Test status as *'gained largely as a result of taking 77 championship wickets in my first full summer of 1964 plus another 50 in the first two and a bit months of 1965. This placed me ahead of my nearest young rivals David Brown of Warwickshire and Jeff Jones of Glamorgan.'*

New Zealand were again defeated comprehensively, Rumsey and Snow bowling well, but with Trueman struggling to make his usual impact. It was to prove his last Test, his two wickets taking his total Test wicket haul to 307, a figure not to be beaten for another 10 years.

The Test ran from 17 to 22 June. On 16 June Northants began their championship game against Somerset. David Steele views the match as a good example of David's sustained bursts of pace where he could be almost unplayable: *As always at Wantage Road we batted first on winning the toss and with rain during the day were happy with 266 for 7 declared, Brian Reynolds having made a fine century. Bill Alley was the only*

Somerset batsman to handle David's pace and bounce as he took 4 for 28 in the first innings. The wicket became really evil on the last day, David taking 8 for 28 as Somerset were bundled out for 95 to lose by 131 runs. Colin Atkinson, the Somerset skipper, when thanking Keith Andrew after the game, said he was very pleased to come away with his players in one piece.

On the team coach to Leeds that evening for the match against Yorkshire David reflected on that second innings performance – the best bowling figures of his life – and the elation he had felt as he ended the match by dismissing the last six batsmen for five runs in only 19 balls. But tomorrow was another day and who knew what it would bring?

It brought a very shaky start for the county, struggling from six wickets down for 55 to a meagre total of 139 thanks to a gritty 41 from Jim Watts. Yorkshire with their nine Test players against Northants' two – David and Keith Andrew – looked good, but then came their turn to bat. With their score on seven David had England batsman Phil Sharpe leg before, and followed with the wickets of Padgett, Hampshire, Illingworth and Nicholson, a tally of five for 43. The *Guardian* correspondent described his pace as 'greater than Yorkshire have faced for a long time.' Declaring their second innings at 189 for 6 Northants set their hosts 178 to win in 135 minutes. Bowling off only a 12 pace run and keeping more control than in the first innings. David moved the ball off the damp wicket, resulting in all his wickets falling to the close catchers, Peter Watts taking three and David Steele two. With just 10 minutes to spare Yorkshire were routed for 119, David finishing with seven for 37.

Ray Illingworth batted at number six: *David Larter played a blinder against us taking 12 wickets in the match, including mine in both innings. He was excellent in that match – almost unplayable. He was tall and strong with an excellent action. He was fast – in my view as quick as John Price and Jeff Jones.*

His real strength was getting the ball to rear up off a length. He didn't bowl too many bouncers – he didn't need to. One of the most difficult balls to play is a near full-length ball which takes off. Not too many bowlers can master that art these days, but Larter could. He also had an excellent out-swinger which got him a few wickets. His strike rate was probably better than most of his competitor pace men because of his bounce and speed. He had trouble with his run-up on occasions and this impacted on his accuracy. He played a big part in Northants' success in the mid-1960s.

David had taken 24 wickets in two matches at an average of 5.6 per wicket. *'Even Test selectors notice that'* wrote Engel and Radd.

Here is Jim Watts's recent recollection of that time: *Against Somerset David was pretty frightening for the opposing batsmen and he did the same thing at Headingley, which he won on his own. My view is that no one on the county circuit really looked forward to facing him.*

With David now fourth in the bowling averages with 54 wickets at 12 the county moved to the top of the championship table with a victory, at Kettering on June 29, over Leicestershire. Brian Crump's seam bowling garnered eight wickets and Peter Watts' leg-breaks six, as Leicestershire crumbled to 113 chasing a target of 256. That target owed something to the batting of Northants' tail-enders Malcolm Scott and

David who, both hitting a pair of sixes, put on 27 for the last wicket, David scoring 25 to go with his 19 not out in the first innings.

At this point in the season *The Cricketer* magazine asked Colin Cowdrey to contribute to their series *'A letter to a young cricketer.'* Cowdrey addressed his letter to David. It contained a number of interesting observations and advices. Here are some excerpts:

'There have not been many very tall fast bowlers who have been consistently successful at Test level… That is why the experts have tended to be a little sceptical of David Larter's chances of breaking through in Test cricket. He has had an interesting career to date and we can all learn from it.

From an early age he has eaten, slept and dreamt fast bowling, longing for the day when he may be England's No.1 fast bowler. Northamptonshire saw him producing fast, very hostile spells a few years ago and his promise attracted the England selectors. He has been to New Zealand with an MCC A side and since then to Australia and to India. He has experienced a fair measure of success, intermixed with irritating periods of injury and some erratic spells. In fact he has known all the ups and downs of a first-class cricketer.

Two things have never deserted him. First a determination to achieve his ambition and, secondly, the drive and enthusiasm to pursue that end. He has always worked extremely hard at practice and on the field he is a stern self critic. What spectators sometimes take for a show of temper, thumping his leg in anger as he walks back, is invariably disappointment with himself. In Australia 1962/63 we often talked about the mental approach to bowling and he was only too aware that too often he was being denied ultimate success through the frailty of his own temperament.

…I have a feeling Larter began this summer in a rather different frame of mind. Complete fulfilment still eluded him and it was all becoming rather frustrating. Time was running out for a genuine fast bowler cannot expect a long life after 30. This might be his last chance to establish himself. All this has brought greater maturity and a more balanced philosophical view of things.

He sets out to be fast and hostile, but he has learned that this does not necessarily involve tearing up and putting everything into each delivery. He is finding himself able to bowl for longer spells and is just as fast as ever before, with less demands upon himself. He has hit upon a more measured and better approach to the wicket. Bowling, like batting, depends upon timing and he keeps surprising himself with the amount of speed he is getting from an easy rhythm.

Timing… I am sure that this is what he has found with more consistency. We all know what it is even if we cannot describe it. We can all point to instances when on going for the big hit or throw, whatever it might be, we have mistimed through pressing too hard.

It is extremely difficult for a powerful, fast running quick bowler who is straining at the leash to be aggressively hostile to learn to relax in order to hit this perfect rhythm. But without timing, as David Larter hastened to assure me, you will always be left very short of top speed.'

> The reference to my thumping my leg is perfectly true. Anybody who played with me will say that I was always grumbling away at myself, and even slapping my leg as I walked back if I had bowled a loose delivery. I was indeed a stern self critic; I would however dispute that this amounted to a frail temperament, and indeed no-one ever made that suggestion to me.

The question of timing as a key to bowling at one's fastest, and its elusiveness, is well illustrated by a story concerning England fast bowler Devon Malcolm. It was said of him, as it was said of David, that when he got everything right he was very quick. It was not every day that everything was right – but on some days all the mechanics were well oiled and in perfect harmony, and the ball came out of the hand faster than usual. Interviewed by James Coyne in *The Cricketer* Malcolm reckoned that his fastest spell ever was at the Oval in 1993 against Australia: *'Micky Stewart was the manager and he said to me "you've got one spell, you've been resting all day thinking about it, just go out there and do it". And boy, everything just clicked. The body was not aching at all. I was so rhythmical, I just hit the crease and it flew. You ask plenty of fast bowlers, you just look for those spells.'*

Bryon Butler wrote in the *Telegraph* that the town of Northampton was a happy place what with the football club, at their end of the Wantage Road ground, having been promoted to the First Division in May, and now, at their end of the ground, the cricket club sharing top place in the championship with Middlesex. He might have added that the rugby club was also on the rise, and that just to confuse things their second row forward was a tall man called Larter. 6'4" forward Peter Larter – no relation – went on to play for England and the Lions.

The cricketers' joy was to be brief however as Surrey, with John Edrich scoring 188, beat them at Wantage Road by an innings and 134 runs. This was followed by a draw with the New Zealanders, playing the last match of their tour, a game notable for two things. It was Mushtaq Mohammad's first game for the county, in the midst of his two-year qualification period. He had first been approached by Denis Brookes and Ken Turner in June 1963 when as a 19 year old he had taken a century off Northants for the touring Pakistan Eaglets side. He declined the offer, being reluctant to spend the two years qualifying in the county's 2nd XI. He did however indicate interest in an approach from Denis Compton and was disappointed that Middlesex then failed to follow that up. In November of 1963 Keith Andrew, a member of Alf Gover's Commonwealth tour to Pakistan, renewed Northants' offer at the tour's Karachi match (Mushtaq this time scoring 178) and the deal was done, to use Stephen Chalke's words, *'in a Karachi bazaar'*.

Mushtaq's Northants' debut was also the occasion of David's return to the Test squad for the third Test, announced on the Sunday of the match, July 4. Buoyed by this news, David was at his fastest against the tourists on the Monday, bowling Graham Dowling, getting Jarvis taken at short leg and after having Morgan dropped twice, dismissing him with the new ball, ending the day with three for 46.

'Trueman dropped for Larter' was the headline on the front page of the Daily Telegraph.

EW Swanton described Trueman's omission *'as the most momentous change in the team... Is this the hour of his Nunc Dimittis?'*

Overlooking the fact that Trueman was probably incapable of departing in peace from any endeavour, Swanton answered his own question in the affirmative: *'One assumes so, but it depends on the rest of the field. It would obviously be foolish on several counts to take him again to Australia, but as regards the South Africa series one can but hope that someone is found to open the bowling. Larter equally deserves a chance to fill the bill. He has disappointed certainly after the early hopes of him, but he has a better record this season than any fast bowler except Statham, he probably has the best physique, and at 25 should be at his strongest and most fit.'*

TRUEMAN OUT OF THIRD TEST

F. S. Trueman, the England fast bowler who has taken more wickets in Test matches than anyone else, is dropped from the side to meet New Zealand at Leeds, his home ground, in the third Test beginning on Thursday.

He said last night: "I couldn't care less." He has played in 67 Tests. His place in the 12 named yesterday is taken by J. D. F. Larter. K. Barrington, who was left out after his slow batting at Edgbaston, is back in the team.

Larter engaged

Soon after Larter was selected yesterday to play in the Test it became known that he was engaged to Miss Thelma Hawkins, a nursing sister at Northampton General Hospital. None of his cricket colleagues knew about the engagement.

E. W. Swanton – P10

Denys Rowbotham thought that the most interesting selection was David: *'whose hostile potential in terms of speed combined with steep lift has never been in question. What has prevented him from realising his potential has been his less than strict control of length and direction. He now lies fourth in the national averages with 50 wickets at 13 each, and the reports of opening batsmen suggest that control has now come to him. If it has, he becomes a candidate immediately for Australia where he improved so markedly three years ago but not quite soon or convincingly enough to earn him a late Test match place.'*

David's happiness was not confined to his cricket. There was great domestic joy as well. David's parents released the news from their home in Framlingham that David had for seven weeks been engaged to be married to Thelma. None of David's cricketing colleagues knew and nor did most of his family. Ian Wooldridge claimed that the 25-year-old David had once told him *'cricket comes first. I shan't get married until I am 30.'* A pledge happily broken.

On Thursday July 8 David donned his England whites for the first time since Calcutta 17 months and 14 Tests ago. England batted first on a good Headingley wicket and John Edrich, on his recall to the side, became only the eighth batsman in the history of Test cricket, and the first Englishman since Hutton in 1938, to score a triple century. His magnificent 310 not out included a five-hour partnership with Ken Barrington, also recalled to the side, who made 163.

David shared the bowling honours with Ray Illingworth with four wickets each as New Zealand were dismissed for 193. Swanton was impressed: *'perhaps the most interesting aspect of New Zealand's innings was the bowling of Larter who maintained a useful pace and control over two spells of little short of an hour each. The only criticism was that his length was rather too full. It does hit the pitch, however. One feels the mechanism is there if only it could be given a really expert tuning, and if of course the mind behind it were really ardent to bring the utmost out of it. Larter was given the breeze from mid-on, and it was a very good ball which moved from the off stump towards the slips that enabled him to have Dowling caught behind. Sinclair hit a full toss from Larter crisply off his toes only to see Smith at short leg just in front of square shoot out his right hand and make a clean catch.'*

MJK Smith, who had already been confirmed as England captain for the three-match South African Test series which would immediately follow the New Zealand series, was widely acknowledged to have a gift for welding disparate talents and personalities into a Test team that would follow him to the end of the earth. He was also, in Swanton's view, defensive by nature (as, he said, were Dexter, Close, Cowdrey, Bailey, and Titmus on indifferent English pitches); Swanton quoted, as an example in the New Zealand Test, Smith's disinclination to give David a third slip when a number of nicks might have gone to hand.

Following on, New Zealand were bowled out for 166, giving England victory by an innings and 187 runs. Titmus took four wickets for no runs in one over, and five in all. In Wooldridge's eyes David was *'a yard faster than last season, finding lift and fire and taking two wickets.'* David's match return was a satisfying six for 120 from 50 overs. Not all commentators were complimentary about England's fielding, JJ Warr in the *Telegraph* observing that Rumsey *'swooped on the ball like Richard Dimbleby, and Larter is not likely to be invited to join the Royal Ballet.'*

Ray Illingworth remembers the match not just for Edrich's magnificent innings but also for *some strange field placings by captain MJK Smith, who – it has to be said – was not a master tactician. He stationed our two big and cumbersome fast bowlers, Rumsey and Larter, at cover point for each other's bowling, and gave them no support – so they were covering most of the off-side by themselves. The New Zealand batsmen were happy to play a number of cover drives to, or towards, the boundary, leaving Rumsey and Larter to chase after the ball when they weren't bowling. Eventually their grimaces and glares, both at each other and towards their captain, sank in and MJK changed the field. The rest of us thought this was hilarious.*

On the credit side David moved swiftly and threw well to effect a run out, as Melford recorded: *'Pollard glanced Illingworth wide of Larter at square leg and there seemed a comfortable run particularly to Larter, but Pollard was stranded several yards out.'* David was a good catcher, dropping very few chances, and although his long legs gave him an ungainly look, he was far from the problem WG Grace experienced during his last season, encapsulated in the complaint he made to Charles McCartney: *'it's the ground, Charlie; it's too far away.'*

England having won the New Zealand series 3-0, speculation started as to whether the selectors would pick David and Rumsey for the forthcoming Ashes tour to Australia. The *Daily Mail* pointed out that David had not been picked for a Test on the 62/63 Ashes tour when he had been a *'withdrawn, self-conscious figure of 22 years of age.'* The paper quoted a selector as saying that too much had been expected of him too early…*'we aren't now expecting him to be an express. What we are looking for is hostility, a bit of nastiness if you like.'*

David had reduced his run-up but Rumsey, perhaps fearing he would lose his hostility, was still operating off a near 35-yard run. Don Kenyon, Rumsey's former Worcestershire captain and now an England selector, had spoken strongly to his fellow selectors against Rumsey going to Australia on the grounds that his body would not stand up to the demanding schedule - with hard grounds, tropical temperatures and eight-ball overs.

When asked years later in interview by *The Cricketer* magazine if he thought he should have played more than his five Tests Fred Rumsey answered in the affirmative: *'I didn't seem to get on well with some of the selectors. I played one game at home against Australia in 1964 and didn't play again until 1965 at home, all three Tests against New Zealand and one against South Africa. I was picked for the next, but I had an injury during the rest day. I reported it because I was concerned. It was then all right on the day and I declared myself fit but I was talked out of it by the chairman of selectors, Doug Insole, who suggested that if I went out and broke down that would be the end of my England career. So I withdrew. It was the end of my England career anyway.'*

Fred, a Somerset player, was driving himself to Taunton after the Test for the championship match against Northants the next day. He offered to lead the way for David who was also planning to drive there.

> He had an MGA twin cam and I had a 3.8 Mk.11 Jaguar. It ranks as one of the hairiest journeys of my life! I have never known anyone drive so consistently fast for 200 odd miles (no M5 then).

An enclosed, intimate, arena overlooked by two imposing church towers to the south and the Quantock hills to the north, Taunton was a welcoming ground with a real country feel. It was here that WG Grace in 1895 scored his 100th century, Jack Hobbs in 1925 equalled Grace's total of 126 centuries, and Graham Hick in 1988 scored his 405.

No centuries were however scored at Taunton in the match starting on July 14. Put in on a drying wicket, Somerset were bowled out for 121 by Jim Watts, with six for 18. Fred Rumsey then got through 37 overs capturing four for 72 as Northants took a lead of 162, Milburn thrashing 63 out of a stand of 83 in 75 minutes. Somerset's batting failed again, David this time doing the damage with five wickets. An innings victory for Northants, putting them back to the top of the championship table.

David was now fourth in the national bowling averages. Keith Andrew was a happy captain. He was also an unassuming but brilliant wicket-keeper, proved, if proof were needed, by a remarkable statistic discovered by chance by the Northants' scorer: during the last seven championship matches Andrew had not conceded a single bye whilst 900 overs had been bowled (175 of them from David) and over 2000 runs had been scored – a world record.

For the first Test against the South Africans, the 100th between them, at Lord's starting on 22 July, David Brown was given his debut in place of Snow, who was omitted despite having recovered from the injury which had kept him out of the last New Zealand Test. David opened the bowling with Rumsey against a strong South African batting line-up, but it was Brown who caught the eye, being lively and quicker than the others, taking three for 44 as South Africa were bowled out for 280. England gained a first innings lead of 58 which would have been greater if Barrington on 91 and Parks on 32 had not been run out by brilliant fielding from Colin Bland in the covers.

Bland's fielding, which Denis Lindsay, the South African wicketkeeper, estimated saved as much as 50 runs per match, had become a talking point across the country. In their first match after the Test, the start of the South Africans' game at Canterbury against Kent was delayed by rain. To quieten a restless crowd Kent captain Colin Cowdrey handed Bland six balls on the outfield, challenging him to throw them at the stumps from 25 yards, in front of avid spectators and TV cameras. He hit the stumps with his first throw, missed with the next two, lifted two stumps out of the ground with his fourth and laid the remaining single stump flat with his fifth. David had played both with and against Bland:

> Colin Bland almost singlehandedly elevated fielding to the important part of the game that it is today. A true athlete and a very capable batsman.

Back at Lord's, second time around South Africa were dismissed for 248, Rumsey and Brown again taking three wickets each. David's 17 overs were expensive, but he did not have much luck. Shortly before leaving the field with a strained ankle, he had Lindsay caught at the wicket, having had Bland, who went on to score 70, dropped on 20 by Titmus at first slip. Set to make 191 runs to win in just under four hours, England were well short of the target with seven wickets down when the match ended. The weather had been poor throughout the Test but the appetite to watch an attractive South African side remained - 90,000 people went through the gates.

David missed two county matches whilst on Test duty and he was to miss a third, a vital top of the table clash with Middlesex, due to his ankle. That match was drawn, grimly defensive cricket being played by both sides. On August 3, bank holiday Monday, David returned to the side at Clacton against Essex, where declarations by both captains enabled a result to be achieved in a rain-affected game. David's pace, allied to a strong breeze from behind, made the ball rise sharply, and he gave away only 23 runs in 20 overs, with three wickets. Brian Crump, *'the tiny Staffordshire lad who trains on milk'* in Alex Bannister's description, with seven wickets in the match and left-armer Malcolm Scott with five put Essex out for 88 in their second innings with less than an hour to spare; a crucial win.

Barry Knight, batting at number six for Essex, still remembers how he lost his wicket to David in the first innings: *I played forward, but David brought it back into me and knocked my off stump right out of the ground. Every time I played against him, I found him a handful, making me play the whole time with hands high. He had so much potential and should have played a lot more Test cricket than he did, having a natural edge on other fast bowlers. He was at the time the tallest man to have played for England, but he was also quick, quicker than the later tall West Indians, Ambrose and Garner, and thus he presented a unique difficulty to batsmen. The pity was that he was injury-prone which prevented him playing many more Tests.*

The second South Africa Test was held at Trent Bridge on August 5. It brought about England's first defeat in 15 matches under MJK Smith.

The match was important for those English cricketers harbouring hopes of imminent selection for the Ashes tour and the leading young fast bowlers Snow 24, David 25, Jeff Jones 24 and David Brown 23 were all aware that only two of the four of them would get the nod. The squad of 12 for the Test also contained Tom Cartwright, recalled because a rainy forecast for Trent Bridge suggested the pitch might be a seamer's paradise. As Swanton said, '*Cartwright, completely ineffective abroad (for MCC in South Africa last winter), for Illingworth, is a selection designed solely to win this Test, and not to prepare for the Australia tour. Personally, I would*

Fred Titmus, Peter Parfitt, Bob Barber, John Snow, JDFL, Tom Cartwright, Geoff Boycott, Dennis Amiss (12th man).
Jim Parks, Colin Cowdrey, Mike Smith, Ken Barrington.

prefer to see one place go to fringe candidates, such as Jones or Higgs.'

The selectors took some criticism for sticking with the same attack as in the Lord's Test, but then things changed. Brown, an unlucky sufferer from injury on the previous winter's tour to South Africa, missed out again with injury, to be replaced in the 12 by Snow. Then Rumsey became doubtful and Jeff Jones was called up. On the morning of the match both left-arm bowlers, Rumsey and Jones, were omitted, leaving the opening attack in the hands of Snow and David.

South Africa batted on winning the toss but were in straits from an early stage against David and Snow. Cartwright then broke through and the visitors struggled to 80 for five soon after lunch. Then 21 year old Graeme Pollock reigned supreme for 70 minutes while he lashed the bowling, with square and cover drives, for an astonishing 91 out of 102, in the course of which he became the youngest player to score 1,000 runs in Test cricket. He reached his century in only just over two hours until he was out for 125 out of 160. The innings was in Swanton's view *'fit to rank with anything in the annals of the game. There is an obvious comparison with Frank Woolley in the style of his batting.'* For *Wisden* it was one of the finest Test displays of all time, and Melford believed that *'old men in 60 years' time will tell their grandchildren I was there to see Pollock's innings.'* One youngster was present who would remember it for the rest of his days: an eight-year-old David Gower, taken by his father to his first Test match.

> '...an eight-year-old David Gower, taken by his father to his first Test match.'

John Snow was later to write *'I was opening the bowling in that Test with David Larter of Northants. Unfortunately, I felt the brutality of Pollock more than anybody, my one wicket in that innings costing 63 runs from my 22 overs. I did better the second time around taking three wickets but that did not save me from the firing squad when the team for the last Test was announced. Larter took five wickets and it did not spare him.'* Snow's recollection was faulty. David was not dropped for the last Test; he, like Cartwright, was injured. David fortuitously did not bowl all the time against Pollock, but did put in a very tight spell of one for 25 from 17 overs, the lift which he drew from the pitch giving Pollock more difficulty getting him away than he did with Snow.

In response to South Africa's 269 England struggled to reach 240, thanks to Cowdrey's 105. On the Saturday another crowd of 20,000 saw South Africa batting again. Cartwright having broken his thumb could not bowl, so Smith called on

Boycott who did a good containing job for his skipper as a stock bowler. Alan Ross felt that David in an opening spell of eight overs *'bowled considerably better than at Lord's or on the first day here. He kept the ball well up on the off stump and got enough movement either way on a placid pitch to disconcert Lindsay, Bacher and Barlow in turn.'*

Swanton provided the details: *'Larter had already taken a wicket, after missing Bacher's stumps by a whisker, when he got Lindsay caught by Cowdrey at second slip off a very good ball that left the bat. His first spell was a good one whereas with Snow everyone in the pavilion was saying "pitch it up". After lunch Larter in his first over brought one back to have Bacher lbw [for67]. Larter then had Pollock out pushing a length ball perhaps a shade early to Titmus at mid-on [for 59]. Both Larter and Snow's tails were now right up, and their performance in this last phase was one of the more heartening episodes of the summer. Larter and Snow maintained their effort for nearly 2 hours, including tea, Larter reverting without much loss of pace to a shortened run.'*

David had felt his hamstring tighten in his spell after tea. He began to limp, but he wasn't going to give in to it, seeking to preserve it by shortening his run. Melford saw him bowl Botten, a formidable number nine, and then *'he kept going for 70 minutes after tea, hammering away at Peter Pollock and McKinnon:'*

> I was determined to play through the discomfort of the hamstring injury. That probably did not greatly help its recovery. It never actually tore. I saw Mike Dilley at Northants tear a hamstring and I thank the Lord it did not happen to me – he was on the floor screaming. Anyway, it was a real nuisance and took time to settle down.

South Africa had reached 219 for four when David and Snow took the new ball. So well did they do that the last six wickets added only 60 runs. Snow ended with three for 83 from 33 overs and David five for 68 from 29, 'probably his best performance to date for his country' according to *Wisden*.

One of David's five wickets was lucky. Peter Parfitt explains: *I took probably one of the best catches of my life off David. He bowled one short outside off. Peter van der Merwe, the South African captain, hit it with everything he had got. I stuck my left hand out at gully and it hit me on the heel of my left hand and bounced from there straight into my left armpit where it stuck. Benaud said 'that's got to be the greatest catch I've ever seen in the gully'. No-one in those days would come running up to you to congratulate – and we just walked off to lunch.*

That was Pollock's Test. His was magnificent batting: a fine player, strong. Fred Titmus went to his grave swearing that he had him plumb lbw before he had scored 10. David bowled

29 overs in that second innings. Bowled well – he got the bounce we were talking about.

Needing 319 to win England were well beaten despite a fighting 86 from Parfitt, Peter Pollock completing a match haul of 10 wickets. David was the last man to go having shown some unexpected strokes in a final flurry before falling to a catch at mid-off for 10. South Africa's first Test win in England for ten years was witnessed by 71,000 spectators.

The hamstring didn't feel too bad after four days' rest, and David declared himself available for the home match against Kent on August 11. He bowled the first over of the Kent innings just after tea. After only four balls he felt the hamstring go. He completed the over and limped off, desperately frustrated, fearing that he would not be able to bowl again in the match, and possibly also in the next match. Without him Northants swept Kent out of their championship path with seven wickets each from Crump's aggressive seam bowling and Haydn Sully's off-spin. Crump had now taken 100 wickets for the season. Ian Wooldridge noted that throughout the summer the team had always pressed on with the game at such a rate – even with the longer run of David in their ranks – that they exceeded 20 overs per hour – *'a fact which on its own was close to deserving the title.'*

David was if anything over-keen to return to the fray, not doing his recovery any good by joining the team on the coach the next day as one of 13 players bound for the Lancashire game at Old Trafford. He then sensibly decided not to play and was again not missed as Northants achieved a 10 wicket victory within two days, thanks to some top-class off-spin bowling from Haydn Sully, who took 11 wickets supported by outstanding close catching from David Steele and Peter Watts. The county was now 28 points clear at the top of the championship.

Trueman now reached his 100 wickets for the season, taken at 14.96 each, in sixth place in the national averages just behind David in fifth with 85 wickets at 14.92. Such figures were of some, albeit limited, importance to the selectors who were to meet on August 15 to pick the party to tour Australia.

Northants had two matches left to play. The first was against Worcestershire who were coming up on the rails very fast, from a long way back. They had to win that game to retain their slim chance of keeping the title. The reason why Northants had played several more games than the chasing pack was their ground-sharing arrangement with Northampton Town football club. This required the cricketers to finish their season early to permit the footballers to start their season on the adjoining pitch.

Colin Cowdrey's article in the September edition of *The Cricketer* that year described the season's denouement: *'The whole championship hinged upon the match between Northamptonshire and Worcestershire in the middle of August. Victory for Northants must eliminate Worcestershire and leave Gloucestershire with far too much to do. The wicket was a fast one and David Larter was the one who could turn the match. Disappointingly a hamstring muscle which had been troubling him for some time, while hampering him in the Test match at Trent Bridge, pulled him up soon after the start and with his retirement went that chance of winning. It was just the encouragement Worcestershire needed.'*

David had bowled 17 overs in the first innings of the Trent Bridge Test without trouble. He then got through 29 overs in the course of the huge effort which he and Snow put in during the second innings. At the end of that day he was limping from discomfort in the left hamstring. The muscle was damaged again in his first over two days later against Kent. He then had six days rest before a serious test in the nets before the start of play at New Road, Worcester. That test would determine whether skipper Keith Andrew thought it safe to pick David for one of the most crucial matches in the county's history.

Andrew concluded, as recorded in later conversation with Stephen Chalke, *'I had to pick Larter. There was no question about that.'* The pitch was quick and uneven; David was their one fast bowler and he had had a glorious summer, high in the national averages and now an established member of the England side. But who should make way for him? Nervous of dropping a batsman, Andrew determined that it had to be off-spinner Haydn Sully, notwithstanding his 27 wickets at 11 apiece in the last three matches.

The toss went in Northants' favour for the 11th time in 12 matches and, following their established preference, they batted. They struggled to 211. In the post-tea session of August 18 David bowled the first over of the Worcestershire innings to their captain, Don Kenyon. Immediately the Northants' team's confidence increased: David extracted pace and lift from the wicket. Andrew recalled his shock at taking his first ball – *'as quick as anything I'd seen all season.'* From the third ball Kenyon was caught at slip, nearly taking slip's hands off. David completed two more overs, very quick indeed according to David Steele, and just as he was beginning to look lethal in Keith Andrew's words, he pulled up lame on the first ball of the fourth over.

> I had had 40 minutes flat out in the nets on Tuesday without feeling a twinge. Now this had to happen on the fastest pitch I have played on this season. The trouble is at the back of my left leg, but this time the damage is in a different place – previously it was at the top of the muscle – now the middle of the muscle has gone.

Brian Crump recalls the surge of disappointment which ran through the entire team. We all thought *bloody hell*, said David Steele. Keith Andrew then gambled. He persuaded David not to go off the field but to carry on bowling off three walking paces and to stand in the gully between overs. Keith's thinking was that David might still take a wicket and that he could relieve the other bowlers. Extraordinarily David managed 15 overs in this mode, and did get the wicket of England batsman Dick Richardson, caught by Crump, but went for 57 runs in doing so, inevitably also giving away some runs because of his immobility in the field.

To heap misery on to misfortune the New Road wicket then favoured spin as much as pace. Without Haydn Sully to help, Malcolm Scott's left-arm spin accounted for five wickets as Worcestershire were dismissed for 217. Their lead was only six runs. But then Worcestershire's two left-arm spinners Norman Gifford and Doug Slade exploited the turning pitch and bowled Northants out for 130, Jim Watts contributing a fighting 55 to add to his first innings 67. With Malcolm Scott and David Steele unable to replicate the dominance of Worcestershire's spinners, Graveney, Ron Headley and d'Oliveira eased their side to victory.

David would probably have won the game for us on that bouncy wicket, is Jim Watts's view. *Even at my pace I was getting the ball to bounce quite high. I have to say I thought Keith was unkind in getting David to continue bowling when injured, virtually on one leg. I felt sorry for David at the reaction of some people at the club, frustrated at our getting so near to a title win. He was a 100% trier and did his best at all times. Of course on some days the ball did not come out as quickly as on others. That is the same for all bowlers. It is important to remember David was still very young in those days, and was learning his trade. Look for example at Jofra Archer today – one day he is bowling at high speed and the next he is relatively innocuous.*

David never complained about his injury at Worcester. He never made a fuss, and in fact was quite a solitary figure in the dressing room, being quiet and uncomplaining.

Northants were still at the top of the table and if they gained 10 points from their last match of the season, starting on August 21 against Gloucestershire, they were likely champions. If they failed to make those points, Worcestershire still had an uphill task ahead - needing to beat Surrey, Hants and Sussex to pip Northants to the post, and Glamorgan similarly could take the trophy if they won their last three matches.

Haydn Sully duly replaced David for the Gloucestershire match at Wantage Road on August 21. Lady Luck continued to decline to smile on the county. Although Andrew won the toss yet again, rain prevented any play until tea on the first day. An astonishing innings of 152 not out from Milburn, with seven sixes and 15 fours enabled a declaration. Arthur Milton then carried his bat through both Gloucestershire innings for a very valuable 86 and 43 as rain ended the match with Gloucestershire 87 for one chasing 181. Worcester meanwhile thrashed Surrey by an innings thanks to a remarkable eight for 38 from Len Coldwell and six for 33 from Norman Gifford.

Worcestershire still had to win their last two matches to take the title, Glamorgan having missed out. They won the first of those, defeating Hampshire at Bournemouth in a controversial match of three dramatic declarations, a result which is no doubt still talked about in the members' bar at Wantage Road. Brian Reynolds, Northants' senior pro, had been playing golf with skipper Keith Andrew when the news came through. Hampshire captain Colin Ingleby-Mackenzie having declared 146 runs behind, Worcester's Don Kenyon had responded by declaring after only one ball, setting Hampshire a victory target of 147 in 160 minutes on a wet pitch. Ingleby had completely misread the weather situation as unexpected hot sun then turned the wet pitch into an old-fashioned sticky dog, on which Hampshire were skittled out by Jack Flavell and Len Coldwell in just over an hour for just 31 runs.

NORTHAMPTONSHIRE COUNTY TEAM
COUNTY CHAMPIONSHIP RUNNERS-UP 1965
Standing (left to right): Malcolm Scott . Haydn Sully . Jim Watts . Peter Watts
Colin Milburn . David Steele . Brian Crump.
Seated: Albert Lightfoot . Roger Prideaux . Keith Andrew (captain) . Brian Reynolds
Insets: Mike Kettle and David Larter

WITH THE COMPLIMENTS OF 'NORTHAMPTONSHIRE EVENING TELEGRAPH'

On August 31 Worcestershire won the third of their must-win three final games away at Sussex, Jack Flavell, for the first time in his career being injury-free throughout the campaign, dismissing seven Sussex batsmen in the first innings. This win, their tenth in eleven matches, sealed an astonishing championship for Worcestershire, never having topped the table throughout the season, by a mere four points from Northants.

David's hamstring injury prevented him playing in the drawn third Test against South Africa at the Oval starting on 26 August. Snow was dropped, Brown was restored after injury, Ken Higgs, picked for the Australian tour, was brought in for his debut and Brian Statham, who had had such a productive season with the ball, was recalled after a gap of two years. The chairman of selectors declined to say if Statham would have played if David Larter had been fit, although he did, strangely, say that David Brown and Jones were a little too inexperienced to open the bowling. Higgs on debut had a fine match with eight wickets and Statham finished his Test career with seven wickets to give him 252 wickets in 70 Tests, a tally only exceeded by Trueman's 307.

> Brian and Fred were always associated in public parlance and affection. On the field the partnership was utterly complementary, but off the field they of course spent time together but also went their own ways. Calm and easy-going Brian was just as happy with anybody as long as a pint glass was somewhere near. He was not one of those who wanted to talk technical cricket, but was a good general conversationalist. Brian had more than a hint of looseness, with a double-jointedness to his bowling action. His party trick would demonstrate this. He could pick up a full pint glass with his right hand and stretching backwards behind his neck, without spilling a drop, offer the pint to his mouth from the left side. This would be followed by his inimitable lopsided grin.
>
> He was the perfect foil for Trueman – his comrade in arms 35 times in Fred's 67 Tests. He was a great bowler.

It was important that David's fitness for the forthcoming tour to the Antipodes was tested well in advance of departure. He withdrew from two of the Scarborough Festival matches – TN Pearce's XI to play the South Africans at Scarborough on September 4, and an England XI against the Rest of the World on September 8 – but was fit enough, after 23 days of recuperation, to play on September 11. He opened the bowling with Brian Statham for an England XI against the Rest of the World at Lord's. Rain reduced the three-day match to a single-innings 70-over game, which

gave David eleven overs, which he negotiated without problem, much to his and the selectors' relief.

David's season ended with him in seventh place in the first-class averages with 87 wickets at 15.32 from 589 overs, following Rhodes, Jackson, Statham, Cartwright, Trueman and Flavell. He played in only 17 of Northants' 30 first-class matches. He again topped the Northants bowling with 71 wickets at 13.5, from only 433 overs.

Hanif Mohammad, Pakistan's leading batsman in the first decades of the country's existence, played in both the Rest of the World matches. He was the second oldest of four brothers all of whom played Test cricket. The third oldest, Mushtaq, had now settled in UK as he completed his Northants' residential qualification. It must have been something of a shock for Derbyshire's 2nd XI playing their last match of the season at Derby to find two Pakistani Test cricketers batting together against them, Hanif for practice and Mushtaq for his future.

1965-66 ASHES TOUR

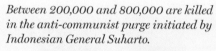

Between 200,000 and 800,000 are killed in the anti-communist purge initiated by Indonesian General Suharto.

On Sunday August 15 1965 three former England captains of Australian tours, Messrs Allen, FR Brown, and May together with Alec Bedser and the tour manager Billy Griffith, plus three men who had never been to Australia, Messrs Insole, Kenyon, and the captain MJK Smith, sat round a table at Lord's to choose an MCC party to defeat Australia. England had won only one Test there in the last ten. The tour would contain 74 days of cricket as against 83 in 1962/3.

The selection of bowlers was critical to success. Fred Trueman had left the Test scene; Brian Statham was on the wrong side of 35 to withstand another winter of Australian wickets (his successful Test return at the Oval was not to take place for another 11 days); and Don Kenyon was of the view that Fred Rumsey would not stand up to the demanding Antipodean schedule. The MCC selectors had to find a new attack from the younger brigade.

An anonymous selector was quoted as saying '*it took us 2½ hours to decide on three fast bowlers for the last Test, so who knows how long we shall need to find four for Australia.*' Selection predictions were coming from all sides of the press spectrum. Swanton was clear that in-swing and seam bowlers with rich harvests on English pitches, for example Len Coldwell and Tom Cartwright, would likely have no success there. His 16 would include '*11 certainties: Smith, Cowdrey, Barrington, Graveney, Barber, Titmus, Parks, Edrich, Murray, Allen and Larter.*'

Michael Melford picked out Larter who he said was now bowling better than ever and whose height alone would give him extra bounce. '*Although he did not play in a Test match, he was not entirely ineffective in Australia in 1962/3 and he took 39 wickets at 24 apiece on the tour, compared with Statham's 33 at 31.*' He would pick Cartwright, Snow, Larter, Brown and Jones.

EM Wellings was against picking a medium-pacer, '*who would be quite useless on Australian pitches... Coldwell went to Australia three years ago and Cartwright to South Africa last year. Their ilk are not for export. It is difficult for any side to dominate in Australia without good genuinely fast bowling.*'

Robin Marlar, not for the first time, was contrary: not only would he select Trueman but also Rumsey and Statham, although the latter might decline the invitation (which indeed he did); some workhorses were needed - Cartwright plus Smith of Gloucestershire or Higgs. '*Larter has done consistently well in more than one season of late, but Brown wins the vote – if he breaks down in an up-country game, he will be on the next plane home.*'

David had his own views:

> David Brown was in my view an obvious candidate for one place. He was a good solid bowling partner, who never gave up trying and who you could rely on to keep up the pressure and make the batsmen work for any runs. Ken Higgs was a probability for another slot after his eight-wicket appearance at the Oval. Ken was a good foil, in the Brian Statham role. Whilst he was more of a fast-medium English-conditions bowler you rarely got a bad ball from him; this left two places open between me, John Snow (a very good bowler, quick and straight, a slightly out of the ordinary character whom I never really got to know) and Jeff Jones, the latter not having yet played a Test match but with the advantage of being a left-armer.
>
> I had got back into the England XI against New Zealand and South Africa with reasonable success, and I felt that in 1965 I was at near peak fitness and indeed ability. Keith Andrew reckoned that when the rhythm was right, I was

hitting his gloves harder than Frank Tyson used to, and I came to realise that I did not fear any batsman anywhere. Good players would still get runs against us but as a county side we knew we could beat anybody.

In the event Brown, Higgs, Jones and David got the nod, with John Snow being the one left out. He was bitterly disappointed: *'Brown, Jones and Higgs I could accept but I thought I had a better claim than Larter who had toured Australia before and returned home with a poor record, the hard wickets affecting his legs. The same thing was to happen again.'*

JT Ikin (asst mgr), DJ Brown, JDFL, K Higgs, Jack Jennings (physio);
PH Parfitt, G Boycott, WE Russell, RW Barber, IJ Jones, BR Knight, JH Edrich;
JM Parks, FJ Titmus, MC Cowdrey, MJK Smith, SC Griffith, KF Barrington, DA Allen, JT Murray.

From Sydney former Australian captain Bobby Simpson issued a challenge to MJK Smith to play more attractive cricket than Dexter's team had done in the 1962/3 series. He thought Titmus and Allen would be the main bowlers *'and Larter might do well too. He wasn't quite Test class last time, but I've always thought he had the potential to be a more than useful Test bowler.'*

On August 15 David was playing at Southport in a benefit match. An announcement came over the tannoy at the tea interval, naming the touring party for Australia in the winter.

> My name was included in the announcement. I am being quite serious when I say that I was probably the most surprised person on the ground. I really had thought that India had finished my touring days and I could play a few more years in county cricket and then gracefully retire. Little did I know that retirement was in fact to be even sooner.

For Swanton there were no surprises in the party. He dismissed Higgs's reported reaction of *'you must be joking'* on being told of his selection, with the comment *'He will be fine – he is very fit, having previously been a centre half for Port Vale.'* The 1965 season's figures of the four chosen pace bowlers were pored over: David Brown had 60 wickets at 24, Higgs 106 at 20, Jones 57 at 17, and Larter 87 at 15 apiece.

One major difference from the 1962/63 Ashes tour was the mode of travel. Then it was stately progress in an ocean liner, now it was fast forwards on a Comet airliner. Not fast by 21st century standards – the flying time from London to Perth would have been 60 hours, with stops. As was customary there was a stopover at Colombo in Ceylon, to accommodate a couple of warm-up matches before landfall at Perth on October 21 where there were six days to acclimatise before the first one-day warm-up match.

With net practice, where the touring party were helped by Richie Benaud and by Peter Loader, the Surrey fast bowler now resident in Perth, as the main activity, the interests of the cricketing press strayed elsewhere. Even to David's sleeping arrangements: the manager of the City Motel in Perth made the sports pages with this: *'we just have not got a bed big enough for him. Many other hefty sportsmen have stayed here, but I have never been called upon to find a bed for such a big fellow.'*

David looked forward to this career opportunity:

> After the surprise of selection, I realised that the 65/66 tour was my chance. No Fred or Brian and a couple of the others were not there. Just me, David Brown, Jeff Jones and Ken Higgs as pace bowlers. I mostly roomed with Jeff – a great lad, but the only Welshman I have met who cannot sing (unfortunately he thought he could). All started well and we stirred up varied Australians in Perth before we moved East.

The opening first-class match of the tour started on October 29. Kelly, having scored a century for the home state in the first innings, retired hurt in the second with his score on three, after being hit on the head by a ball from David. He returned at the fall of the third wicket to score a second century. David bowled the final over with WA needing eleven to win with two wickets in hand. He castled Terry Jenner and then had Mayne caught at slip off a big out-swinger, to give MCC a nine-run win. Denys Rowbotham felt that MCC's bowling was disappointing *'save for Allen and Larter, with Higgs struggling with his direction and Jones being treated unmercifully.'*

NINE-RUN VICTORY BY M.C.C.

WAN   H11067   8TH NOVEMBER 1965.
A CAUGHT AND BOWLED EFFORT BY M.C.C. PACE
MAN DAVID LARTER. THE VICTIM IS WESTERN
AUSTRALIA'S SKIPPER BARRY SHEPHERD WHO HAS
MADE 11.
THIS INCIDENT OCCURED ON THE LAST DAY OF
THE FOUR-DAY M.C.C.-WESTERN AUSTRALIA
GAME WHICH WAS PLAYED AT PERTH.
THE TOURING M.C.C. SIDE WON THE GAME
BY NINE RUNS. LARTER WAS THE HERO OF THE
DAY - TAKING TWO WICKETS IN THE LAST
OVER.

DAVID LARTER – TWO IN LAST OVER –
TAKES M.C.C. TO 8-RUN VICTORY.

XWXX WAN   H 10879   2ND NOVEMBER 1965.
CABLE PICTURE RECEIVED TO-DAY FROM PERTH

THE TOURING M.C.C. CRICKET TEAM WON THEIR
MATCH WITH WESTERN AUSTRALIA IN AN
EXCITING FINISH AT PERTH TO-DAY (TUESDAY).
FAST BOWLER, TALL DAVID LARTER TOOK THE LAST TWO
    W.A. WICKETS IN THE LAST OVER TO
GIVE M.C.C. AN EIGHT-RUN WIN.
PHOTO SHOWS:

                WESTERN AUSTRALIA BATSMAN
PETER KELLY FALLS TO THE GROUND AFTER BEING
HIT ON THE HEAD BY A BALL FROM DAVID
LARTER (RIGHT) DURING PLAY IN PERTH TO-DAY
(TUESDAY). KELLY LEFT THE FIELD BUT LATER
RESUMED TO BAT. THE OTHER BATSMAN IS
PLAYLE.
THE HEAD OF COLIN COWDREY IS SEEN JUST AT
THE BOTTOM .

CABLE FEES PAYABLE   CABLE FEES PAYABLE.

David paid for his effort on the hard Perth track with blistering of his toes and welcomed being rested for the second Perth match. The tour selectors, anxious to give all the party early game-time, brought in David Brown alongside Higgs and Jones. Higgs had struggled with direction in the first match, bowling 14 out of 16 successive deliveries down the leg side. A fast, true pitch gave the batsmen on both sides domination over the bowlers, although David Brown's energy brought some encouragement.

Three days' rest permitted the party to move on to Adelaide for the match against South Australia on November 12, a victory for the tourists thanks to good bowling by Allen, Brown and David, dismissing the home state for 103 in the first innings on a sticky wicket. The covering of wickets in Australia had been compulsory since the early 1950s and the mixture of rain and sun in this Adelaide match was said to have produced the first sticky since Brisbane in 1950. Brown was good value for his seven wickets in the match. David caught a fine catch, high above his head, from a shot from Hawke flying some 8 feet over the fence. In South Australia's second innings Swanton thought that David, Brown, and Higgs, all came through with much credit. *'Marks, the chief hope, was bowled early in the day by Larter who in the same over set up a great yell for lbw against Sharpe – it could not have been a mile away – and when in Larter's next over Jarman was missed by Parfitt, a difficult chance at short leg, the probable pattern of the day became clear. Larter bowled as well in his first spell as I've ever seen.'*

Geoff Boycott, playing his first match of the tour, having suffered gastro-enteritis in Ceylon, produced a positive 94 to give MCC a lead of over 200.

> I bowled quite a lot at Geoff during my career. Although he never scored much against us at Northants, he set himself targets and achieved them. Not as naturally gifted as the greats but a triumph of perseverance and technique.

From Adelaide the tour wended its way to Melbourne, via a one-day game in Hamilton. The four-day State match against Victoria was lost by 32 runs. Bill Lawry, the state captain, batted for over seven hours in the two innings, taking runs off Higgs, Jones and Brown, who nevertheless did well to claim four wickets.

At Sydney on November 26 in their sixth first-class match, and with two weeks to go before the first Test, MCC's batsmen made hay in the Australian sunshine, declaring at 527 for six in under seven hours. Then New South Wales replied. In the words of Jim Swanton *'MCC began against NSW with some good and fast overs by Larter and Brown. These two having accounted for an opener apiece, MCC were deprived*

Boycott and Higgs off Sydney Harbour.

after two overs of the services of Larter who had bruised his heel and they missed him during the afternoon although Brown was lively and Jones beat the bat quite frequently.'

> David Brown and I each got a quick early wicket. At the start of my third over I ran in to bowl, landing heavily as always on the left foot just before the moment of release. My ankle gave way and I went head over heels on to the pitch, feeling a sharp pain in the ankle area. I did not know it but that was the end of my career – November 27, 1965 at Sydney.

The next morning David was unable to walk, the pain in the foot being severe. He was given treatment all that day in the hope that he might bowl again in the match.

Frank Tyson was reporting for the Observer:

'Larter's... bruised heel and retirement today comes regrettably at a time when he should be approaching his peak for the first Test. The full new length of Larter and Brown was worth two wickets to their side before the interval. Thomas sliced Larter's fifth delivery, an away-swinging half volley, into Cowdrey's hands at second slip. Larter limped off before lunch. Jones struggled hard to merit Larter's mantle, but there was absence of late in-swing and an ability to use the crease. Jones could learn from Alan Davidson.'

With David and Bob Barber out of action, bad became worse when, in the second innings Jeff Jones, who had been bowling very well, was banned from bowling further in the match, for causing damage by following through on the pitch. He became the first bowler in the history of cricket in Australia to be stopped from bowling in this way. The next to go was David Brown, already struggling with two of his toes strapped together as a result of stabbing his foot on the beach, limping off the pitch with strained stomach muscles, and a new diagnosis of a broken toe. Titmus and Allen, almost the last bowlers standing, did a great job in bowling NSW out twice for a nine-wicket win for the tourists.

Tour manager Billy Griffith and his tour selectors Mike Smith, Cowdrey and Barrington called London for a fifth fast bowler. Statham was said to have been discreetly approached about coming out despite having earlier turned down the trip to be with his family. Barry Knight was the choice, flying out as standby cover for the first Test. There was some good news: Boycott rejoined the party having again been recuperating from illness in Adelaide.

David had before his injury been the favourite to open the bowling in the first Test, on December 10 at Brisbane, two weeks away. He was told that an x-ray revealed severe bruising to the heel and ankle. The doctor 's advice was that he should not bowl for two weeks, on the assumption that two weeks should suffice for even a severely bruised ankle to mend itself. When two weeks went by and became three weeks, sympathy turned to concern.

> I never accepted the diagnosis of a bruised heel. It was too easy. I still think it was more like the modern front foot injury where the foot twists with full body weight on it and grinds away at the cartilage components of the ankle until it literally wears out a section and the joint becomes bone on bone.

From Sydney the party moved to Brisbane where on December 3 there would be one state match against Queensland, before the first Test on December 10. David did what he could during those games in and around the dressing room to support the team. He did so a little more impoverished than he had hoped. On arrival at Brisbane he, Billy Griffith the manager, John Murray and Bob Barber found that they had been robbed in the hotel during the night:

> The thief was a cheeky devil. He apparently came into our rooms at night, in my case emptying my wallet not 18 inches from my face, and did several more. We reported it and by the end of the day the police had arrested an habitual

hotel bedroom thief. Around six of us, including Billy Griffith, lost £30 or £40 each, but the insurance did eventually pay up.

Eric Russell scored an elegant 110 against Queensland, cementing his place in the first Test, but sadly suffering a cracked thumb in the process. For the first Test England's bowling attack, without David, comprised David Brown and Ken Higgs, who, in a rain-affected draw, took five of the Australian wickets to fall in a total of 443 for six declared. Russell's injured thumb allowed him to play but misfortune struck again when he split the webbing on his right hand while fielding: *When I came off Billy Griffith asked David to take me to hospital to get the webbing sewn up. David must have regretted doing me that favour because he fainted when he saw the needle go in!* Russell's two hand injuries were to keep him from selection for all the remaining Tests.

Poor fixture scheduling meant there were four consecutive one day up-country games within 5 days, followed by a single state match, against South Australia, in the two weeks which would elapse between the first and second Tests. On December 17, three weeks after the injury, and having successfully negotiated several net sessions, David played in the first one-day game, against the Australian Prime Minister's XI at Canberra.

Bowling at three-quarter pace from his shorter run he had two spells of three overs each, in the first of which he bowled Wes Hall, batting at number six, and in the second had Benaud caught by Edrich for 45. On the face of it two for 43 was a reasonable return for his efforts but the reality was that it was painful and unsatisfactory.

He was picked for the following three one-day games in the hope that he would be in good enough shape for selection for the second Test. In those three matches he again bowled in spells of three or four overs at a time, at half to three-quarter pace. His 3 for 31 in the last game might have appeared to offer some hope that the injury was now behind him. However, as in the previous three games, his left foot jarred with each landing. A further medical examination found that in trying to avoid undue pressure on the heel he had been landing so uncomfortably on a toe that now the side of the foot was injured. Back to the physio. David was in familiar hands – the MCC masseur/physio was Jack Jennings of Northants.

Jack was a great bloke, but looking back now, perhaps a bit old-fashioned. He was also the Northampton Town Football club physio and worked with English amateur football. He knew the difference between footballers and cricketers, but modern ideas like x-rays and ultra-sound were foreign to him.

Everybody was desperate for me to get back into action. I had x-rays, scans, hot wax treatment – all to no avail. Nobody could tell me what I had done. The nearest to a diagnosis was that I had damaged, destroyed, misplaced or worn out some bits of cartilage in between some of the many bones that make up the ankle.

It was clear that David could not be selected for the state match on December 23, which would have provided a proper cricket examination before the second Test on December 30. David Brown's pulled stomach muscles had still not mended and, although keen to play, he then contracted a form of housemaid's knee, leaving the attack against South Australia, played over the Christmas period, in the hands of Jones and Higgs with support from Barry Knight, who had just arrived from London. It proved to be a high-scoring match which MCC won by six wickets, Knight excelling with 79 and 46.

England's fast bowling misfortunes continued into the second Test at Melbourne, with Higgs going down to a virus, joining David and Brown on the sick list. Jones and Knight, in another high-scoring draw, did well to keep Australia's batsmen from dominance with four and six wickets respectively. The third Test followed, back to back, on January 7 at Sydney and produced a splendid win for England, who batting first totalled 488, before Brown, fit again, with five wickets in the first innings, and Titmus and Allen with four wickets each in the second, brought England a win by an innings. Titmus scored his 1000th run and thereby completed the Test 'double' in his 40th Test match.

I stayed with the tour, doing what I could, helping out with the baggage and acting as a general procurer of things for the lads. It was a bit grim trying to keep polite, never mind cheerful, as I saw my future rapidly changing. I was kept for the whole Australian leg but came home before the New Zealand part.

David Brown sympathised with David:

I had more than my fair share of injuries in my career – mostly major ones rather than niggling ones – a ruptured stomach muscle, a cyst in the shoulder and ankle and foot injuries. It was such a shame that David broke down. I don't now recall the incident against New South Wales when he fell but I do recall him being in considerable pain and taking a long time to recover.

I roomed with David a couple of times on the tour. It took me a little time to get to know him as he was quite reserved, but I found him to be a very good team-mate, very laid back, and I liked him a lot. We had all been really looking forward to Arty Larter taking on the Aussies on bouncy Australian wickets. In fact, apart from Perth the wickets weren't quite as bouncy as they traditionally were. He had all the attributes of a fine opening bowler – pace and bounce with the great advantage of height. He was quick – I would say not far off John Snow's pace.

The team was sympathetic to David. Of course, on occasions it was natural that some might be frustrated that our great hope was having to sit out the matches. I remember during the fifth Test, on which the series depended, when Lawry and Cowper batted together endlessly, with Cowper scoring 307 over 12 hours, when we came back into the pavilion for each interval inevitably pretty exhausted and frustrated, a few jokey comments would be made as we spotted David sitting on the top deck with a cigarette and a soft drink can in his hand. I suspect none of us appreciated how serious the injury had been. It must have been very depressing for him. There is of course much more management of fast bowlers these days and he would today have been looked after far more closely.

Sitting down for signing duties.

David was picked for the first two of the three games between the third and fourth Tests. Against Northern NSW Country Districts, a non first-class three-day game, he got through 19 overs in the match, in short spells, with one wicket to his name. Swanton described David as being in sparkling form with the bat, adding 45 with Barry Knight in 20 minutes: *'He made a rare appearance at the crease and unburdened himself of some most respectable drives, including a six over long on.'*

He struggled through 20 overs in the second game, against Tasmania at Launceston. For David, in discomfort after more than four or five overs, it was simply a question of getting through these matches without causing embarrassment to his colleagues. He remained in Peter Parfitt's view a good team man, prepared to join in and very amiable. The Middlesex trio were examples of the members of the tour party who would have fun when the opportunity arose. The Australians played their part, in Eric Russell's opinion being generally very hospitable. He remembers a party at the home of one of the Australian players at Launceston. As the evening wore on JT Murray decided it was time for a challenge. *He knew that Arty Larter was one of those people who could drink a yard of ale – or in this case a four pint goblet – in one draft – and JT invited the opposition to bet money on David being the fastest to down the drink. David took it all down in one and everybody roared with laughter as the Australians failed to match it.'*

Jeff Jones can still remember the timing: David sank it in six seconds.

The fourth Test saw Australia execute a complete reversal in form by winning by an innings, in four days. Jones and Brown opened the bowling, with Higgs and Knight standing down. Ken Barrington, making his final Test appearance at Adelaide, scored 60 and 102, completing a run of ten consecutive 50s in first-class matches on the ground in the course of the 1962/63 and 1965/66 tours. Australia, superior in all departments, scored 516, thanks to Simpson's 225 and Lawry's 119.

Jeff Jones achieved his best Test match figures with a very hard-earned six for 18. Adelaide was memorable for him for that but also for other reasons: *The food we had on the tour was great. Our Adelaide hotel food was memorable: David and I enjoyed steak with two eggs for breakfast every morning.*

There was yet again only one first-class match before the fifth Test. In the return match against New South Wales Simpson and Thomas led the state to 488 on a good Sydney batting pitch. Ray Robinson for The *Guardian* watched good bowling by the England pace men on a cool and windy day. David managed 23 overs in short spells, taking one for 95. Higgs also bowled 23 overs, going wicketless for 86 whilst Knight did well with three for 81. Eric Russell, restored from the hand injuries incurred at Brisbane, made an attractive unbeaten 101 as MCC, forced to follow on, scored a mammoth 449 runs on the last day.

With the series level at one all, the fifth Test at Melbourne was all-important. It proved to be an anti-climax. The opening attack of Jones, Brown, and this time Knight, got through 96 overs and the spinners Titmus and Barber 58 overs, in a vain attempt to dislodge Australian batsmen booked in for bed-and-breakfast. Bob Cowper led the way by batting 12 hours for 307 and Bill Lawry clocked up his third ton of the series. The match was doomed to a tedious draw - both sides fearful of losing. This attitude was exemplified by Boycott. Although out of touch he opened the match by taking 60 of the first 80 balls bowled, from which he scored 15 runs, a really poor start to the contest compounded by his calling for a hopeless run from the last ball of an over to retain the strike, thereby running out Barber. Jeff Jones witnessed the repercussions:

As this was the third time that he had been run out by Boycott on the tour, Bob Barber, Gentleman Bob, lost his rag and gave Boycott an earfull upon his later return to the pavilion. The manager Billy Griffith used to say to me: 'Jeff – do you mind rooming with Boycs?' As all he talked about was cricket, he was not outstanding company, but I agreed.

Geoffrey stirred emotions amongst all his cricketing colleagues. Acknowledged by everyone as one of England's greatest run scorers, of high value to the English cause – only 20 of his 108 Tests ended in defeat – there was a general view that his drive for perfection was often born of self-interest rather than for the benefit of the team. Those who played against him when he started his career, batting number six for Yorkshire, saw nothing out of the ordinary, but noted how he was dedicated to improvement, always last out from the nets, and in time he made himself into a hugely successful player, made not born.

When Peter Parfitt described how some of the great batsmen had the skill to manufacture a single off the last ball of an over in order to retain the strike he did not include Boycott as having that facility. But he was most certainly good enough to bat all day against any opposition, frustrating every stratagem by the bowlers. On occasion, umpiring intervention was the only way to dismiss him. Robin Hobbs recalls one case: *Essex playing Yorkshire at Colchester in 1971 with Boycott on 233 after batting all day. A hopeful appeal from me for lbw was immediately accepted by umpire Sam Cook, muttering 'we've had enough of him today.'*

Billy Griffith was a popular manager. Eric Russell had first met him when as a boy on the MCC ground staff he was gently admonished by Griffith as MCC's assistant secretary for sneaking off to play cricket when he was meant to be on Lord's gate duty. On this Ashes tour the party stopped off in Hong Kong for two more matches on the way home: *We were staying in the Hong Kong Hilton. At around midnight I went to the bar on the top floor and saw Billy Griffith sitting in a corner on his own. I went across and joined him for a glass of white wine. 'Now Eric', he said, 'about that Lord's gate duty'. All those years ago and he had not forgotten. He was a very fair and reasonable man.*

Captain MJK Smith was one of those who thought David vulnerable to injury on very firm Australian pitches: *There's always a fair chance of a chap that size breaking down out there. David was a good bowler without doubt. The major bonus of his height enabling him to get bounce was also his problem – at 6 feet 7 you are more likely to break down. David was a good tour member. His was not an outgoing personality, which meant that one didn't know what his thoughts were – the opposite of course of Fred Trueman! It was such a pity the medicos couldn't sort out the problem.*

In the first-class matches played in Australia David bowled only 99 overs, taking 12 wickets at 34 apiece. David Brown in 221 overs did well with 29 wickets at 31 apiece and Jeff Jones also with 34 wickets at 36 apiece. Ken Higgs's 24 wickets in 279 overs cost 41 apiece.

> I said when describing my feelings about the 1964 tour to India, that by my poor performance I felt I had let people down, and by association my captain, Mike Smith. My feelings after the 1965-66 Ashes tour were different, in that it all started well, but ended abruptly in Sydney. But I felt the same niggling feeling of having let people down, and by association the captain, for whom I had the greatest respect.

THE TWILIGHT YEARS

— 1966 —

England win the Football World Cup,
1.5million attending the 32 matches.

Interviewed by *The Cricketer* magazine in March 1966 Doug Insole was asked if the selection of David Larter for the Ashes tour had been a calculated risk in view of his susceptibility to injury. Insole commented *'not really – he was the most formidable-looking fast bowler in England last summer, and his figures were good. He has always been a bit prone to injury but no more so than he was and his record in Australia was good.'*

Since his return home in February David had visited a local osteopathy consultant six times and had also travelled to London to see a senior consultant there. No one could give him an answer to the continuing issue of pain in his left ankle after bowling some five or six overs. But David retained some hope, having tried out the ankle in the Wantage Road nets:

> The strange thing was that given a week or two of rest my ankle felt fine and I could bowl properly in the nets.

The programme of rehabilitation in the outdoor nets continued, with David operating from a new run-up. Like Frank Tyson on the 1954/5 Ashes tour David had learned on the trip to Australia that a shorter run-up could with practice and technique sustain a fast bowler's longevity. In mid-April he was quoted in the press as having shortened his 22-yard run up with the hope of regaining his 1963 form when he took 121 wickets.

> It will take time and I will lose two yards in pace. It will take me at least 250 overs before I know if the switch has been successful.

Training suffered a significant but wonderful interruption when on April 23, 1966, at St. Mary's Church, Harborne, Birmingham, the eve of his birthday, David married Thelma.

I had known Thelma for some three years and did not need any prompting to make an honest woman of her! (I am joking – she was a damn sight more honest than I was). We set up home in Northampton and waited to see what happened to the cricket. Thelma carried on as a ward sister at Northampton General Hospital and we set about being the model married couple.

My best man at the wedding was Albert Lightfoot, a lovely fellow and the best quaffer of draught Guinness that I saw outside the Emerald Isle. A big gangly left-handed batsman and a very useful right-arm medium-pacer. Albert used to love taking care of Thelma if I was actively involved in a game. She loved the attention and felt very safe when with him.

There was a Bass pub called The Bear in central Northampton, where the landlord was a huge cricket fan. A small group of us – Albert, Colin Milburn, Malcolm Scott, Gus Williamson, and sometimes Mick Kettle - would spend many an innocent hour there. Albert was unofficial head barman. We always thought that was good training for the future and so it turned out. Albert later became groundsman, clubhouse steward and much else at a club called

Northampton Saints (not the rugby club). He then moved back to the county ground as head groundsman, moving on eventually to a similar role in the Manchester area.

The Northants camp emanated confidence that Mushtaq Mohammad, having completed his two-year English qualification, would play an important part in sustaining the county's push for championship honours, following the third and second place finishes in the two previous years. That optimism was reinforced by the news that David had recovered from his ankle injury.

David changed into his whites for the first match of the season with some trepidation but with excitement at the renewal of the annual challenge. At Wantage Road on May 1 the opponents were Glamorgan in the first round of the Gillette Cup. It was a disaster. Northants were bowled out for a paltry 67, David's MCC tour room-mate Jeff Jones proving almost unplayable as he took four for 12, *'just as accurate as he had been in Australia'* in Michael Melford's view, *'bowling a controlled fast-medium with the odd faster ball in reserve.'* Glamorgan had no difficulty in chasing down the target for the loss of only one wicket. David got through five overs without great discomfort and with good accuracy.

The county ground at Derby was the venue for the first championship match of the season, played under the new rule of limiting the first two innings to 65 overs each. It was a draw, ruined by rain but enlivened by a fine 130 from Milburn. David did well, opening the bowling with Brian Crump, tying down the Derbyshire batsmen and removing two of the four Derby wickets to fall for 24 runs in 16 overs. David did not suffer much adverse reaction to his efforts in that game and was included in the team for the next match, away to Sussex.

At Hove Sussex were beaten by 10 wickets. David removed both openers, Suttle and Lenham, but not before they had put on 100. Another powerful innings from Milburn with 137 was followed by Northants off-spinner Haydn Sully breaking the back of the Sussex innings with seven for 29, a career best, one of his wickets, that of Pataudi, being *'brilliantly caught by Larter at deep square leg.'*

David Steele recalls a catch in the next match, on May 13 at Wantage Road on a pitch enlivened by rain: *After a late start Northants were shot out for 72, leaving Gloucestershire's openers Arthur Milton and Ron Nicholls three quarters of an hour to bat until the close of play. It was important to achieve an early breakthrough. With the team yet to score Nicholls unexpectedly glanced a ball from David. I was at leg slip, as I normally was to David, and the ball flew to my right. I dived full-length and caught it, putting the opposition a vital man down before a run had been scored. David said to me 'That's a bonus – it didn't feel like a wicket ball!' Brian Crump took six wickets as Gloucestershire were all out for 66, but they managed to creep home to victory by one wicket.*

The high hopes held by David and by the county that the ankle injury was a thing of the past had always had an element of crossed fingers for luck about them. In each of the four matches he had felt pain after a few overs. There was not much point in those circumstances trying to keep up with the unforgiving championship schedule of six days a week cricket. He spoke to Keith Andrew and to the physio Jack Jennings. He felt it was in the county's interest that he should stand down from the side, get back to the physiotherapy table and start again in the county second team.

After two weeks of rest David was at Witham playing against Essex seconds, getting up some good pace and taking four wickets. He played in the next match, a home fixture at Corby against Derbyshire seconds on May 30 and 31. He got through 15 overs, taking another four wickets.

The success of those two games gave David the confidence that he could manage a three-day game, and he was accordingly picked on June 4 for the county against Cambridge University at Fenner's, a first-class fixture. David looked forward to it, playing alongside new team-mates in Mushtaq Mohammad and 16-year-old Peter Willey on his first-class debut. The Cambridge team was of a good standard, captained by Deryck Murray, West Indian Test wicket-keeper, and included off-spinner David Acfield, soon to join Essex.

David had never previously been picked to play against the University sides. Although of first-class status they were not championship matches and Northants had always taken the opportunity to give him a rest. Quite the opposite for a number of old professionals: Fred Trueman for example not only played against the Universities but bowled flat out on the basis that wickets taken in those matches counted towards the first-class averages. His view was clear: *'when the selectors were picking the Test team they were not interested in who you got out, but how many.'*

David's 17 overs, in three spells, produced three undergraduate wickets, giving him his 650th wicket in first-class cricket. But it was painful, and his three wickets cost him 71 runs. He bowled only one over in the second innings.

Jack Jennings then persuaded David to try a plaster cast on his lower left leg. After three weeks it was removed and he opened the bowling at Horton, for the seconds against a Middlesex seconds team. David again got through 15 overs in several spells, this time for 18 runs and the wicket of Clive Radley. From Horton the seconds went straight to Old Trafford where David took one wicket, that of opener

Harry Pilling, from 11 overs. Things were not so good in the second innings, his 14 overs costing 74 runs for one wicket. Next it was to the Oval, where David demolished the Surrey second eleven batting, taking five for 21.

Back at Wantage Road for a one-day fixture against Huntingdonshire, David took five wickets as the visitors were rolled over for 39. Things seemed to be going well but two days later against Warwickshire seconds the ankle pain meant David had to stop bowling after only three overs. It was July 8.

There was no point in continuing a losing battle. It was his last game of the season. It was of no interest to David that his three first-class matches left him third in the county averages, his five wickets costing 29.6 each, or that for the 2nd XI he was second in the averages with 20 wickets at 13.15 apiece.

> Northants, to give them their due, kept me on a full contract for 1966, but I played very little cricket, and when I did turn out back came the pain. The county did arrange for some treatment, part of which involved sticking a plaster cast on my lower leg for several weeks. Off came the cast and I played in a second team game. Back came the pain! The injury manifested itself as a deep, jarring pain in my left ankle after say 6 or 8 overs. This continued off and on for the whole of 1966 with no progress at all.

For the county the great hopes of going one better in the championship were snuffed out. With David's first-class season terminating in May, and left-arm spinner Malcolm Scott sustaining a season-ending injury in July, the team lacked the firepower necessary to dismiss opponents with sufficient regularity. There was a splendid win over the visiting West Indies and a double over champions Yorkshire, and, in the circumstances, a fifth place finish was very satisfactory. Colin Milburn had a wonderful season, first in the country to 1,000 runs he made five centuries for Northants, struck the most sixes, 31, and made the season's fastest century in 82 minutes. His talent was finally recognised by England selectors, and justified by a fine century at Lord's in his second Test.

> I spent the 66/67 winter in partnership with a larger than life character who was convinced that double glazing was the future. We set up a small company manufacturing and fitting the product, and the venture proved to be useful for me if only for the experience it provided.
>
> It was short-lived, fortunately not financially embarrassing, and I walked away from it amicably in April 1967.

— 1967 —

In November Labour devalues sterling by 14% – Wilson's 'pound in your pocket' speech.

Having rested the ankle over the winter, David gingerly tried it out in the spring. The pain was still there but minimal: good enough for another try at resuming his career. The county club was understandably cautious:

> The one-day 60 overs competition, the Gillette Cup, was beginning to make its mark and it was thought I could last for the maximum permitted 12 overs per bowler. The club offered me a match fee contract. Having no sensible alternative, I accepted.

To fit the Gillette Cup fixtures into an already crowded championship schedule, the Cup games started in April, which by the standards of the time was very early. It was April 26 when David opened the bowling against Bedfordshire in a match which Northants won by 83 runs, thanks to Milburn's man of the match performance. In his twelfth and final permitted over David dismissed Bedfordshire's last man to wrap up the game.

> The ankle gave way in that match, a game I had been hoping would open up a good season for me. That hope was well and truly dashed. I decided to announce my retirement.

On May 9 David handed his resignation letter to the club committee and spoke to the press. The *Daily Telegraph* quoted him:

> It was useless trying to carry on. I played only four games last summer because of a damaged left ankle and it broke down again in our Knockout Cup match against Bedfordshire at Luton. If I can't stand up for one match it's pointless trying to play in three-day games. My ankle will just not stand being jarred.

David was perhaps himself a casualty of the changes in the club.

> It began to dawn on me that I was rapidly becoming a liability in the eyes of the Club, and yet I was not being offered any help or guidance. No more treatment of the ankle was offered, and nobody from the Club seemed to be taking much interest in me. The same was true of the MCC. In fact, I have never heard another word from them or any successor body to this day. It seemed that I was a bit of an embarrassment that they hoped would quietly go away.
>
> There was no question of a benefit, nor of any form of compensation. My resignation letter to the Northants committee was accepted without question, with no personal contact and no hint of gratitude for whatever I had done. By this time, I was 27 years old, literally out of a job and not at all well off.

I could understand David's unhappiness at the way his career ended, says Brian Crump: *There were a number of players who would not come back to county reunions for the first few years after retirement, whilst they were settling into their next stage of life. But there were some who would never come back, and this has been a bit of a problem at the county. If David was not very impressed by the county's handling of his serious ankle injury in late 1965, I can sympathise with that: the county was rather cruel on its cricketers in those days, having evidently set themselves a rule of getting get rid of players once they reached the age of 32: Brian Reynolds and Albert Lightfoot were cases that immediately come to my mind.*

The mention of Mick Norman having been told by Freddie Brown that it was time for him to find another county, is another example of the county's man-management skills. Mick was my close friend in the team and we would do everything together, often in the company of my cousin David Steele. Neither I nor Mick were drinkers, but we would often go out for a meal together – once, Mick being a serious Roman Catholic, to a monastery where we had an excellent meal provided by the monks. In my own case I lasted until I was 34 and was then surprised to see my name on the 'not to be retained' list, the day after I had scored a century at Chesterfield in the last match of the 1972 season. My disappointment at this treatment meant that I did not for many years, and perhaps not until the last 10 or 12 years, become an attender at the annual reunions.

Jim Watts remains unhappy at the manner of David's career ending. *David's career record was a fantastic 666 wickets at only 19 apiece. Those figures show his commitment and effort. He could hardly have done any better. But sadly his career was, at least in the eyes of some at the Club, marred by the 1965 championship-determining match at Worcester, when he suffered a hamstring injury, causing frustration and perhaps for some even annoyance. In my opinion that hamstring injury was a turning point in the Club's view of David, and the subsequent ankle injury in Australia only entrenched their view.*

David was not yet forgotten by the press. On July 12 at Portsmouth Marshall and Reed put on 233 for the first Hampshire wicket against visitors Northants. The *Daily Mail* lamented *'it is clear that Northampton badly need another Larter.'*

He could not bring himself to give the game up entirely.

> I turned out for some non first-class games when the other lads got injured and odd games for Rothmans Cavaliers and the Lord's Taverners. These were usually £50 a time outings and enjoyable in that I got to meet some of my fellow cricketers. The International Cavaliers played on Sunday afternoons at club grounds around the country, featuring some of the best players in the world, before large crowds. Rothmans were great sponsors of these televised games throughout the 60s. Their initiative sowed the seed for the advent of the Sunday league in 1969.

On July 27 David was asked to help out the county second team in the game against Leicestershire seconds at Wantage Road. He did well. The *Daily Mail* picked up on this news, giving it a headline *'Larter returns with three wickets for Northampton second XI.'* Opening the bowling with Roy Bailey, in two spells of four overs each, David took three for seven, adding another three wickets in the second innings. David commented to the press:

> I am not contemplating playing for the first team again. The county is short of fast bowlers and I turned out just to make up the number.

A mid-August game for the Lord's Taverners against Leicestershire at Grace Road was an enjoyable outing in the company of old friends: Mick Norman was now playing for Leicestershire along with Tony Lock, whilst the Taverners side included his original Northants mentor Jock Livingston, three more Australians Bobby Simpson, Richie Benaud and Ben Barnett, Khan Mohammad the Pakistan fast bowler, and Barry Knight and Jack Robertson.

Robertson was an elegant stroke player who opened the batting for Middlesex and occasionally for England in the 1940s and 50s. He was cool under pressure, an attribute neatly summed up in the well-known anecdote of the match between the Army and the RAF at Lord's in 1944. The former England captain RES Wyatt was about to bowl to Robertson and had just started his run in when the drone of a doodlebug was heard overhead. All the players fell flat on the ground, but the flying bomb missed Lord's, detonating some 200 yards away in Regents Park. Still clutching the ball Wyatt scrambled to his feet, ran in and bowled. Robertson calmly pulled it for six into the Grandstand and the match continued. Sang froid in action.

> An interesting fact is that I was bowling quicker than ever. In that Sunday Taverners game I was feeling good and decided to open up. After about three deliveries Richie Benaud ran all the way from first slip to tell me that the old Australian wicket-keeper Ben Barnett, who was a bit past the first flush of youth, was in some trouble trying to see and catch the ball! I was by this time at peak strength and in short bursts I knew it was quick, but I also knew that the ankle would not stand a long spell.
>
> Richie Benaud was often around during my career and was a frequent participant in benefit and exhibition matches in England in the late 60s. He and Ben Barnett were popular figures in both Australian and English cricket.

Barnett played in the 1938 Test series in England, keeping wicket when Hutton made his record 364. He made just one mistake, but it was one he had to live with for the rest of his life: when Hutton had made 40, he was stranded a yard out of his ground beaten by the flight of Fleetwood-Smith's delivery. Barnett fumbled the stumping. As has been noted by writer Robert Bagchi, if the stumping had been made then Hammond's 336 made in 1933 would have lasted 25 years as the world record, until Hanif Mohammad made 337 in January 1958 and Sobers 365 a month later. The misery of Barnett was equalled if not exceeded by Chris Scott of Durham when he dropped Brian Lara at Edgbaston in 1994 when he had scored 18. He went on to score 483 more. Barnett made his last first-class appearance at the age of 53 in

1961, at the Hastings Festival. David's *a bit past the first flush of youth* was a little over-polite. Barnett was a hearty 59 when David decided to bowl thunderbolts at him.

> On several occasions over the next year or so playing for the International Cavaliers, I was asked by my fellow Cavaliers why on earth I was not still in the first-class game, and a few times I was asked to tone it down a bit.

The 1967 season saw Northants slip from fifth to ninth in the championship. The summer of love contained a number of comings and goings. David retired, Jim Watts accepted a job as a teacher, robbing the side of a key all-rounder, Milburn and Mushtaq Mohammad both missed matches through Test calls, and left-arm spinner Malcolm Scott was banned by the MCC for the last couple of fixtures when his bowling action was questioned. Keith Andrew retired to be replaced as captain by Roger Prideaux who himself went down with shingles, leaving senior pro Brian Reynolds – '*the perfect pro*' in Arlott's eyes – to stand in.

There was some good news. As Andrew Radd, journalist and Northants' archivist, noted: *'Keith Andrew's retirement finally gave Laurie Johnson an extended run behind the stumps – a challenge he prepared for by spending the winter months repairing the splintery wooden green seats (now blue and plastic of course) between the old Ladies Stand and the signal box.'*

— 1968 —

Wimbledon tennis goes open with professionals now able to take part.

I played some 5 or 6 games for Rothmans Cavaliers. Interesting and fun but very much a sense of joining the 'has-beens'. Guess who was captain for most games? One ER Dexter, but by then the past was forgotten and there were no problems.

David recalls a game at Banbury, which tells a little about Fred Trueman and about 'my lovely Thelma.'

I had taken Thelma for the day and Fred was on our side. It was the cricketers' custom to wrap one's watch around one's wallet, threading any rings on to the watch strap before handing it to the 12th man who was responsible for taking the team's valuables to the office. I noticed Fred seeking out Thelma and giving her something as we prepared to take the field. She quickly came across to me and opened her hand which contained a very fat wallet and, in her words, 'a diamond ring which would make ten of the one I had happily presented to her on our engagement.' The cricketers' habit was hard to break and Fred was looking for someone trustworthy to look after his bundle, even though it was a Sunday game. Fred did not trust the locals, but our Thelma was alright by him!

Fred was in many ways a really good friend, and his private persona was quite different from the public version which he liked to act out. The stories are legion – here are a couple: the visit to his opponents dressing room before a match: '*I need nine wickets from this match and you buggers had better start drawing straws to see who I don't get.'* At the Sportswriters Association dinner: *'I'm here to propose the toast to the sportswriters. It's up to you whether you stay or not.'*

Apart from those recollections David retains little recall of the one-off matches over the 1967/68 seasons.

> That may I suppose be the result of some mental blocking reaction. By that time, I was working at other jobs and using holiday time and goodwill to take time to play.
>
> Why I did not retire absolutely I cannot say. I, and some people at Northants, had thought there was still a glimmer of light at the end of the tunnel, but it slowly became clear that the ankle was not going to get better. These days it would be fairly routinely sorted (Freddie Flintoff seemed to have the same problem), but I was not offered a solution. I was never given a definitive diagnosis, and to look at me wandering around nobody would guess I had a problem. The pain never recurred in ordinary life.

Flintoff, the 6'4" pace bowler, did indeed have the same left ankle problem in the early 2000s. Scans failed to find the cause of the severe pain, which left him struggling to get through even four overs. Four operations in four years, to remove bone causing compression on a tendon, and subsequently to remove bone fragments, enabled him to continue playing until 2009 when ankle and knee problems forced him to retire from Test cricket.

Jim Watts quotes a modern day equivalent: *'Current England fast bowler Mark Wood has had continuous trouble with his ankles, but with modern treatments has been able to play many times for England. If those treatments had been available in David's day he would have had a much longer career.*

If one watches Stuart Broad bowling (in my view better today than he's ever bowled before) one can see the force with which the front foot lands in the delivery stride, putting a huge strain on that joint. No wonder David on hard Australian wickets suffered that front ankle injury.'

18

THE SEARCH FOR A JOB OUTSIDE CRICKET

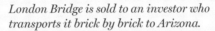

London Bridge is sold to an investor who transports it brick by brick to Arizona.

Looking back to 1967, I have to admit that I was still living in a dream world where I did not have to serve in a shop, work in an office or dig holes in the road. I was still earning odd amounts playing cricket, but the end was in sight. I realised that I needed to forego my determination to be independent and self-employed and that I should look for a job – welcome to the real world!

David had always been a car enthusiast and had owned a fair few of them. What would have been a dream job with Aston Martin at Newport Pagnell faded away when a cost-cutting exercise or the like ended that dream. He then worked for a year as a trainee factory manager until the summer of 1968.

I talked myself into a job close to my heart – in road transport. I knew one of the wealthier Northants members who ran a substantial transport operation. I actually went to ask him for a job as a driver and came out of our meeting as a trainee training officer. The Industrial Training Act 1968 had just come into force and he saw me as his answer. I learnt enough and saw enough to realise that this was an industry sorely in need of training and organising as I set up the framework of a training plan for him.

It was a satisfying job, but something was nagging away at David.

Thelma thought I was silly, but I knew I wanted independence. A few words with Father and in the autumn of 1968, I bought another lorry, a 14-ton gross Leyland Comet flatbed, and set about conquering the road transport business. I enjoyed myself and relished the sense of achievement attained when jobs were done well, but I knew there was a long way to go.

As most of the work was agriculturally based it became increasingly obvious that David needed to locate nearer to the source. With some misgivings from Thelma they moved in early 1969 to Suffolk, to a rented house in Albert Road, Framlingham, just by the  College, taking with them David's prized possession – a Jaguar XK150.

Thelma's misgivings proved grounded because she found no opportunities for work, and we relied on what I could earn. I then made a couple of rash decisions.

Through various odd chats and visits for tea, it became apparent that Framlingham College was trying to open the door to us. My old cricket master Norman Borrett, still running it at the College, made it plain that I could become the cricket professional in succession to John Harris, who was off to pastures new, and that Thelma would be ideal as the School Matron, a post which was shortly to become vacant. I have to admit to being pig-headed, refusing even to consider the idea. Looking back at it I had looked the proverbial gift-horse in the mouth.

Another bigger and better lorry, a Leyland Super Comet 16-ton flatbed, kept things going, but David felt some diversification was necessary. He established a commercial tyre re-treading operation in his transport premises.

We were keeping the wolves from the door, I was back in my home territory, and I felt settled. I had kept fit, doing some bowling at the Framlingham Town nets without pain in the ankle, and in the early months of 1969 I began to wonder whether I could now stand up to more serious cricket than the Cavaliers matches which I had enjoyed but which were not really serious tests of skill or competition.

What David had in mind was the new Sunday league competition, sponsored by John Player and Sons, the tobacco firm. The Gillette Cup had been a success and the public was eager for more instant cricket. The Players Sunday league starting in 1969 comprised one 40 over innings per side and - this was the important bit for David – each bowler could bowl no more than eight overs, with the run-up limited to 15 yards. All the counties signed up to it and that meant 16 Sundays of play. Gate money was now permitted on Sundays – previously funding had been achieved by donations from spectators.

> I took the plunge, asking Northants if they would be interested in my playing in the coming summer. The response was positive, the club offering me a renewed match fee contract. Without much hesitation I accepted.
>
> I recall I was paid about £100 per game plus minimal expenses. The money was not my motivation – it never had been. Can you imagine cold grey post-war GB and someone asks do you want to play cricket for a living?

That was in fact a fair sum, compared with the £650 David earned when capped in 1961.

> The 1962 Aussie tour brought in around £1,000 with a set of kit and blazer – you buy everything else. Sponsors were nowhere to be seen. I tell a lie – Gunn and Moore gave me two bats – remember I was a fast bowler so they did not get much exposure! I think the 1965 Aussie tour was around £1,500 with kit and blazer.
>
> I loved it and when on top of my game my earnings were better than modest. As I recall for the years 1964 and 1965 I grossed about £2,500 (£40,000 today) from cricket. I was happy with this as my two brothers in law, who were skilled men in the motor industry, earned just over half that sum.
>
> Today's millionaire players are in another world! It's called progress.

19

A FINAL FLING

1969 Rupert Murdoch gains control of the News of the World.

So, against all the odds, there I was on Sunday April 27 opening the bowling in the Sunday league for the county for whom I had not played for two years, against Glamorgan at Wantage Road. I was nervous but at the same time very pleased to be back in the environment with old colleagues – Colin Milburn and Mushtaq, Roger Prideaux, Brian Reynolds, Laurie Johnson, Brian Crump, young Peter Willey and the South African Hylton Ackerman. Glamorgan were a strong side with Majid Jehangir, the Pakistan Test player, Peter Walker and Tony Lewis, the English Test cricketers, in their ranks.

Northampton collapsed to the bowling of their old rival Don Shepherd, all out seven runs short of their target of 139. David had two productive spells of four overs. *Wisden* recorded that *'former England fast bowler, Larter, back after two years, deserved his four wickets.'*

Northants achieved their first victory on May 11, beating a Worcestershire side which included Basil d' Oliveira and Tom Graveney by 66 runs. David was happy with his work, conceding only 24 runs in his eight overs for the wicket, caught and bowled, of Ron Headley. The next day Northants again lost to Glamorgan, this time in the first round of the Gillette Cup, David completing his full 12 overs, clean bowling Tony Lewis and Malcolm Nash.

The Sunday afternoon format was quickly generating enthusiasm from the spectators but also from the players. Roger Prideaux, captaining Northants, was quoted as saying that *'there was more tension in half a day than you normally get in a month of county cricket.'*

On May 25 Northants were at Lord's. It was an unhappy day.

> It was really hard to concentrate on the cricket as our thoughts were on Colin Milburn, whose life-changing car accident had happened the evening before. I came on second change and prised out Mike Smith and their top scorer Clive Radley for 22 in my seven overs. If Colin had been playing, we would have made much more of a game of it. As it was, we were dismissed 35 runs short for 101, in my case stumped by John Murray off Titmus for six.

It was announced there would be a benefit match for Milburn in South Africa in November. John Arlott who had enjoyed dinner with Milburn only hours before the crash wrote: *'As he took a match in his hands and by vivid power reshaped it according to his own unique designs, he lifted the heart as perhaps no other batsman has ever done – not simply a cricketer to admire, but a man to enjoy.'*

After a month of cricket David was feeling back to his best.

> I was now happy with my bowling – the old rhythm was there – and I was doing well enough to be asked to play in the next championship match against Warwickshire.

So, against all predictions, particularly his own, on June 14 David started his first championship game for three years, at Peterborough. Roger Prideaux, as agreed, used him in short spells, enabling him to get through 22 overs in the first innings and 12 in the second.

> I started well, with three quick wickets at the start of the match, Ibadulla, Jameson and Amiss, all three Test cricketers. The second innings was even better – I took four wickets for one run in my first six overs including Amiss again. Dennis was a very good player and went on to do great work for Warwickshire and the ECB after retiring as a player. I admired his stand over helmets: he was the first to wear one – an adapted motorcycle helmet – in the World Series matches in 1978.

The *Daily Telegraph* picked up the story of David's return to the first-class game: *'The third day's play was enlivened by a hostile spell of fast bowling from Larter. Larter, who had been dogged by Achilles tendon trouble* [sic]*, at one stage had taken four Warwickshire wickets for one run, three of them in one devastating over. The former England bowler made full use of his considerable height to obtain life and movement on a responsive pitch, Abberley, Amiss and Cartwright all departing to agile close catches, whilst Warner gave Larter a simple return catch. When Warner and Cartwright had gone to successive balls, Larter had the chance of his first hat-trick in first-class cricket. Timms in fact had flicked the next delivery into the hands of backward short leg, but the umpire had called no-ball for overstepping. Larter was called eight times in all. Northants hope he will agree to make further three-day appearances.'*

Dennis Amiss recalls David as *a marvellous fast bowler with great height, quick, and moving the ball away from the bat. The steep bounce made him one of the hardest of fast bowlers to play. My long experience at Warwickshire meant that I saw far more of David Brown than I did of David Larter. Browny was not as quick as David, and perhaps a bit more round-arm, and one of the best triers ever, whether or not the odds were stacked against him. It was such a shame that David Larter was so unlucky with injuries – he had the ability to be one of the best ever.*

Having bowled 22 overs in the first day of that match, the Saturday, David was worried at the further test the ankle would go through on the Sunday. The Players league fixture, this time against Lancashire, was thankfully also at Peterborough. David took the opening wicket, that of Farokh Engineer, in an economical spell of seven overs for 16 runs. By the Tuesday end of the championship match he had bowled 41 overs in four days. The ankle was sore but stable.

He was rested from the following championship match away at Kent but continued to play in every John Player Sunday game, meeting old opponents and new. Against Hampshire he found himself opening the bowling against the most formidable opening partnership in English cricket that season – Hampshire's Test stars South African Barry Richards and Roy Marshall from the West Indies. David's eight overs and one for 21 was a good return but was not enough to prevent Hampshire winning by six wickets.

On Saturday June 28 he played his second championship game, a draw with Lancashire at Wantage Road, opening the bowling opposite the promising Peter Lee. Lee turned in a fine performance with six wickets whilst David chipped in with two. In the second innings 22-year-old David Lloyd, revisiting the ground where as a 17-year-old he had first played in 1964 for Lancashire seconds, scored freely for a

Wantage Road for the last time.

well-made 96. Lloyd remembers the match and the Wantage Road characters:

I remember that there was a small shed to the left of the pavilion and when we were batting in the middle, we could hear the conversation of two old fellows sitting there. I heard one say to the other as Lee came back for another spell: 'Oh I see Boards is coming on – What do you mean 'Boards'? – This young chap Lee – when he comes on, they shout 'boards' – as the batsmen hit the ball into the boundary boards.'

It was the first time I had faced David Larter, his comeback season. On the county circuit the bush telegraph soon picks up on someone who is pretty quick. So I knew I had to watch out for him. In that particular game he was I would say similar to Colin Croft, very tall, not express, but with extra bounce. It was obvious that when he was fit, he would be a real handful – certainly quick enough to trouble most batsmen with the added advantage of that bounce.

He put a lot into his bowling and was far from being a metronome in terms of accuracy, but you don't need your strike bowler to be a metronome if he gets early wickets. An example was David Sayer of Kent – very quick but he really did spray the ball about. I would say a lot of tall fast bowlers get injured, particular with hamstrings and other leg strains. Chris Tremlett was a good example, as were Colin Croft, and Bob Willis who of course had to run a long way to get himself going.

If David had been playing in the present day, he would have been closely managed and would be rested if his fitness got close to the red zone. He was unlucky that in those days little or no physiological management took place.

If there was intended to be some geographical synergy linking the venues chosen for championship fixtures and those for the intervening John Player Sunday league, it often failed to show itself. After his 27 overs on Saturday June 28 at home David and the rest of the team transferred by coach to Derbyshire. The Sunday league game was in the pleasant surroundings of Queen's Park, Chesterfield, an attractive parkland ground with ducks on the lake and spectators on the grassy banks, overlooked at 238 feet by the strange twisting spire of All Saints. The ground had gained notoriety, and embarrassment for the groundsman, in 1946 when the county match against Yorkshire had to be stopped for the length of the pitch to be measured – and found to be two yards too long at 24 yards.

David's two for 24 runs in his eight overs helped Northants to a six-wicket win. Then it was back on the coach to Northampton for the resumption of the Lancashire championship match.

On July 12 David was at Hove for his third championship match. He bowled 19 overs in each of the Sussex innings, downhill, carefully nursed by skipper Roger Prideaux, ending with five for 111 in the match. His wickets included captain Mike Griffith and, satisfyingly, Tony Greig, whom David found *noisy and unnecessarily aggressive*, caught behind by Laurie Johnson for six.

It was to be David's last championship match. The first wicket he took in the second innings was that of Sussex opener Mike Buss, caught by Johnson off David for a duck. His last was Mike's brother Tony, dismissed the same way for 83, his career best score. When Northants batted, Hylton Ackerman, their South African overseas player, made an excellent 145 and David was out for a duck, caught and bowled by John Spencer. Northants were four-wicket victors over the seasiders, their first win of the season. It was July 15.

In David's three championship matches he had taken 14 wickets at 24 runs each, putting him second in the county averages for the season behind Mushtaq. *Wisden* wrote: '*the former England fast bowler, Larter, who had previously retired owing to ankle injury, played in the occasional game. He still took wickets and would have been an asset had he appeared more regularly.*'

I did not qualify for the county until 1966, reflects Mushtaq. *Therefore, apart from my 1965 county debut against New Zealand, the only championship games I played alongside David were the three he managed in 1966 and in 1969. I had of course played against him in 1962 on Pakistan's tour, when he bowled very well against us for Northampton at Wantage Road, and then for England in the Fifth Test. It was a big disappointment that his ankle trouble disrupted his career. I thought he was a great fast bowler in the 1964/5 seasons, a great asset for both county and country. I liked him a lot. When I joined the county as a 23 year old he looked after me and became a good friend. A reserved and gentle man.*

The final John Player fixture was at Bradford on August 31. David started the match by bowling Yorkshire's opener Leadbeater with only three runs on the board, the last wicket he was to take in top cricket. He ended with one for 33 in seven overs, as Northants subsided to a 39-run defeat. In a full season of 15 John Player fixtures, David finished with a respectable 19 wickets for 19 runs each.

Hat-tricks in limited overs cricket were rare. The first was David's against Sussex in 1963 at Northampton. It was not for another 33 years, in June 1996, that John Emburey, the ex-Middlesex and England off-spinner, matched that in the 60-over Gillette competition against Cheshire, also at Northampton.

Ray Illingworth, amongst others, commented that David would have flourished in 21st century one-day cricket, with his good strike rate and economy rate. The only statistical support for this idea is the minimal evidence of David's Gillette Cup experience from 1963 until 1969 – 27 wickets costing only 14 runs apiece, putting him fifth best in the country in that era. The scoring rate in those early days of one-day cricket was pedestrian when compared to 21st century rates – in the 1960s 57.7 runs per 100 balls was not hugely greater than the then first-class rate of 44.4.

So that was it. David had tried the comeback. It had been worth that final effort, but the ankle had beaten him. Now he had to move on to a new career. It would take time for the disappointment to dissipate.

Jeff Jones, who was forced to retire at 26, knew about that feeling of loss: *It was terrible to give up at the age of 26 with elbow and shoulder problems when I had what a lot of people felt was a bright cricketing future ahead of me. For the first two years the loss hurt me so much, but we all get injuries in cricket and we have to live with the risk they may be serious.*

20

WEST TOWARDS WALES

UK inflation reaches 24%. Top rate of tax 83%. The Three Day Week. The winter of Discontent.

With the birth of their son Jonathan in 1971 David and Thelma commenced building a big, modern bungalow on part of his father's land near Framlingham at Coles Green.

> We moved in in 1973, settling in for the good life. Not so, as Ted Heath and the three-day week in 1974 bringing fuel shortages and lack of work, forced a big change of direction. I looked around and had a go at several jobs. One interview was for the job of Secretary of Essex CCC. Doug Insole was the interviewer, and I think he was just being kind to me – but no job!

In late 1974 David took it into his head to spend a long weekend with Thelma's parents in West Birmingham and to have a look at the job market.

> To keep it short, I was offered a job, and could I start Monday? Big decision – obviously could not start immediately but did so the next week. I left Thelma in Framlingham with the task of selling the bungalow (Father was not best pleased) and I became the transport and warehouse manager for a small international

operation in Halesowen. My certificates of competence, operator's licence and HGV licence helped me to be very hands on, and I was soon enthusiastically tackling groupage work (many consignments – 'grouped' onto one trailer – now called logistics) and customs procedures – mainly for the near continent. We also warehoused for Cadburys, mostly with nuts from the Middle East.

Thelma did well and the bungalow went in around six months and she came up to Birmingham, she and David landing on her parents 'for a few weeks' – which turned into nearly 9 months – until a house was found in the Worcestershire countryside and they began a new life.

> Very few people knew who I was, but one or two who did said that I should not be messing about with big dirty trucks, and that I would make a great salesman. So, in Autumn 1981, dressed in suit and tie, off I went to work for Hambro Life Assurance as an associate. Yet another mistake! I stuck it for around a year and then had to admit that I did not even believe in what I was selling, let alone like it.

By now the three of them had forsaken Worcestershire for Shropshire, living in Bridgnorth for what proved to be a much more settled period, with David working for Telford Development Corporation as the Manager of their Youth Training Scheme. It was a fantastic eye-opener:

> Telford was a New Town and had lots of problem youngsters, some 500 of whom we placed with local industry, along with some craft workshops we ran ourselves. Although I enjoyed the role, road transport was still my love, so when the Road Transport Industry Training Board offered me a position as a management trainer at their training facility north of Telford, I went for it. It was April 1985. At long last I had found my niche.

'At long last I had found my niche'

> I concentrated on trans-European transport matters, liaising with other European training organisations and even negotiating courses for Russians and running RTITB exhibitions at international events. This took me right through the 1980s until the Training Board was disbanded in 1991. My redundancy came with a good package, and I left one Friday in January 1991 to start up as an independent consultant the next Monday. I could not believe

it – I found myself doing exactly the same work with what was the successor body to the RTITB – another government quango after all! Self-employment held no fears and with my established contacts I was soon working for the household names of the industry – TDG group, BRS, Exel and others.

2003 saw a move to Wales, only four miles over the border, the house price differential at the time making it very attractive. Jonathan, his wife Katherine, Thelma and David pooled their resources and settled into a much-extended Welsh long-house with the youngsters at one end and the parents at the other. David gradually ran down his consultancy work, using the time to develop the house. They are still happily there, in their own four acres with its many natural features. Jonathan has inherited David's practical nature and the four of them literally do everything for themselves.

David, Katherine, Thelma, Thelma's sister Pauline, and Jonathan.

My passion for cars saw me own several quick Ford XR4i cars and a Jensen Interceptor in the 80s and 90s. I remember once getting to 145 mph on the M1 (before limits) in a factory demonstrator model Aston Martin DB4 GT. In 1998 and 2000 I purchased a Jaguar Sovereign and then a Jaguar Sport (I never did get to an E-type Jaguar) before switching to the first of a series of Ford Mondeos. In 2013 I acquired my current car, a Range Rover, and a 1949 Ferguson TEA20 tractor – a real trip down memory lane, my having first driven one of these in 1956.

This car stuff leaves a lot of people cold, but it may help to explain me. Both the cars and the cricket satisfied my interest in speed. That desire has worn off somewhat now in my dotage, but I look back with very happy memories on those twin passions, which gave me so much fun.

David's wife Thelma with grandson Matthew driving the Ferguson.

21

REFLECTIONS

The common approach adopted by cricket writers in summarising David's career is exemplified by his entry in *England Test Cricketers* by Bill Frindall: *'Fast bowling imposed too great a burden on his elongated frame and an assortment of strain-related injuries curtailed and finally ended his career.'*

David's first-class career lasted effectively only six seasons – from mid-1960 to the career-terminating ankle injury in November 1965. He was to play only six more first-class matches, three in 1966 and three in 1969. He missed only some 22 matches over those six seasons – not an inordinate proportion of his 182 matches. He had injuries which were 'strain-related' – a back injury cost him five matches in 1961, torn intercostal muscles six matches in 1962, and hamstrings three in 1965. All fast bowlers suffer strain injuries but do not tend to be defined by them as David has been. That he was so defined can be explained.

David had damaged his hamstring on August 9 in the second South African Test. Nine days later he damaged it again after three overs in the critical championship game at Worcester – an injury which attracted great publicity given the importance the press had attached to David being the man who would ensure Northants of their first-ever championship title. Then, when only three games into the Ashes tour, David suffered the ankle injury which effectively rendered him a passenger for the rest of the tour. The perception was that this was another example of a strain injury.

That perception, conflating the two hamstring injuries in England with a trauma injury in Australia, was assisted by the fact that the seriousness of the ankle bone injury was not diagnosed and consequently was not communicated. The press was variously informed it was merely bruising, of the heel or the ankle, and it was therefore variously written up as a strain or even as Achilles tendon damage. Worse for David was the fact that the injury only caused him real pain after he had bowled a few overs; off the field he displayed no sign that he had sustained, unknown to everyone, a career-ending trauma. EM Wellings, writing *Wisden's* summary of the tour, as much in the dark about the nature of David's injury as anyone, was unforgiving: *'Larter was a passenger for most of the venture. When he suffered a bruise or a muscular strain, he spent an unconscionable time recovering. When he was in action, his bowling was short of resolution and purpose. Brown was also injury prone…'*

If David, not wishing to let the team down, had instead left the tour and returned home, greater understanding might have followed him. As earlier stated, his misfortune was to have sustained an injury which would have been managed, and no doubt cured, if it had occurred a decade or so later.

As Jim Watts has said earlier both Flintoff and Wood have in recent times suffered similar ankle injuries. In his view the injury was hardly surprising when one considers the force exerted on the ankle when the front foot lands, particularly on hard Australian wickets.

Whilst his career ended on a low, refusing to concede defeat to his ankle condition by trying again both in 1966 and in 1969, David is entitled to reflect with pride on the highs he achieved in his six years in the upper reaches of his profession.

In English domestic seasons he took 100 wickets twice – 101 in 1962 at an average of 19 and 121 in 1963 at 16.7 – and was within four wickets of a third occasion in 1964. For Northants in that 1963 season his figures were 112 wickets at 16.1. To find an average lower than that for a Northants bowler who took 100 in a season one has to go back to George Thompson in 1912. David was one of the top eight bowlers in the national averages in four of his six seasons.

He was invited to tour each winter from 1960 to 1965 except for 1964. His wickets in the calendar years from 1960 to 1965 were 53,106,126,150,110 and 99. In 1966 he took eight more and then 14 in 1969, giving him a career total of 666 wickets at an average of 19.53. 550 of those were captured in England at 18.85 apiece and 116 on overseas tours at 22.80.

Those 666 wickets at 19.53, in the opinion of Jim Watts set David apart: *He was special, and a character all of his own. A very fine fast bowler with a very good strike rate.*

David's own view of his best performances is perhaps not what one might expect:

> Although my best performances statistically were the 24 wickets in
> consecutive games against Somerset and Yorkshire in June 1965, and the six

for 26 against Worcestershire in my sixth game in 1960 was a real thrill, my most satisfying was the subduing of Lancashire in the Old Trafford game in August 1962 when I took seven for 48.

My best performance in Tests has to be the nine for 145 against Pakistan at the Oval: my first Test – 22 years old – with the Australian tour coming up – a schoolboy's dream come true.

The other Test performance which meant a lot to me, although the 1965 Trent Bridge five wickets against South Africa runs it close, was the 1963 seven-wicket match haul against New Zealand in Auckland, straight after Australia. It gave me a quiet satisfaction to make the point that not having been picked for a Test in Australia I could do it when given the chance.

In 2001 David was named by Northants cricket club historian Andrew Radd as one of the *100 Greats of Northamptonshire County Cricket Club*:

'A laid-back character but with a cricket ball in his hand he set a stiff examination for county and international batsmen, albeit for a disappointingly brief period. When Northamptonshire near as dammit won the county championship title in 1965, they owed much to their towering fast bowler, David Larter. Although called up for three of that summer's six Tests, the six-foot seven-inch paceman collected 74 county wickets at 13.59, including match hauls of 12-56 and 12-80 in successive games during June, against Somerset and Yorkshire respectively. Larter's immediate reward was a second tour to Australia in 65/66: but sadly, his Northamptonshire career was virtually over.

His brief return to the game in 1969 when he claimed 14 wickets in three championship outings and bowled economically in the new Sunday League, served to underline what a major loss he was to Northamptonshire.'

Engel and Radd considered that David might have lasted longer *'if there had been less pressure on him to be the new Tyson and if he had concentrated on bowling slower, shifting the ball and conserving his fitness. Though he failed to make the Test team on the 1962/3 Ashes tour, the Australians were impressed by what they called 'Sky Balls' and he did his reputation no harm. The next summer he took 110 wickets in the championship alone. Tyson had never taken 100 wickets in a season for the county.'*

Ray Illingworth also expresses a widely held view: *We felt David had bad luck with injuries. He was a wholehearted competitor and was an excellent cricketer on his day. A fast bowler is inevitably liable to get injured, it comes with the job. They put more pressure on their bodies than spinners. It was desperately bad luck for him, and for Northants and England, that injuries ended his career at a comparatively young age.*

Fletcher, Amiss, Gifford and Knight, amongst others, agreed that David would have played more Tests if his career had not been cut short, including of course on that second Australian tour. Some, Amiss being one, thought he had the potential to be one of the best.

Reflecting on a career which both promised and delivered much, despite being cut off in its prime, David, understandably, is left to wonder what might have been:

> Did you know I was a Trivial Pursuits answer? Who was the only English Test cricketer to tour Australia twice without playing in a Test?
>
> The ankle has not given me any problems since those days, in my non-cricket life, so in that respect I am fortunate. But inevitably I look back at the cricketing part of my life with disappointment and a lot of frustration, because I felt the job was only half done.
>
> Some things I might have done better in my life, some I am quite happy with. I did harbour a resentful attitude to cricket in general when and just after I finished, and I turned my back on it all and even found myself thinking of it all as a failure. Time has however changed that belief, and now if I indulge in wishful thinking, I imagine what another 7 or 8 years might have brought: perhaps a score or more Test matches and a few hundred more first-class wickets.

Appendix

Thanks to the skills of Andrew Samson, the distinguished cricket statistician to the Test Match Special team, a comparison appears below of the figures of the 22 English seam bowlers who took at least 650 first-class wickets in the 1960s decade.

The traditional yardstick of a bowler's success is the average cost in runs conceded for each wicket taken. This measure shows Statham, Trueman, Flavell, Shackleton, Cartwright, Rhodes, David and Wheatley, in that order, as the eight bowlers who averaged under 20 per wicket. Six were pace men, Shackleton and Cartwright being medium-paced seamers.

Looking at strike rate, the number of deliveries bowled for each wicket taken, which tells something of a bowler's potency, six of the 22 had a strike rate less than 50. Trueman topped that list followed by Statham, Flavell, David, Snow, and Butch White. Cartwright's rate was 53 and Shackleton's 58.

On the measure of wickets per match in the period the top six are headed by Shackleton with 4.64, followed by Flavell, Statham, Trueman, Cartwright and then David and Coldwell both with 3.66.

As for David's batting suffice it to say that he was one of a distinguished band of bowlers who took more wickets than the runs they scored when batting – in David's case 639 (at an average of 6.08).

Between David's first Test, against Pakistan in August 1962, and his last, against South Africa in July 1965, 34 Tests were played by England (16 at home and 18 away). 13 pace or seam bowlers formed the new ball, or support attack role, in those matches. Of those 13, using the traditional benchmark of average runs per wicket, in all Tests played during their career – not just in the 1960s decade – Trueman at 21 is way out in front, followed by Statham at 24, David at 25 and Snow on 26.

English seamers with 650 first-class wickets in the 1960s – by average

	Name	M	Balls	Runs	Wkts	Avg	RPO	SR	BB	5I	10M
1	JB Statham	249	46144	17711	1034	17.12	2.30	44.62	8-37	63	7
2	FS Trueman	311	52776	21731	1222	17.78	2.47	43.18	8-36	65	17
3	JA Flavell	213	41763	16684	935	17.84	2.39	44.66	9-56	55	12
4	D Shackleton	267	73014	22434	1239	18.10	1.84	58.92	9-30	91	18
5	TW Cartwright	263	53448	18563	1007	18.43	2.08	53.07	8-39	58	13
6	HJ Rhodes	255	45145	16591	886	18.72	2.20	50.95	7-38	37	4
7	JDF Larter	182	31379	13013	666	19.53	2.48	47.11	8-28	27	5
8	OS Wheatley	240	45190	16611	840	19.77	2.20	53.79	9-60	46	5
9	LJ Coldwell	225	42103	16688	823	20.27	2.37	51.15	8-38	50	5
10	KE Palmer	243	38960	15970	775	20.60	2.45	50.27	9-57	44	5
11	NI Thomson	194	41111	14590	707	20.63	2.12	58.14	10-49	29	3
12	JA Snow	179	31653	13538	654	20.70	2.56	48.39	7-29	34	4
13	JD Bannister	206	38085	13718	651	21.07	2.16	58.50	7-52	25	3
14	TE Bailey	234	40524	15553	686	22.67	2.30	59.07	7-40	33	3
15	K Higgs	289	55346	22366	985	22.70	2.42	56.18	7-19	33	5
16	DR Smith	261	50886	20290	892	22.74	2.39	57.04	7-20	36	5
17	DW White	291	50574	23584	1021	23.09	2.79	49.53	9-44	52	5
18	A Buss	229	40908	18138	754	24.05	2.66	54.25	8-23	36	3
19	BR Knight	326	52097	23297	968	24.06	2.68	53.81	8-69	40	6
20	CT Spencer	258	41166	18124	721	25.13	2.64	57.09	8-88	26	3
21	C Forbes	220	39553	16680	662	25.19	2.53	59.74	7-19	23	2
22	AS Brown	260	42002	18249	691	26.40	2.60	60.78	8-80	32	5

Minimum 650 wickets, ordered by average

English seamers with 650 first-class wickets in the 1960s – by strike rate

	Name	M	Balls	Runs	Wkts	Avg	RPO	SR	BB	5I	10M
1	FS Trueman	311	52776	21731	1222	17.78	2.47	43.18	8-36	65	17
2	JB Statham	249	46144	17711	1034	17.12	2.30	44.62	8-37	63	7
3	JA Flavell	213	41763	16684	935	17.84	2.39	44.66	9-56	55	12
4	JDF Larter	182	31379	13013	666	19.53	2.48	47.11	8-28	27	5
5	JA Snow	179	31653	13538	654	20.70	2.56	48.39	7-29	34	4
6	DW White	291	50574	23584	1021	23.09	2.79	49.53	9-44	52	5
7	KE Palmer	243	38960	15970	775	20.60	2.45	50.27	9-57	44	5
8	HJ Rhodes	255	45145	16591	886	18.72	2.20	50.95	7-38	37	4
9	LJ Coldwell	225	42103	16688	823	20.27	2.37	51.15	8-38	50	5
10	TW Cartwright	263	53448	18563	1007	18.43	2.08	53.07	8-39	58	13
11	OS Wheatley	240	45190	16611	840	19.77	2.20	53.79	9-60	46	5
12	BR Knight	326	52097	23297	968	24.06	2.68	53.81	8-69	40	6
13	A Buss	229	40908	18138	754	24.05	2.66	54.25	8-23	36	3
14	K Higgs	289	55346	22366	985	22.70	2.42	56.18	7-19	33	5
15	DR Smith	261	50886	20290	892	22.74	2.39	57.04	7-20	36	5
16	CT Spencer	258	41166	18124	721	25.13	2.64	57.09	8-88	26	3
17	NI Thomson	194	41111	14590	707	20.63	2.12	58.14	10-49	29	3
18	JD Bannister	206	38085	13718	651	21.07	2.16	58.50	7-52	25	3
19	D Shackleton	267	73014	22434	1239	18.10	1.84	58.92	9-30	91	18
20	TE Bailey	234	40524	15553	686	22.67	2.30	59.07	7-40	33	3
21	C Forbes	220	39553	16680	662	25.19	2.53	59.74	7-19	23	2
22	AS Brown	260	42002	18249	691	26.40	2.60	60.78	8-80	32	5

Minimum 650 wickets, ordered by strike rate

David Larter: First-class Career

Total First Class

	Matches	Overs	Maidens	Runs	Wickets	Average	S/R	Econ
Bowling	182	5,229	1,338	13,013	666	19.53	47.11	2.48

	Matches	Innings	Not Out	Runs	HS	Average
Batting	182	162	57	639	51*	6.08

Test Matches

		Matches	Overs	Maidens	Runs	Wickets	Average	S/R	Econ
1	Pakistan 62	46.1	4	145	9	16.11	30.8	18.87
2	NZ 62/3	40.1	15	77	7	11.00	34.4	11.52
3	NZ62/3	21	3	70	0			20.00
4	NZ 62/3	44	13	91	3	30.33	88	12.41
5	India 64	30	5	95	0			19.00
6	India 64	15.3	2	48	2	24.00	46.5	18.82
7	India 64	26	4	88	3	29.33	52	20.31
8	NZ 65	50.1	16	120	6	20.00	50.2	14.37
9	SA 65	43	12	114	1	114.00	258	15.91
10	SA 65	46	13	93	6	15.50	48	12.13

	Matches	Overs	Maidens	Runs	Wickets	Average	S/R	Econ
Bowling	10	362	87	941	37	25.43	58.7	2.59

	Matches	Innings	Not Out	Runs	HS	Average
Batting	10	7	2	16	10	3.20

First-Class

In England

	Matches	Overs	Maidens	Runs	Wickets	Average	S/R	Econ	Nat Posn
1960	16	352.2	108	750	46	16.30	42.4	2.13	5th
1961	25	649.2	172	1729	77	22.45	50.6	2.66	27th
1962	24	814	215	1924	101	19.05	48.4	2.36	7th
1963	25	820	226	2028	121	16.76	40.7	2.47	8th
1964	28	839.1	200	2043	96	21.28	52.4	2.43	33rd
1965	22	589.2	169	1333	87	15.32	40.6	2.26	7th
1966	3	75.1	16	220	8	27.50	56.4	2.93	
1969	3	108.4	24	341	14	24.36	46.6	3.15	
Total	**146**	**4,221**	**1,130**	**10,368**	**550**	**18.85**	**46.1**	**2.46**	

First-Class continued

Overseas

	Matches	Overs	Maidens	Runs	Wickets	Average	S/R	Econ
NZ 60/61	9	241.2	77	534	36	14.83	40.2	2.21
CW Feb 62	4	96	29	228	8	28.50	72.0	2.38
Aus 62/3	7	186	17	700	29	24.14	51.4	2.82
NZ 62/3	3	105.1	31	238	10	23.80	63.1	2.26
E Af Oct 63	1	33.2	15	57	7	8.14	28.6	1.72
India 64	7	151.3	27	477	14	34.07	64.9	3.15
Aus 65/6	5	99.2	12	411	12	34.25	66.2	3.11
Total	**36**	**912**	**208**	**2,645**	**116**	**22.80**	**52.2**	**2.6**

Note 8-ball overs in the two Australian tours. Econ rate is based on balls bowled.

List A Matches

Total List A Matches

1963/69	26	1424	40	782	48	16.29	29.7	3.29
Batting	26	16	6	60	27	6.00		

Gillette Cup

1963/69	11	789	26	421	29	14.52	27.2	3.20

John Player County League

1969	15	635	14	361	19	19.00	33.4	3.41

Minor Counties Championship
Suffolk

1958	4	531	17	285	14	20.36	37.9	3.22

Acknowledgements

This book would not have seen the light of day without the generous help of a large number of people. Grateful thanks are due to the following for their kindness and interest.

From the Larter family: David, whose patience and enthusiasm I have frequently tested, and his family who have supported him through the process, Thelma, Jonathan, Katharine and David's late mother whose scrapbook of David's cricketing progress has been put to good use.

From distinguished cricketers who gave generously of their time in interview: Mike Brearley, David Brown, Brian Crump, Ted Dexter, Graham Dowling from New Zealand, Keith Fletcher, Norman Gifford, Robin Hobbs, Ray Illingworth, Jeff Jones, Laurie Johnson, Barry Knight, Alan Knott, David Lloyd, Micky Norman, Mushtaq Mohammad, Peter Parfitt – who opened the batting for me - Jim Parks, Eric Russell, Alan Smith, Geoff Smith, MJK Smith, David Steele, Jim Watts.

From lovers of the game who gave help, advice and encouragement: friend and fellow cricket tragic, Yorkshireman Robert Beaumont, for undertaking the Ray Illingworth interview; David 'Bunbury' English CBE for his interest; Stephen Chalke who gave so much valuable advice, David Frith, Rob Kelly, Ivo Tennant, Huw Turbervill and his colleague James Coyne of The Cricketer magazine, Martin Chandler, Patrick Ferriday, Andrew Hignell, Andrew Samson who kindly provided the 1960 decade statistics, and the font of all Northamptonshire cricket information, Andrew Radd who was a constant source of information and photographs; Fraser Stewart of the MCC, Clive Radley, NMK Smith, Neil Burns from the London County Cricket Club, Denis Petropoulos, and Sean Armstrong.

From the world of publishing: Bill Ricquier, podcaster of 'From the Pavilion End', author Colin de la Rue and Clare Calnan of the Dartmouth Bookseller.

From Framlingham College: Principal Louise North for supporting the book launch; senior staff Mark Robinson and Marcus Marvell for photographs; the Society of Old Framlinghamians led by trustee Chris Essex, for very generously sharing the financial burden, OFs Norman Porter, Andrew Lillie and the late Chris Subba Row for their help, and Robin Anderton, David Boulton, Derek Moss, John Rankin, the late Michael Spencer and David Turnbull for sharing their school memories of David.

I am indebted to David Gower for graciously agreeing to write the foreword to this book; to two devoted editors, Paul Taylor and Jon Elvey (not forgetting Sandra) whose patience and literary skills were so valuable. Thanks too to my son Jim for his numerous thoughtful contributions.

Above all I thank Chris Keeble whose great talent as a book designer is fully evidenced here. He has laboured mightily but fruitfully; his inventive layout and design skills have in every way enhanced this publication.

Georgina Sayer has been far more patient, encouraging and supportive than any husband is entitled to expect.

I make grateful acknowledgement to the authors and publishers of the many books, newspaper and magazine articles listed hereunder, from which I have quoted. My thanks go to the staff of the British Library, and to the newspapers I was able to study there, including the Guardian, the Daily Telegraph, the Daily Mail, The Times, The Times of India, Northamptonshire Evening Telegraph and the East Anglian Daily News.

I have made regular use of Wisden Cricketer's Almanack, The Cricketer magazine, MCC Annual Reports, Playfair Cricket Annuals, Cricinfo, the splendid Player Oracle of CricketArchive, and the following books.

Bibliography

Addis, Ian and Radd, Andrew	The Bank Clerk Who Went to War	Chequered Flag Publishing	2018
Barker, Jack	Summer Spectacular	Collins	1963
Batchelor, Denzil	The Test Matches of 1964	Epworth Press	1964
Bowes, Bill	Aussies and Ashes	Stanley Paul	1961
Brearley, Mike	On Cricket	Constable	2018
Brearley, Mike	On Form	Little Brown	2017
Carman, Arthur	The Cricket Almanack of NZ 1963	Sporting Publications	1963
Chalke, Stephen	Micky Stewart	Fairfield Books	2012
Chalke, Stephen	Guess My Story – The Life of Keith Andrew	Fairfield Books	2003
Chalke, Stephen	Summer's Crown	Fairfield Books	2015
Clarke, John	Challenge Renewed 62-63	Stanley Paul	1963
Clarke, John	With England in Australia 65-66	Stanley Paul	1966
Engel,Matthew & Radd, Andrew	The History of Northamptonshire CC	Christopher Helm	1993
Fay, Stephen & Kynaston, David	Arlott, Swanton and the Soul of English Cricket	Bloomsbury Publishing	2018
Frindall, Bill	England Test Cricketers	Willow Books	1989
Frindall, Bill	The Wisden Book of Test Cricket	Book Club Associates	1978
Hoult, Nick	The Daily Telegraph Book of Cricket	Aurum Press	2007
Indian Express Brochure	MCC Visit to India 1964	The Indian Express	1964
Kelly, Rob	Hobbsy	Von Krumm Publishing	2018
Ledbetter, Jim	Frank Tyson	ACS Publications	1995
McLean, Roy	Pitch and Toss	Howard Timmins (Pty) Ltd	1957
Midwinter, Eric	The Illustrated History of County Cricket	Kingswood Press	1992
Moyes, AG & Goodman, Tom	MCC in Australia 1962-63	Angus & Robertson	1963
Murtagh, Andrew	Touched by Greatness – Tom Graveney	Pitch Publishing	2014
Parks, Jim	The Commonwealth Book of Cricket	Stanley Paul	1963
Percival, Tony	Suffolk Cricketers	ACS Publications	2018
Radd, Andrew	100 Greats Northamptonshire CCC	Tempus Publishing	2001
Roberts, RA	The Fight for the Ashes 1961	Harrap	1961
Ross, Alan	Australia 63	The Sportsmans Book Club	1963
Rumsey, Fred	Sense of Humour, Sense of Justice	Fairfield Books	2019
Rutnagur, Dicky	The Indian Cricket – Field Annual 1963-64	Rutnagur	1964
Sandford, Chris	Tom Graveney	Witherby Ltd	1992
Sheppard, Rt Revd David	Parson's Pitch	Hodder and Stoughton	1964
Snow, John	Cricket Rebel	Hamlyn	1976
Steele, David	Come in Number 3	Pelham Books	1977
Swanton, EW	Swanton in Australia with MCC 1946-1975	Collins	1975
Swanton, EW	The Ashes in Suspense	The Daily Telegraph	1963
Trueman, Fred & Mosey, Don	Cricket Statistics Year By Year 1946-1987	Guild Publishing	1988
Turbervill, Huw	The Toughest Tours	Aurum Press	2010
Waters, Chris	Fred Trueman	Aurum Press	2011
Wilde, Simon	England – The Biography	Simon & Schuster	2018
Williams, Charles	Gentlemen & Players	Weidenfeld & Nicolson	2012
Wooldridge, Ian	The International Cavaliers Cricket Book	Purnell	1969
Wyne-Thomas, Peter	England On Tour	Hamlyn	1982

Index

F

G

H

I

Index continued

David finally hangs up his cap in 1969.